W9-AEF-146

More Than a Game

One Woman's Fight for
Gender Equity in Sport

Cynthia Lee A. Pemberton

with a foreword by Donna de Varona

Northeastern University Press
Boston

Northeastern University Press

Library of Congress Cataloging-in-Publication Data
Pemberton, Cynthia Lee A., 1958–
    More than a game : one woman's fight for gender equity in sport / Cynthia Lee A. Pemberton ; with a foreword by Donna de Varona.
        p. cm.
    Includes index.
    ISBN 1-55553-525-9 (pbk. : alk. paper)—
    ISBN 1-55553-526-7 (cloth : alk. paper)
    1. Pemberton, Cynthia Lee A., 1958–   2. Linfield College.
    3. Sports for women—Oregon.   4. Sex discrimination in sports—Oregon.   5. Sex discrimination in education—Oregon.   6. Sex discrimination against women—Oregon.
    7. Women athletes—Government policy—Oregon.   8. College sports—Social aspects—Oregon.   I. Title.
    GV709.18.U6 P46 2002
    796'.082'09795—dc21   2001059193

Designed by Janis Owens

Composed in Stone Serif by Coghill Composition, Richmond, Virginia. Printed and bound by Edwards Brothers, Inc., Lillington, North Carolina. The paper is EB Natural, an acid-free stock.

MANUFACTURED IN THE UNITED STATES OF AMERICA
06   05   04   03   02   5   4   3   2   1

To women and girls in sport

Contents

Acknowledgments

If there is one thing I've learned over the course of my Title IX ordeal, it's that nothing is truly lived or endured without the love and support of others.

There are many people to whom I owe a debt of gratitude. Certainly there were friends in and around Linfield who offered support and comfort, often at considerable professional risk to themselves. You know who you are: thank you.

To the Seven Sisters, thank you. Our friendship and the times we shared were an important part of my ability to get through each day. You helped keep me grounded and were constant reminders that the world is a big and complex place, that there was life beyond Linfield.

To those who helped me try to make sense of it all and worked with me and for me, personally and professionally, Etta Martin and Kenton Hill, thank you. I am a better person because of our time together.

To my family, who I know often felt left in the dark and sometimes had difficulty understanding what was happening, and why I persisted when it clearly caused me so much pain, thank you. You stood by me, loved and supported me, and didn't ask for or expect the explanations I couldn't give.

To Michelle Barber, my swimmer, my assistant coach, and above all my friend, the person who lived the day-to-day realities of my Linfield life, thank you. Thank you for reading and rereading the early drafts of the manuscript. Thank you for insisting I go beyond the story and include the person who lived it. You will never know how important your friendship and support were and are.

To Idaho State University, the College of Education, and Department of Sport Science, Physical Education, and Dance, the support I have received to pursue this writing and, most important, to speak and teach about gender issues and social justice has been invaluable in the writing of this book and the healing process I am still working through. I have found a professional home, and for that I am very grateful.

To Sherie Dulaney, my dear friend, your careful reading of the early manuscript helped me shape it into something presentable. Thank you for your thorough attention to detail and candid feedback. I miss the "snake" but know you were right.

To Louise Schultz, the first person not involved with my Linfield life to read the manuscript, thank you. Your fresh view and heartfelt response gave me confidence to move the work forward.

To Linda Carpenter, my colleague and friend, whose interest in me and this story opened the door to publication, thank you.

To Elizabeth Swayze, my editor at Northeastern University Press, whose call that fall morning put a smile on my face that I carry today, thank you. Thank you for taking the project on and working with me to shape what started as a cumbersome diary of events into a readable memoir of the whistle-blower reality I lived. A special thanks also to the copy editors for their efforts to improve the manuscript's readability. Jimmée Greco, you especially are amazing!

And finally, most important, to my friend, my partner, and my husband, Tim Cheney, thank you. Thank you for your selflessness and understanding. Thank you for your patience, for your willingness and ability to hold our life together when I had neither the strength nor the energy to act other than selfishly. You were and are my life support. Tim, your role is mentioned little in the story itself. This is not an oversight or a slight, but a reflection of impossibility. Your support, advice, comfort, and understanding were anchors in an otherwise overwhelming storm. Every piece of the story, every day, every incident, every moment of pain and joy, you were, and are, a part of it all. I stand tall and strong in the constancy of your love. "I am not unaware," and, even though I like to ask, I know how you know, because you show me in the life we live every moment of every day. I love you.

Foreword

Although there is a considerable age difference between Cynthia Pemberton and me, in many ways our lives have paralleled each other. As a child of the seventies and a swimmer in college, Cynthia benefited from Title IX of the Equal Education Amendments Act. However, she later found inequities as a collegiate female coach and sports administrator.

I was a child of the sixties who at seventeen years of age, after having won two Olympic gold medals, was forced to retire for lack of opportunity. In my era, male athletes were offered scholarships to the best universities in America, while female athletes were left out of the system. Indeed, until the passage of Title IX, which made it illegal for federally funded educational institutions to discriminate against women, elite college sports were for men only.

My entire life has been devoted to sports. As the daughter of an All-American football player and rower at the University of California, I spent many fall weekends squeezed into the season ticket holder's section of Cal's football stadium beside my father. My father, who came from a broken home, used his exceptional athletic ability to earn his way through college. Sport opened doors for him, and he wanted his children to benefit from the same experiences. My father played an important role in my life, especially in the sixties, when there were daunting obstacles to overcome for women and girls interested in becoming elite athletes. Both my father and mother were the ultimate supportive sport parents. Shortly after I competed in my first Olympics at the age of thirteen, they moved our family forty miles north to Santa Clara, California, so I could train with George Haines, who at that time was recognized as the most outstanding swim coach in America. In 1964 I qualified for the U.S. Olympic Team for a second time, and brought home two Olympic gold medals. Then, after breaking eighteen world records and setting numerous world best times, I ran into swimming's "glass ceiling." While Don Schollander, who won four Olympic gold medals, packed his bags for Yale University and continued training with his sights set on the 1968 Mexico City Olympics, I had no place to go and retired at the "ripe, young age" of seventeen.

In looking back, I find it difficult to believe how I just accepted the roadblocks that prevented me from continuing to compete. Sometimes I wonder what I could have accomplished had I been able to participate in further Olympic competition. For a while I considered playing water polo, but what was then a natural step for male swimmers was not an option for women. Water polo would not become an official sport for women in the Olympics until the Sydney games of 2000.

In the winter of 1965, shortly after representing the United States in an international meet in Bremen, Germany, I decided to leave the sport I loved while I was still on top. I realized that without a collegiate program to nurture my talent, I could not maintain a winning edge. My biggest concern as a "washed up" Olympian was how to pay for my college education. There simply weren't sport scholarships for women—no matter how many gold medals they won. Fortunately, fate intervened in the form of a wonderful person and benefactor, Bill Beckenhauer. Bill took a personal interest in me and offered me a scholarship to the university of my choice.

Bill changed my life with his generosity, and I promised myself that when opportunities presented themselves I too would help others. In the fall of 1965 I entered UCLA, and during the following summer I began to make good on that promise. I accepted a position to work in an experimental inter-city program for Vice President Humphrey. One of my work colleagues was the late and great American track star, Wilma Rudolf, who won three Olympic gold medals during the 1960 Rome Olympics.

Working in the hot and volatile cities of the Civil Rights Era taught me unforgettable lessons, lessons of hope and of despair, of prejudice and violence, of fear and hatred. But most important, it taught me not to be afraid to fight for what I believed in.

In 1967 Vice President Humphrey's "Operation Champ" program did not make it past congressional budget cuts. Even so, in 1968 Wilma Rudolf and I went out onto the streets of America, traveling with the Olympic skier Suzy Chaffee, judo expert Ben Nighthorse Campbell (now a senator from Colorado), and runner Billy Mills. Our challenge was to take the Operation Champ message, that is, the power of excellence in achievement through sport, to America's youth. Later (in the late sixties and early seventies) Suzy Chaffee and I would again team up. This time we targeted Congress, and championed "Operation Champ," "Olympic Reform," and Title IX of the Equal Education Amendments Act.

Those were driven times and we were driven people. Our dedication was fueled by the political climate of the era. The Civil Rights Movement, equal rights, feminism, and the protests over America's involvement in Vietnam created an environment ripe for change. It was an era of great idealism. It was also an era of cynicism, colored and marred by the assassinations of President John F. Kennedy, his brother Robert, and Martin Luther King, Jr. Even so, we remained hopeful that we could find purpose and reason in a world that often seemed to have lost its way. Wilma, Suzy, and I sought strength from our beginnings in sport. Through the Olympics we had found a global community, a community that embraced us, and although that same community exhibited great prejudice toward women, each of us appreciated the opportunity we had been given to experience, for however brief a time, equality through excellence. We wanted to share that opportunity with others. We wanted to feel pride in ourselves. We wanted to matter.

In 1972 our activism became more defined. Title IX of the Equal Education Amendments Act, which eventually helped revolutionize women's sports, became federal law. What began as a battle cry for equality in the classrooms of America became a war over the rights of female athletes to gain entry into the locker rooms and playing fields of American sport. NCAA lobbyists and football coaches stormed the halls of Congress claiming support of women's sport would bankrupt the collegiate sports system. Other arguments focused on the ability of the female athlete to produce revenue. Fortunately, during the early years, when the NCAA spent millions of dollars trying to defeat Title IX, the law was not compromised. However, knowing we were not safe from being undermined (nor are we even now), Suzy Chaffee and I realized that we needed more allies. In 1974 we found them, and the seedling of the Women's Sports Foundation took root.

I'll never forget the Billie Jean King and Bobby Riggs tennis match, "Battle of the Sexes." It was so much more than a sporting event. It was a contest that represented the rhetoric of the times. As feminists fought for equal pay for equal work, Billie Jean King played the theme out on the tennis court. When Billie Jean beat Bobby on national television I called Suzy and asked her to set up a meeting with all of us, and soon after we met in Suzy's New York apartment. We discussed women's sport, the role of the amateur athlete in the Olympic games, and the struggles women in sport were facing. A few months later, at the request of Billie Jean's husband, Larry King, I flew out to California and outlined my idea for a Women's Sports Foundation, and how it might function. Shortly after, Billie Jean donated money to help set up the organization. Although slow in finding a direction at first, the foundation has since become a powerful force in women's sports.

Since those early days, much has changed for women and girls in sport. In 1972, one in twenty-seven high school girls played sports; today one in three does. In 1972 only 15 percent of the participants in the Munich Olympics were women. In the 2000 Sydney Olympics, 40 percent of the participants were women. Yet despite impressive gains, in 2001 university men received $160 million dollars more scholarship money than university women. Beyond participation numbers and scholarship dollars, perhaps the most disappointing fallout of Title IX is the war that has ensued between women and men in sport. Too often the victims of this battle are the women who raise their voices in support of the law of the land. And, unfortunately, even though it is their right to speak out, they are often ostracized, harassed, and slandered. Some even lose their jobs or have to change careers.

While these brave individuals make an often thankless sacrifice, women across the nation benefit. Without these pioneers, the American sporting landscape would be quite different. Imagine 1999 without Mia Hamm and the awe-inspiring women's World Cup soccer event, which has often been characterized as the most successful sporting event in history, for which fans purchased over 650,000 tickets! Imagine the 1996 Olympics void of the gold medal efforts of America's female swimmers, gymnasts, track and field athletes, synchronized swimmers, fast pitch baseball and basketball players. Imagine the Sydney games of 2000 without Dara Torres or Marion Jones. In fact, just try to imagine an Olympics without women.

As the mother of a young son and daughter, I want both of my children to have an opportunity to experience the joys of competition and benefit from the lessons learned through sport. I will never understand the "disconnect" between some men and women over the issue of Title IX. Resources need to be shared, not hoarded. The success of women's collegiate basketball, which has become a moneymaker for the NCAA and a spawning ground for the WNBA professional league, is just one example of what is possible when support is provided.

The role of educational institutions where sport is concerned is not only to help athletes who want to become professionals, but to provide all student-athletes with opportunities for growth. It's not about men versus women or boys versus girls. It's about both, and there is no place for comparisons of value between a collegiate football player who wins the Heisman Trophy and Olympic gold medallists like the track star Marion Jones or the wrestler Ruhlon Gardner. All are special, and "no person in the United States" should be excluded from, denied the benefits of, or subjected to discrimination under "any educational program or activity" on the basis of sex.

This foreword is dedicated to a woman who had the courage to fight for what she knew was right and her willingness to risk everything in the struggle.

Donna de Varona

September 2001

Prologue

"You don't know how to read?!"

So you don't know how to read?!" That's what Pam Jacklin, Linfield's mousy-looking, middle-aged attorney caustically asked as we labored through my multiday deposition. I could only assume her question had to do with my testimony, and that despite my educational and athletic background, I hadn't known about Title IX prior to the summer of 1992.

Title IX is a federal gender-equity law that's been in place since 1972. As an athlete competing in high school and college, I wasn't aware Title IX was responsible for the opportunities I enjoyed. As a coach at the age group, high school, and collegiate levels, and later as an athletic administrator, I didn't know Title IX was the reason I had female athletes to recruit and scholarships to offer. The truth was I'd been ignorant, uninformed, and naive. I'd benefited personally and professionally from twenty years of Title IX, and I didn't even know it existed.

That was one of the hardest things to get a handle on: the issue of truth. To me it was all about truth and only about truth. It was about doing what was right because it was right. It wasn't about me; it was never about me. It was about women in sport and educational equity. It was about treating people fairly and allowing both women and men the opportunity to benefit from sport. That idealism was not, however, what played out.

For Linfield College, the various administrators, faculty, and coaches, it was about saving face and not losing. And for the attorneys on both sides, it was about winning. Equity and truth were lost asides.

Depositions are awful things. They are long, personal, and insulting. They aren't about the truth. They're played out as a relentless cat-and-mouse game, where every query seems an attempt to incriminate. They're about digging for dirt and twisting the truth to use as a weapon wielded to destroy and strip dignity and credibility. Depositions are ugly experiences.

But I should probably back up a bit and tell how I came to be sitting in a room, with lawyers on either side, responding to the question "You don't know how to read?!"

Part I

Introduction

My History

My name is Cynthia Lee A. Pemberton. I was born October 2, 1958, which made me thirty-three at the time my Linfield Title IX ordeal began. I am the oldest of three children and spent much of my adolescence in a single-parent household helping to raise my brother and sister.

Many of my early school memories are not good ones. I attended parochial school through the third grade and did not do well. What I remember most was having a hard time paying attention and often getting in trouble. The nuns were not terribly tolerant or patient, and I spent a lot of time in front of the class with my nose in a corner or pounding erasers during recess. Nowadays my restlessness would probably be blamed on attention deficit disorder; back then I was just considered inattentive and disruptive.

When I was ten I tried out for the local swim team. It took three summers of tryouts for me to make the team. The first summer I broke my arm attempting to ride a neighbor's horse, and the second summer I fell off the monkey bars, was trampled by some kids playing chase, and broke my collarbone. Finally, the third summer I succeeded, and from then on things began to look up for me.

I started doing better in school and began to excel in swimming. I loved swimming. I loved racing and I loved winning. My family became very involved in the sport and the lifestyle that accompanied it. All our friends were swimmers and their families. It wasn't long before swimming became the center of our family universe.

My parents divorced when I was thirteen, and I remember being glad. Although I have many good early family memories, the Cleavers we were not. Prior to the divorce we'd lived a fairly middle-class lifestyle; but divorce in the early 1970s was particularly tough on women with children. As a result, our middle-class lifestyle quickly deteriorated, and I was ruthless in blaming my father for the discomfort that resulted. It was difficult for my father too, but at the time I was too young and self-absorbed to consider his pain and problems.

My mother didn't have a college education, and job opportunities for uneducated divorcées were limited, and careers almost unheard of. My mother worked two jobs, over time working her way up from straightening greeting-card racks in the local Payless store to becoming a regional greeting-card manager, and eventually the greeting-card buyer for the entire chain. She was on the road and gone a lot, which is how I came to be the primary caregiver for my brother and sister. My mother became the family breadwinner, and eventually we settled into our respective family roles, with me playing mom and mom playing dad.

After high school I went to college at Willamette University. Willamette is a small, liberal arts college with selective admission criteria and a hefty price tag. At that time it simply wasn't possible for my mother or father to contribute to my college costs. Fortunately, I received academic and need-based scholarships, as well as student loans. I held down a work-study job during the school year and worked summers coaching swimming, teaching swim lessons, and cleaning swimming pools. It was tight, but between these various sources, I scraped together enough money to finance my college education.

I flourished at Willamette. I loved school and excelled academically and athletically. I graduated in May 1980 with a Bachelor of Science degree, a double major in Biology and Psychology, an undergraduate, award-winning publication from my senior thesis, and four years of All-America swimming honors.

The fall after graduation I had an opportunity to go to Hawaii. I lived in Hawaii a little less than a year. It was a wonderful time. I coached swimming, taught swim lessons, worked as a scuba diver, and enrolled in graduate study at the University of Hawaii, Manoa, working with the Dolphin Language Learning Program.

Late spring 1981 I left Hawaii and returned to southern Oregon. The graduate program in Hawaii had lost some of its funding, and I had to move on. I coached swimming and resumed graduate work at Southern Oregon State College (now Southern Oregon University). In August 1983 I completed a Master of Science degree in Interdisciplinary Studies with content areas in physical education, psychology, and nutrition.

The day after my degree was conferred I married my college sweetheart, Michael Anderson, and we moved east to Virginia Beach, Virginia. We were there a little less than a year before we moved again, this time west to Reno, Nevada. In Reno we both coached swimming, and over time my coaching roles expanded to include the master's swim team (adult swimmers), a high school team, and later the University of Nevada—Reno (UNR) women's team. I also taught classes at the local community college and the university and began work on my doctorate in education. The restless, hyperactive kid I'd been had grown into a woman seemingly incapable of juggling fewer than a half-dozen balls at one time.

1

"If a fish were an anthropologist . . . "

I came to Linfield College in the early summer of 1989. Originally, I had no interest in the job. The job advertisement was for a facility director, swim coach, and instructor. At the time I was married, living in Reno, busy working my six different coaching and teaching jobs (at least half of which were full-time jobs by themselves), and taking doctoral classes at the university. In one of my classes I was doing a project on the interview process, and when a couple of opportunities presented themselves, they seemed to provide a valuable perspective, enabling me to write my term paper while being an interviewer (serving on a search committee in the university athletic department) and an interviewee (applying for the job at Linfield). As far as I was concerned I was applying as part of a class assignment, with no intention of actually pursuing the position. One thing led to another: I became an applicant, interviewed, turned down the first offer, and, after some negotiation, accepted the position.

Although it meant living apart from my husband and taking a considerable pay cut, there were many reasons why it seemed to make sense. First, it was an opportunity to work just one job in one place. This was something that greatly appealed to me. It was also an opportunity to work full-time in academics. And for me, it was moving home. I'd grown up in Oregon. My mother and sister were living in the Portland area; and although it would be a bit of a commute, I would be able to live with my mother and keep expenses to a minimum. The pieces fell into place, and in June 1989 I left Reno towing a U-Haul.

Within the first week of the job, the women's athletic director resigned, and I presented myself to the athletic director stating my interest in the vacated position. Shyness has never been one of my traits. I felt I was qualified for the job and eager for the challenge. After some administrative rearranging, I became the assistant athletic director for women's sports, aquatics director, head women's and men's swim coach, and an instructor in the Health, Human Performance, and Athletics Department (HHPA). It would be another year before my position was again changed and reclassified as tenure track, which meant I was no longer an instructor but an assistant professor. To say I was pleased and excited would be an understatement. I had a keen interest in academics as well as athletic administration and leadership. I felt I'd landed exactly the job I wanted.

It wasn't long into my early years at Linfield that my marriage began to unravel. As I look back, I think the chance to escape my marriage was an underlying motivation to take the Linfield job in the first place. I'd been with Michael off and on since I was seventeen. We'd gone to college together, swum together, and basically grown up together. Our marriage was a working partnership. We'd coached and taught swimming together in Virginia and Nevada. It was in many ways an ideal match, but it was also an impossible match. We were simply too much alike. Too often it was like having two captains trying to steer the ship, both entirely capable, willing, and able, and both highly competitive, stubborn, and domineering, often to a fault.

Professionally, I don't think I could have been happier. I've always been a hard worker and an overachiever. Those first years at Linfield were wonderful and fed my insatiable need to be challenged. I was enamored with my job, especially coaching, and readily put in the work needed to excel.

I loved working with college athletes and enjoyed coaching both women and men. I worked like a crazy person. I'd leave for work at 4:30 in the morning and come home between 10:00 and 11:00 at night. Most of the time I worked six to seven days a week, and I thrived on it. In just a few short years, the Linfield swim program grew from a fledgling start of two women and four men, with no national qualifiers, to one of the premier small-college programs in the country. It was an exciting time.

In my role as assistant athletic director, I was left to my own devices. For the most part, the athletic director (Ad Rutschman) was preoccupied with coaching football, and what time and attention he had to spare were directed toward administering the men's sport programs. Even though I was technically his assistant, we operated independently. We'd meet periodically; I went to him with questions from time to time, but for the most part he left me to do the job of administering and directing women's athletics, which was fine with me.

I don't work well when I feel I'm being controlled. I am a self-starter and an independent worker. I'm good at solving problems and figuring out how to get something done, whom to contact, what resources are needed, and how to get them. I like being given general guidelines about what is to be accomplished and then turned loose to do it. For a while that was Ad's and my mode of operation and, as a result, early on we were quite compatible. It wasn't until a few years later that I realized our relationship was dependent upon my willingness to agree with him, and didn't have much to do with compatibility.

An early example of my willingness to agree with Ad involved a discussion about athletic shoes. The question was whether I had a problem with the men's basketball team being given team shoes while the women's team had to buy their own. I don't remember whether the shoes were being donated, or whether the department was going to purchase them. What I do remember was my response. I said, "If and when the women's basketball team starts making money, they too can have shoes, but until then as long as the men's programs are making the money, it's okay with me that they get more." It's embarrassing. No, it's more than embarrassing; it's appalling that I thought, said, and believed those words. That was me then.

I'd spent my athletic life benefiting from Title IX, and I hadn't had a clue it existed, let alone what it was about. I wasn't a women's sports advocate; I was one of women's sports' worst nightmares, and I didn't even know it.

I'd swum on my high school swim team (1972–76), then been recruited to swim in college (1976–80). It never occurred to me that women hadn't always had opportunities to participate on high school teams and compete in college sports. I didn't know that the opportunities I enjoyed were in all likelihood a result of Title IX, a 1972 civil rights statute designed to address issues of educational equity.

As I look back, it seems odd that I never questioned why I swam in three different nationally affiliated intercollegiate championships: the Association for Intercollegiate Athletics for Women (AIAW), the National Association for Intercollegiate Athletics (NAIA), and the National Collegiate Athletic Association (NCAA). I didn't know that this competitive upheaval represented the bloody aftermath of a gender-equity war waged against women's sport governance.

Since its inception, the NCAA and NAIA had opposed Title IX. By the late 1970s, after efforts to lobby Congress and legal challenges failed to limit Title IX's applicability, the NCAA, and to a lesser degree the NAIA, embarked on a mission of merger and acquisition to gain control of women's sports. It never dawned on me that Willamette switched national athletic affiliations because the AIAW, the smaller and financially weaker women's sport organization, was being driven out of existence by the NCAA and NAIA.

I knew nothing of the history of women's sport, how recently the opportunities I enjoyed had come about, or that in response to Title IX, in large measure, women's sport leadership and self-determination (the AIAW) would be lost. Undeniably Title IX resulted in gains for women in sport, but those gains came at a price.

As a university swim coach at Nevada—Reno, I hadn't realized that Title IX was the reason I was able to recruit and offer female athletes scholarship money. In fact, in the mid-1980s the university athletic program was facing budget cuts and the two women's sports under consideration for being dropped were softball and swimming. I remember putting together a case, based on performance outcomes and success, that addressed why swimming should be spared the ax. Swimming was spared and softball was the women's sport eliminated. This all took place during the time that a Supreme Court decision called *Grove City v. Bell* had effectively limited Title IX compliance to school programs that were direct recipients of federal funds. As most athletic programs were not direct recipients, schools felt comfortable ceasing women's sport program expansion efforts and even making cuts. Fortunately, in 1987 Congress overrode the *Grove City* decision and, over a presidential veto, enacted the Civil Rights Restoration Act. This act effectively put the Title IX umbrella back over all programs in an education institution.

I'd been a female athlete, and later a college coach, riding the wave of Title IX, and I hadn't known it existed.

Title IX is fairly succinct and direct. It states simply: "No person in the United States shall, on the basis of sex, be excluded from participation in, be denied the benefits of, or be subjected to discrimination under any education program or activity receiving Federal financial assistance."

Originally, athletics wasn't even a part of Title IX; it had been quietly added, as more of an afterthought, by Oregon congresswoman Edith Green. According to Indiana senator Birch Bayh, a Democrat and the principal Senate sponsor of Title IX, it was put forth as "a strong and comprehensive measure [that would] provide women with solid legal protection from the persistent, pernicious discrimination which [was] serving to perpetuate second class citizenship for American women." In other words, Title IX was designed to proactively address the historical wrongs associated with culturally embedded gender discrimination and thereby ensure gender equity in educational opportunities, such as admissions, housing, and scholarships. It just so happened, thanks to Edith Green, that it also included athletics.

The legislative and legal evolution of Title IX has come to include rules and regulations, policy interpretations, a 1980 Office of Civil Rights (OCR) Investigator's Manual, clarifications and interpretations by the OCR, and a barrage of women's sport court cases in which women have predominately prevailed.

The Office of Civil Rights is the chief governmental agency responsible for enforcing Title IX. The ultimate consequence for noncompliance is the loss of all federal funds. This includes student financial aid, which would effectively shut down almost any college or university. The reality, however, is that Title IX compliance, assessed based on athletic financial assistance, the accommodation of athletic interests and abilities, and equity in "other" program areas, has most often been enforced in response to legal action brought by female student-athletes and their parents. To date, the OCR has never levied the ultimate consequence.

According to Title IX, athletic scholarship dollars must be allocated in amounts that mirror athletic participation numbers. In reality, allocating scholarship dollars in amounts reflective of existing participation is not terribly progressive and does little to encourage growth in women's sports.

With regard to the accommodation of interest and abilities, Title IX prescribes compliance with one of three conditions. An institution must (1) demonstrate that its athletic participation opportunities for females and males are provided in numbers substantially proportionate to its enrollment; or (2) show a history and continuing practice of program expansion that is responsive to the developing interests of the underrepresented sex (typically women); or (3) demonstrate that it is fully and effectively meeting the expressed interest and abilities of the underrepresented sex (again, typically women). This compliance area has been, and continues to be, a topic of heated debate.

What has come to be called the three-prong test originated not with a group of rabid militant feminists, as some would like to believe, but with the National Collegiate Athletic Association (NCAA) and the American Football Coaches Association (AFCA). Women wanted things split down the middle and shared equally between boys and girls, women and men. The NCAA and the football coaches' association came back instead with the three-prong test and the notion that meeting any one prong would translate into compliance. When the three-prong test was adopted through the Federal Register Rules and Regulations and Policy Interpretations, according to Donna Lopiano—cited in a March 2001 *Ms. Magazine* article, "Title IX: The Little Law That Could"—the men thought they'd walked away with a win.

In the early 1970s men made up the majority of college students (more than 60 percent), so, from a men's sport perspective, the proportionality prong didn't pose a threat. Prong two, a history and continuing practice of program expansion, seemed vague and flexible enough to provide schools with a compliance deadline that could stretch on almost endlessly. Finally, there was, and to a degree still is today, the perception that females aren't as interested in sports as males, so prong three, full and effective accommodation of expressed interest and abilities, wasn't considered an issue.

Impact on the status quo would have been minimal if it weren't for the fact that over the past thirty years females have been enrolling in colleges and universities in ever-increasing numbers. Today, over half of all college and university students are women. As a result, the proportionality prong no longer serves to maintain a male-dominated status quo. Even so, despite a few hard-fought cases, the Title IX front remained relatively quiet between the late 1970s and 1992.

The reality is that law only sets general policy. Therefore, if the consequences for breaking the law can be tolerated or avoided, laws don't compel action. It wasn't until 1992, the twenty-year anniversary of Title IX, that decisions in two landmark court cases, *Franklin v. Gwinnette County Public Schools* and *Tyler v. Howard University*, changed the climate of Title IX litigation.

The *Franklin* case involved teacher-student sexual harassment in a K–12 setting. One outcome of the case was that for the first time, the court ruled that plaintiffs could sue for damages under Title IX. Similarly, the *Tyler* case was the first decision that made clear that employees could sue and win damages under Title IX. The dog could now bite as well as bark.

The combined effect of changing college and university demographics and the potential for damage awards opened the floodgates of Title IX litigation. And the three-prong test was, and remains today, the center of the controversy. One case in particular, *Cohen v. Brown University*, explored the application of the three-prong test.

In the *Brown* case, the debate revolved around whether Brown University could define proportionality on its own terms. In a cost-cutting move, Brown decided to eliminate two women's sports and two men's sports (gymnastics and volleyball, golf and water polo, respectively). Brown's idea of proportionality was grounded in the notion that females have less interest and ability in sport than males. Therefore, Brown reasoned that schools should be allowed to incompletely accommodate interest and ability, as long as they did so in proportion to sex-based levels of expressed interest. For example, if there were 200 men and 100 women who wanted to play sports, Brown's interpretation of proportionality would mean that if, say, 80 percent of the men and women (that is, 160 men and 80 women) were provided opportunities, compliance would be achieved.

The courts didn't buy this argument, calling Brown's perception of Title IX "myopic" and stating that "Brown reads the 'full' out of the duty to accommodate fully and effectively." Ultimately, after a series of appeals that ended with the Supreme Court's refusal to hear the case, Brown was found in violation of Title IX.

Overall, in regard to the three-prong test, the courts have generally held that although not required, substantial proportionality (prong one) creates a sort of Title IX safe zone relative to the accommodation of interest and abilities. Early on, prong two (history and continuing practice of program expansion) was difficult for schools to demonstrate because although many could show a history of program expansion through the addition of women's sports in the 1970s, in many instances those efforts stalled in the 1980s while the Supreme Court and Congress wrangled over the *Grove City* decision and the Civil Rights Restoration Act. Expansion efforts resumed only after the threat of damage awards became clear in the early 1990s. Because of this, the continuing practice part of prong two was and is often found lacking. With regard to prong three (full and effective accommodation of interest and abilities), the courts have held that in order to really know whether interest and abilities are being fully met, the entire statistical universe of potential college and university student-athletes would need to be surveyed. This, as is obvious, would be a logistical nightmare—not to mention the fact that at many schools, unmet interest and ability among female athletes is demonstrated beyond varsity-level sports programs by the existence of thriving club and intramural sports programs. Additionally, females in sport have to overcome significant bias and discrimination just to have a chance to play. Perhaps women and girls really don't want to play sport as much as men and boys. Maybe, given all they have had to overcome, they want to play more!

Finally, Title IX requires that all other opportunities and treatments afforded sport participants be equivalent. It is important to note that equivalent does not mean exactly the same, nor does it imply equal spending. This is a key point that came about as a result of congressional action involving John Tower, a Republican from Texas, and Jacob Javits, a Republican from New York.

During the time that the Department of Health, Education, and Welfare (HEW) was working to develop rules and regulations and later policy interpretations to make Title IX operational (mid- to late 1970s), Congressman John Tower proposed an amendment that would have exempted revenue-producing sports (such as football) from Title IX considerations. Congress did not act on the Tower Amendment and instead passed the Javits Amendment.

The Javits Amendment instructed HEW to make reasonable regulatory provisions considering the nature of particular sports. This language made clear that although Congress was not willing to accept an amendment exempting revenue-producing sports, it did understand that treating sports equitably did not necessitate equal spending. Contrary to popular myth, Title IX does not require equal spending. What it requires is equitable accommodations. Translation: sometimes treating people equitably means treating them differently.

The third broad area of Title IX compliance is a catchall category of other program areas and involves both sport-to-sport and overall program comparisons. Title IX compliance in this area includes equipment and supplies; scheduling of games and practice; travel and per diem allowances; opportunities to receive academic tutoring; opportunities to receive coaching as well as coaching compensation; locker room, practice, and competitive facilities; medical

and training room services and facilities; housing and dining services and facilities; publicity; support services; and recruitment. In
essence, with the passage of Title IX, it was no longer okay to treat
daughters in sport as second-class citizens.

Despite the fact that I'd participated as an athlete during Title
IX's early years, and coached and administrated women in sport
throughout the 1980s, it would be the summer of 1992 before I
gained my first awareness of Title IX. In fact, not only was I unaware, but my behavior even suggested an active state of denial.

Early on at Linfield I received a call from a female faculty member inviting me to be part of a newly formed women's caucus. I
responded to her invitation by telling her that I didn't believe I'd
ever experienced sex discrimination and, in fact, didn't even believe
it existed. I self-righteously informed her that if women would just
work hard and stop complaining, they could and would get what
they deserved. I concluded my sermon by turning down the invitation.

I have thought about the shoe incident described earlier and
that call on many occasions, and I have since apologized to the
faculty member who extended the invitation. Even so, I can hardly
believe I could have been that naive, not to mention how shame-
fully I behaved. Margaret Mead once said, "If a fish were an anthro-
pologist, the last thing it would discover would be water." I was so
immersed in the male-dominated culture, it was so much a part of
everything I knew and understood, so much a part of who I was,
that I wasn't aware it was there.

And so went my early years at Linfield. There were ups and
downs, and some dustups among various staff at times, but overall
the women's sport programs grew and improved steadily. Funding
increased incrementally, and I marched on through my work and
my life, secure in the self-delusion that I was not only doing my
job, but doing it well.

2

If I'd Only Known Then

L infield College is a small, private, liberal arts school, located in McMinnville, Oregon. It was founded in 1849 with historic ties to American Baptist Churches. Linfield boasts an undergraduate enrollment of roughly twelve hundred students, almost all of whom are traditional eighteen to twenty-two year olds. The average entering student has a 3.5 grade point average and an 1,100 SAT test score. The price for tuition, room, board, and fees is in excess of 20,000 dollars a year. The upshot of all this is that students at Linfield are typically either good students from fairly privileged families who can afford to send them or students with excellent academic credentials from hard-working, less-privileged families. There isn't much of a middle class, nor does the student body seem very interested in social justice activism.

McMinnville is a small community, located about fifty minutes south and west of Portland, Oregon. Now the population is just over 25,000, and it was considerably smaller when I first arrived. It is a quiet family town, a place that prides itself on a strong sense of community. It is also a place where diversity is tolerated as long as it is limited to a grocery aisle dedicated to Mexican and Asian specialty foods. There are over eighty churches in the county where McMinnville is located, with more than thirty in the city itself. Sunday spirituality is a staple, followed closely, or perhaps for some even surpassed, by Saturday spirituality, otherwise known as Linfield football. I read a book recently called *Friday Night Lights*. It's a story about football in small-town Texas; it could just as easily have been a story about Linfield football in McMinnville.

Linfield football, with its three NAIA national titles, was and is a local legend tied inseparably to Ad Rutschman. Ad's involvement with Linfield College spanned nearly fifty years. Ad graduated from Linfield in 1954 after earning twelve letters in football, basketball, and baseball. After a stint teaching and coaching at the high school level, he returned to Linfield in 1968 to take over as head football coach. During his coaching tenure Ad led Linfield's baseball team to a national title in 1971 and the football team to NAIA national titles in 1982, 1984, and 1986. Under Ad's leadership the Linfield football program amassed a winning streak spanning almost a quarter century, and Ad, deservedly, was inducted into the NAIA Hall of Fame (1989) and the Oregon Sports Hall of Fame (1993). He was also the recipient of the Slats Gill Man of the Year Award an unprecedented five times.

In short, Ad Rutschman was Linfield football, and in many ways Linfield athletics. He was a local hero and a legend in the minds of many. His success was without match, and his status, influence, and power at Linfield, in the McMinnville community, and in small college athletics were considerable. When I first came to Linfield, various people, sometimes in jest and sometimes in earnest, referred to Ad as the "great god of football." Initially, I didn't realize how fitting that label was. I would come to know differently in time.

During the summer of 1992, I received a copy of the regional newsletter *The Inside Track*, a publication of the Oregon Women's Sports Leadership Network. The newsletter was addressed to the athletic director but was forwarded to me, probably from Ad. That newsletter, along with news clips from the *Oregonian* headlining the twenty-year anniversary of Title IX, marked my first real awareness of gender-equity issues, an awareness that would irrevocably change my life and set off a firestorm at Linfield College. On July 27, 1992, I sent the following memo to Ad:

> Ad, the issue of Title IX and Gender Equity in Athletics is making a strong resurgence as we round the 20 year bend of Title IX implementation. The attached articles talk in some detail about Equity Issues.
>
> It is my belief, that although the financial and opportunity status of women's athletics at Linfield has made considerable strides over the past few years, that we still have a ways to go. I think it will be important for us to work together and stay on top of the issues of Gender Equity and Title IX compliance. It is my hope we will take a positive leadership role in pursuing Gender Equity, rather than waiting for compliance pressures to force us to make uncomfortable changes.
>
> I have ordered a copy of the "Title IX Tool Box," a publication that addresses the "meat" of the law, and compliance. Once I receive it, I will review it carefully and then hope we can meet to discuss where we are and where we need to go with women's athletics at Linfield.

I also sent copies of this memo and the attached materials to Charles Walker and Vivian Bull (the outgoing and incoming college presidents), as well as to various Linfield deans and vice presidents. I proceeded as I said I would. I ordered a copy of the *Title IX Tool Box* and began researching and reading about Title IX.

The more I learned, the more I became convinced that the intercollegiate athletics status quo at Linfield was not okay. I didn't realize that I'd opened Pandora's box, and there would be no going back. I thought that Linfield's gender-equity problems were a result of ignorance and naïveté. I figured that if I hadn't known about

Title IX, its compliance requirements and potential impact, then others probably hadn't known either. I thought that once we all became educated on the matter, everyone would see the obvious inequities and promptly do the right thing.

There is a warning in the *Title IX Tool Box* that reads something like this: before you start inquiring about and/or pushing for Title IX compliance and gender equity, try to imagine the worst possible response scenario. Try to imagine how bad it could possibly be, and then know it will be worse. I probably would not have chosen to act differently, but I would have been more prepared had I heeded that warning.

Throughout the late summer and early fall of 1992, Ad and I met regularly with Scott Carnahan (a practice Ad established shortly after his decision to resign as head football coach and continue full-time as athletic director and professor). Scott Carnahan was Linfield's facility director and head baseball coach. At the time, I suppose I'd have characterized him as a good old boy ex-athlete and a relatively successful middle-aged coach with a slight paunch and a tendency to chew tobacco.

During these meetings I'd periodically volunteer information about my Title IX research and readings. Typically neither Ad nor Scott would respond; they really didn't seem very interested. I repeatedly told Ad I was working on an initial report and expected to have it ready by mid-fall.

For the most part the meetings were congenial and amounted to Ad asking Scott and me to report back to him on various assignments or telling us things he wanted us to take care of. Ad became much more directive in his role as athletic director after resigning as head football coach. This was a change in our working relationship that I was not particularly thrilled about.

During that fall I attended a conference at Lewis and Clark College in Portland, Oregon. It was a women's issues conference, and one of the featured speakers was Dr. Donna Lopiano. Dr. Lopiano is a dynamic, highly energized, and impassioned speaker. I've had the great pleasure to hear her speak on numerous occasions since. She served for a number of years as an athletic director at a major university in Texas and was responsible for the significant development of its women's sports programs. At this time she had left or was leaving that post to become the executive director of the Women's Sports Foundation. Today Dr. Lopiano is recognized as one of the one hundred most influential people in sport.

The information she shared reinforced what I was learning about Title IX, and after her presentation I approached her, asking how she convinced people at her school to pursue gender equity and initiate change. I remember her response quite clearly: she told me it simply had not occurred to her that resistance to gender equity was even relevant. Then, and for some time to follow, I too felt that way. It would be a number of years into Linfield's long and painful process before I realized that discounting, ignoring, and failing to anticipate significant resistance was foolish and naive. It took a long time for me to realize that just because something is right morally, ethically, and even legally doesn't mean others will readily jump on board, especially if doing what's right means questioning the status quo. But questioning is exactly what I did. Questioning was my crime.

As I learned more about Title IX, I began to question Linfield's athletic policies and practices, which just wasn't done under Ad's leadership. To Ad a query was a threat. I found Ad an interesting character: not a bad guy really, just a relic who couldn't seem to change with time. He was a silver-haired ex-athlete, a die-hard football coach with a warm smile and a hot temper who seemed to have grown so accustomed to absolute obedience that anything less was simply intolerable.

An early example of my questioning Ad's status quo occurred in September 1992, and involved a discussion about concession stand use. Our policy and practice then was that a particular men's sport booster (a financial supporter of the athletic program) was in charge of running the concession stand. According to Ad, this booster had funded and built the concession building, and, thus, concessions could be run only when the booster wanted to run them. If the booster didn't want to run concessions during women's events, he didn't have to. The women would simply go without.

On October 5, 1992, I sent Ad, along with various Linfield administrators, my first Title IX overview and program report. The cover memo read as follows:

With all the publicity Title IX has been receiving (attached Time magazine article, Oregonian series July 1992, Inside Track Newsletter Spring/Summer 1992, Franklin-vs.-Gwinnett case Feb., 1992, etc.) it appears timely for all schools to engage in an internal review to assess compliance with the law. I sent for and received the Title IX Tool box, a publication compiled by the National Association for Girls & Women in Sport; and made available through the American Alliance for Health, Physical Education, Recreation Dance. The Toolbox itself is a compilation of information and materials related specifically to Title IX; and includes sections on: 1) the law itself, 2) background historical overview information, 3) compliance evaluation information, 4) guidelines and suggestions for causing change, and 5) support and reference information. The Toolbox does NOT claim to be an all-inclusive Title IX document, but does serve to provide broad-based Title IX information.

The following report is a summary of my readings and conclusions relating to how Title IX and the issue of gender equity, impact Linfield College and our athletic programs at this time. Due to the detailed nature of this information, I have often made reference to the Toolbox itself rather than belabor this report.

Based on my readings, it appears clear that although in some areas our programs may be in compliance, there are other areas where we seem to be dangerously out of line. It is important to note that: 1) the Toolbox repeatedly cites that

under the law revenue sports *cannot* be excluded when reviewing overall gender equity and Title IX compliance; and 2)
compliance is evaluated relative to equity of opportunity regardless of funding sources, (budget, booster monies, etc.). I
am sure we can all agree it is preferable that we work together
with our administration to begin a plan of compliance from
within rather than waiting for outside pressures to force us to
make uncomfortable changes.

The report itself contained sections on what Title IX actually
said; a brief historical overview of its legislation and evolution;
copies of the Federal Register Rules and Regulations and Policy
Interpretations, which detail how Title IX is to be instituted; and
information about Title IX compliance assessment. The report also
briefly identified areas of possible compliance concerns that were
specific to Linfield athletics.

I'd identified areas of concern in almost every compliance assessment category. First, we weren't allocating athletic financial assistance in proportion to athletic participation. Second, I believed
we had problems in regard to the interest and abilities three-prong
test; that is, (1) our athletic participation ratios were not propor-
tional to our enrollment ratios; (2) although various women's and
men's sports had been added and deleted, we could not show a history and continuing practice of program expansion for women; and
(3) we were not fully and effectively accommodating the expressed
interest and abilities of existing female athletes: we had club sports
and intramurals that indicated both interest and ability in varsity
women's sports we did not offer. Third, I identified areas of inequity
in almost all of the eleven program components (equipment and
supplies, scheduling of games and practice, travel and per diem al-
lowance, tutoring, coaches, locker rooms, practice and competition
facilities, medical and training facilities, housing and dining facilities, publicity, recruitment of student-athletes, and support services).

I concluded the report by suggesting that we carefully review our current athletic programs, enact immediate changes where identified inequities could be remedied with minimal cost, and develop a plan to address costlier, long-range change.

My summary statement read:

> While it appears that we do have areas where immediate attention needs to be directed, as well as a need for careful long range planning regarding overall Title IX legal compliance; I am certain we would all agree that Linfield provides the type of environment in which we can take positive steps to assure compliance with the law. By initiating our own evaluative and planful compliance steps, we can avoid the time, cost and negative publicity that an outside evaluation and complaint would entail. Given the current climate of Title IX interest and awareness the likelihood of eventual outside evaluation and intervention could be a definite possibility. I am sure we are all in agreement that it is in the best interest of Linfield College to be in compliance with the law.

Although it would be some time before Ad would acknowledge that he had read the report, some of the people to whom copies were sent were quick to respond. I got a call from John Dillin (the director of college development) expressing concerns about adequate documentation. He wanted to know if I had accurately documented the reality of Linfield athletics. John thought the report was informative, but he also found it to be inflammatory.

A couple of days later Dan Preston (the director of financial aid) called to say that he "probably should have been more involved in the money dispersal" to help ensure equity.

On October 12 Dave Hansen, the dean of students, sent me a memo thanking me for the report and asking if I wanted to send a copy to the chair of the Student Activities Committee. Dave was under the impression that the Student Activities Committee would be the appropriate body to "make sure we [were] in compliance." Obviously, Dave was underassessing the situation. On that same day, during one of our regular meetings, I asked Ad for feedback regarding the report. He indicated he had not yet read it. The next day we met again, and he said he was still "not through it all yet."

On October 22 I talked with Ken Williams, Linfield's faculty athletic representative (FAR), about the report as we walked across campus. The FAR is a person appointed by the college president who serves to represent student-athlete interests at the athletic conference and national levels. The FAR is the second-highest-ranking decision maker in regard to athletics, behind only the president. Ken indicated that he had read the report but planned to do nothing in response to it. According to Ken we (meaning Linfield) were not breaking any laws, and most schools break this law anyway. He went on to say, "we break the law in many areas and nothing happens."

On October 29, more than three weeks after receiving the report, Ad commented, and he was furious! He didn't like copies of the report being sent to others and felt I hadn't followed the chain of command by distributing it as I had. Ad went on to tell me that any Title IX violations at Linfield were my fault, and that it was my job to submit women's sports needs to reflect a move toward equity. In reality Ad was right about my job. Both our job descriptions stated that we were responsible for making sure Linfield athletics complied with federal laws and NAIA rules. Without even knowing it, by reviewing our Title IX compliance and submitting the report, I was doing my job.

I tried to explain to Ad why I wrote the report, how it related to my job responsibilities, and why the people who received copies were and would be important to any broad-based compliance assessment and ultimate change. Ad was not happy with the report and was even less happy with my explanation and rationale. He was, in his words, "pissed off." That meeting ended with my telling Ad I was working on a more-detailed follow-up report in an effort to identify sport-specific areas in need of compliance assessment. Ad demanded the next report be given only to him, a command I fully complied with.

Over the course of the next several weeks Ad expressed his anger through little day-to-day things. He wouldn't share copies of various meeting agendas with me, making my participation at conference and district meetings difficult. He'd demand that I complete various assignments, but not give me the information needed to do so. Both he and Scott began to interrogate the women's sport coaches, asking whether they had seen the report and what contributions they had made to it. People became more than uncomfortable; they were scared.

The afternoon of November 4, Garry Killgore, the track coach, found me in the pool and told me that Ad had met with him about the report. He said the meeting was intimidating and accusatory. He went on to say, "I have a wife and kids, a house . . . I cannot pursue this situation with you." Over time Garry, who was once my friend and colleague, would turn out to be one of my most vehement critics.

Mary Kincaid, the women's basketball coach, came to me very much upset after being probed by Scott about the report. Scott told Mary, "Cindy's misleading you . . . she's setting you up." Laura Kenow, the softball coach, told me of similar incidents. Apparently, Scott had two different conversations with Laura in which he was not only trying to intimidate her, but trying to persuade her that I was wrong about Title IX.

I think these incidents were particularly tough on Mary and Laura. They were both young. Mary had come to Linfield the same year I had, straight from graduate school, and Laura followed a year or two later. Linfield basketball was Mary's first collegiate head coaching position and, given Linfield's long history of basketball mediocrity, posed quite a challenge. Mary is a quiet, soft-spoken woman with a keen sense of propriety and a sparkle in her eye that hints at fun. She is relatively small in stature, yet while growing up had been quite athletic. Mary was the first female in the state of Oregon to play Little League baseball. According to her, her desire to play with the boys caused quite an uproar in the league. She was a trailblazer before she was old enough to understand what sharing the field with the boys really meant. Mary went on to play a variety of sports in high school and then focused on basketball in college.

Laura is a thin yet strongly built woman. Her short brown hair and unadorned looks radiate a healthy athleticism. She has a feisty wit and a fun sense of humor. Like Mary when she arrived at Linfield, Laura was relatively fresh out of graduate school, and assuming the head softball coaching position was her first turn at the helm in collegiate sports.

I enjoyed Mary and Laura very much, and at first one might assume Laura would be the real fighter of the two. However, Mary would be the one who steadfastly rode the storm. Laura would struggle and in the end capitulate in the face of perceived opportunity.

Even now, years after writing the original report, as I reread it I am amazed at the degree to which Ad and Scott were upset. The report was factual; it wasn't inflammatory. I probably should have expected the response I got, but I didn't. I just couldn't understand why they were so upset. Scott stopped talking to me almost altogether. In fact, he wouldn't even acknowledge my presence with a superficial hello. Both he and Ad were openly hostile, suspicious, and accusatory in their interactions with me and about me.

I didn't really understand then what I understand now. The change implied by that first report and all the various reports, consultations, and meetings that followed meant that much of what they believed in, the very foundation of athletics as they understood it and had lived it, was called into question. For Ad in particular—a moral pillar of the community and small college football coaching legend—if I was right about Title IX and Linfield's lack of compliance, then he and much of what he'd done for the past quarter century was wrong. Not to mention that for Ad, it was always a zero-sum game. He couldn't see it any other way. If women were to get more, then men would get less. Less would mean less winning, less glory, less excellence, less, less, less—and that just wasn't an option.

On November 6 I gave Ad my second Title IX report. This report included a cover memo, copies of various Title IX informational documents, and a survey identifying sport-specific Title IX compliance concerns.

I concluded the cover memo with the following paragraph in an effort to assure Ad that I wasn't his adversary.

> I hope that my efforts will be seen as they have been intended . . . to draw to the College's attention that we need to be sensitive to issues of gender equity and Title IX compliance and start to actively work on plans to address compliance concerns. Title IX isn't an issue of Men versus Women, or Ad versus Cindy. It is an issue of providing the best we can, to and for, the folks and programs we all believe so much in and care so much about. I appreciated the frankness of our meeting October 29; and know we can work together to weed through the issues and concerns of Title IX in athletics, and come up with a plan to make Linfield Athletics an even better place for ALL our students.

On November 10 Ad, Scott, and I met. We discussed various items related to athletics, yet neither Ad nor Scott mentioned Title IX, the report, or the secret meetings they were having with various women's sport coaches. Secrecy and innuendo had fast become their standard modus operandi.

On November 13, 1992, we had our first real Title IX compliance discussion. It was a discussion about financial aid during which Ad defended our current allocations as being "close enough" to equitable, and referred to instances in the *Title IX Tool Box* in which "close" was considered compliance. Clearly, Ad had started doing some thinking about Title IX. In a way I was glad about that. I still, down deep, felt certain that Ad would do the right thing once he came to understand what the right thing was. To this day I don't believe Ad is a bad person. I don't believe he or anyone else at Linfield woke up each morning thinking, "How can we stick it to women's sports today?" I think the scope of the potential ramifications associated with gender equity in sport was just something Ad could not, and would not, consider. If I was right about Title IX, then Ad was wrong, and that would be like telling a minister there is no god.

Our next significant Title IX discussion occurred on November 17. This meeting included Ad, Scott, and me, as well as the department chair, George Oja. George is a mild-mannered academic. He's a thoughtful, intelligent man, an ex-athlete and coach, and I believe that, unlike most others in Linfield's athletic department, George was an academic first and a coach second. In fact, he worked for years to be released from his coaching duties to focus full-time on academics and was finally granted that request, against Ad's wishes. Throughout my Title IX ordeal at Linfield, George recognized what was happening and was sympathetic to my situation and the plight of women's sports. He offered what support he felt he could, but George wasn't much of a fighter. He may have been the department chair, and therefore technically Ad's immediate superior, but in reality he was unwilling, or perhaps unable, to stand up to Ad.

During this particular meeting, Ad shared his interpretation of "interest and abilities" as it related to Title IX compliance. Ad felt that we needed to have overflowing interest and demonstrated talent before we could, would, or should begin talking about adding participant opportunities for women. Ad never did get beyond this.

On numerous occasions I laid out what I came to call the cup metaphor. It goes like this: you can take a cup, fill it up, and then, when the first cup begins to overflow, put out another cup (a reactive model). Or, you can start with multiple cups and work to fill them (a proactive model). Ad was a proponent of the reactive model. I preferred the proactive model.

We discussed financial aid allocations again and began to delve into issues of the eleven Title IX compliance program components. Ad asked repeatedly if I thought we were discriminating, and my response was always the same: yes. Based on the information I had, I believed we were. It was a meeting filled with hostility and blame, especially when we touched on the subject of sport program publicity.

Annually, Linfield published a football media guide, a basketball media guide, and a baseball media guide, and women's sports were left to fend for themselves. During my early years at Linfield we had progressed to publishing fall, winter, and spring sport guides that included both men's and women's sports, in addition to a football guide complete with a full-color cover. During a discussion about public relations in general, and sport media guide publications in particular, Ad claimed that he was responsible for the monies used to produce the guides and threatened to put a stop to the guides entirely if I didn't like the way things were. (This turned out to be a threat I would hear in other contexts too. Later, President Bull would tell me how some colleges were handling Title IX compliance issues by dropping athletics entirely. I think this was supposed to scare me into being content with the limited progress Linfield was making toward gender equity.)

In reality, Ad's version of the media guide responsibility and funding wasn't accurate. The College Development Office contributed funds and production power (film, photo processing, layout, typesetting, and so on) to the media guide publications. Although Ad's efforts through athletics had a significant impact, the bulk of the resources needed to support these publications was allocated through the Development Office. I confronted Ad with this clarification and he backed down, admitting that he wasn't entirely responsible for the guide production. Whenever I caught Ad in such inaccuracies he would never really admit he was wrong, but he did back down.

After this heated meeting I was feeling worn down by the hostility and subterfuge that had become the norm. I was emotionally exhausted and frustrated. I remember coming to tears off and on during the meeting and then really breaking down afterward.

I am generally not much of a crier, but over time the mounting strain increasingly brought me to tears. I'd spent my life operating, I thought successfully, in a male-dominated world. Crying was a sign a weakness, a lack of control that got in the way. But I wasn't weak and I wasn't out of control; I was frustrated and mentally and emotionally tired. I was human, and the climate of paranoia, threats, and attacks was wearing me down.

I was in our department workroom after the meeting when Scott came in. He saw I was upset and, to be fair to him, probably thought he was comforting me. He put his arm around my shoulder and told me, "my wife gets this way once a month too." I was stunned. In what he probably thought was his most compassionate moment, Scott had demonstrated that he couldn't get past the idea that all the fuss was because I was an irrational woman. But the fuss was real; we had real problems and needed real solutions, not condescending, sexist attempts to console.

At the time I was so dumbfounded I didn't know how to react or what to do. I remember making note of the incident. (I was fast becoming used to noting dates, times, nuances, and quotes from incidents and interactions.)

Later that winter, in a meeting with President Bull, I told her about Scott's comment, and gave her a chronology of what had been going on in the athletic department. Her response was even more unbelievable than Scott's utterance. Vivian told me that she was sure that he hadn't "meant it that way." I'm not sure how many ways one can mean "my wife gets this way once a month too," and Vivian didn't enlighten me.

I've thought about this incident many times. There is a part of me that wants to see good in the people, actions, and events of that time. But no matter what angle I come at it from, this one just floors me. Did I find his comment condescending? Yes, I did. Was it insulting? Absolutely. Was it inappropriate and sexually demeaning? Without a doubt. But worst of all, when Vivian denied the experience by assuring me Scott probably hadn't "meant it that way," I felt I was without recourse. Vivian was the college president; there wasn't anyone higher on the chain of command to consult.

As fall crept by, we continued various Title IX discussions. Ad always wanted to know if, specifically where and in what ways, I thought we were violating the law. I always answered the same, replying yes, I thought we were in violation, and indicating where I thought we needed to begin looking to assess compliance. I offered information about how we might conduct an internal compliance evaluation. Ad was never satisfied with my response. He wanted specifics that I couldn't give because neither he nor the college ever gave me access to the men's sport information needed to create a complete gender-equity picture. I asked for this access repeatedly and at one point was even told by President Bull I would receive it, but I never did. When it came to men's athletics, budgets, and booster money, Ad played his hand close to the chest.

Finally, in December 1992, exhausted from meetings during which I was attacked for my position on Title IX and grilled to supply information I couldn't provide, I recommended we develop a committee to look at the issue. My idea was that we form a committee composed of the dean of faculty, the faculty athletic representative, the department chair, Ad, Scott, and me. Ad rejected this idea immediately, stating that people outside the department didn't understand athletics. Then, just before finals, he informed me that we would have no further discussion about Title IX. According to Ad, the issue was now in the hands of the administration, and as far as I was to be concerned, the case was closed, end of discussion.

As before, Ad continued to show his displeasure by making my life difficult in countless little ways. He'd go behind my back and act on behalf of women's athletics without my knowledge. He'd question my coaching policies and practices with my assistant coach and athletes. He tried to pressure the women's soccer coach (one of my supporters) to resign. And, while denying requests for athletic training funds for purchasing swimear medication, according to Tara Lepp (the athletic trainer), he appropriated funds from the athletic training budget to cover football training expenses.

In mid-December Ad summoned me to a meeting—immediately. It didn't matter that my day had already been scheduled to the minute, teaching classes, coaching practices, and attending meetings. It didn't matter that I had a recruit-visit scheduled at the very time Ad demanded we meet, with the parents and athlete waiting patiently outside my office. Ad was an autocratic leader, and an immediate summons from him was just that; everything else was secondary. During this unscheduled meeting, Ad informed me that he had met with the president and the dean, and that I was to break down the women's athletics budget request to identify specific Title IX compliance concerns, outlining a request inclusive of Title IX and one exclusive of Title IX (that is, a normal budget request). Further, I was to establish priorities for any increases in the request over a five-year period. Ad outlined guidelines for me to follow, one of which was to delete specific swim team travel requests, and he instructed me to have the task completed over the next two days. This was a tactic Ad would use often: he would give me assignments that required considerable time and effort with unreasonably short deadlines.

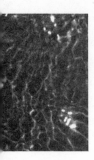

3

The School Year: 1992–93

I first met Dr. Vivian Bull during an open faculty forum as part of her interview for the position of Linfield college president. She gave a short presentation and responded to questions. I immediately liked her and hoped that she would become Linfield's next president. She seemed warm and open, as well as intelligent and reflective. I thought that she would be a good president and that I could learn a great deal from her leadership.

Vivian is a small woman with fine brown hair, worn simply. She likes to wear tennis shoes with her skirts as she walks across campus; although she is a bit quirky, she is for the most part unremarkable in appearance.

On December 17, 1992, I met with President Bull to specifically address Title IX. She informed me that she had read both Title IX reports (obviously Ad had shared the second one with her, as I had given that report only to him) and told me she planned to seek out Pam Jacklin (a Portland-area attorney with Title IX experience, the same woman who would later ask me the question "you don't know how to read?!") and begin work on the issue in January. She was careful to refer to the City University of New York (CUNY) suit in which the university opted to drop its entire athletic program rather than deal with Title IX compliance issues, a not-so-subtle threat that she would repeat from time to time.

I told her about my concerns regarding my Title IX reporting and the fact that Ad couldn't seem to get past his perception that I had stepped out-of-bounds in completing the reports. I recounted the sequence of my Title IX actions. I discussed my concerns with the way I and other members of the women's athletic department were being treated. I gave examples of differential sport treatment and scrutiny, unreasonable assignment demands and unscheduled meetings, open hostility and aggressive accusations by both Ad and Scott, as well as details about our numerous meetings and discussions about Title IX. I told her my reasons for looking into Title IX, and that because it was part of my job, I was obligated to do so. I explained that the reason I hadn't done so before was simply because I'd been both naive and uninformed about the law and its implications.

Vivian responded that Ad had obviously acted under his own rules for quite some time, and she was hopeful that by bringing in an outside person, some of the pressure I was feeling would be alleviated. I remember feeling a great sense of relief. I didn't want to be in the hot seat. I welcomed the idea of someone else being the bearer of bad news.

As winter progressed, Ad's efforts to make my working life miserable continued unabated. If anything, they escalated and became specifically targeted toward my role and responsibilities as swim coach. Under the guise of cost cutting, Ad scrutinized the swimming national travel policies and practices, the point of which seemed to be to keep qualified swimmers from attending the national meet.

He called other conference schools and asked about their policies and procedures (always after he asked me what they were—I suspect he was trying to catch me in a lie or at least an error). He went behind my back questioning swimmers about practice times and requirements, travel practices, and so on. Over the years Ad had received copies of weekly swim team meeting agendas that clearly detailed practice times and requirements. But now, despite my consistent history of sharing information and keeping him informed, he became obsessed with checking up on me. I suppose he was hoping to find evidence that I had violated some Linfield policy or practice. He didn't find any evidence, because there wasn't any.

There was, however, one time when he thought he had me. I'd submitted to the dean a travel request for bus transport. Ad called me into his office with the request in hand, demanding to know why I had submitted such a request and reminding me that only the football team was allowed to take buses to competitions (as per his latest policy adjustment). I responded that I had followed the policy and that although I did not understand or agree with the new football-only bus policy, I didn't see how it affected a travel request based on prior approvals. Ad was flustered by this and said he'd check with the dean and get back to me. He did get back to me, the travel request was processed, and the swim team traveled by bus. It was, however, a hollow victory. The more I did things right, the more obsessed Ad seemed to become with trying to catch me doing something wrong.

Linfield's bus travel policy was a frustrating and disappointing battle. No matter how often I forwarded articles and information about school van accidents, injuries, and even deaths, regardless of the road complications and risks regularly encountered (including a winter swim team trip during which we had two accidents, one resulting in the front end of a van being totaled; Linfield's only response came from the motor pool secretary, asking where the van was) and the extra time away from school for athletes, Ad refused to consider allowing any team but football to travel by bus. President Bull capitulated and offered the following solution. She suggested we hire work-study student drivers to drive the vans for nonfootball teams. Her reasoning was that the athletes and coaches would then be relieved of driving responsibilities. The fact that her plan would result in even more students missing class, needing lodging and food, and taking unnecessary road risks just didn't seem to register. After all, she was the president; so I suppose from her perspective it must have been a good idea. When people paint themselves into a corner, they'll grab at almost any ridiculous idea to get out. The decision made me very sad and frustrated, and it created an ongoing risk and liability to the students and the school, a risk that to my knowledge still exists.

Another example of Ad's quest to find fault in my work had to do with our women's basketball team playing a partial junior varsity (JV) schedule. In our seasonal *Ladycat* sports newsletter I commented on the growing success of our women's basketball program and highlighted our inaugural season of JV play. That didn't go over well with Ad. It seems ridiculous now, given what would later be revealed as Linfield's Title IX deficiencies, that an opportunity to promote women's sports would have been anything but cheered. But Ad wasted little time in making clear to me that I'd been wrong to state or imply we had JV women's basketball. Ad went on to say that if he'd had the decision to make over, he would not have allowed JV women's basketball games to be played. He felt the women's basketball participation numbers were inadequate to justify play.

Winter moved into spring and Ad continued to rearrange and redefine policies and practices, and his propensity for inconsistency was becoming obvious. He talked of instituting squad limits, eliminating Linfield's historic no-cut football policy, while in the same breath claimed that there never had been a no-cut policy. He grasped for control of every aspect of Linfield athletic administration, and my approval as assistant athletic director was no longer adequate to process requisition requests, travel itineraries, or fundraising requests for women's sports. Contrary to what I had been doing for more than three years, coaching vacancies were to be handled by Ad, and everything, absolutely everything, was to go through him. Anyone foolish enough to question his complete control was simply told that he or she could look for another job (something Ad said directly to the softball coach, Laura Kenow, in February 1993).

About this time I was working through the process of requesting a leave of absence. I had decided (before I raised Title IX issues) that I wanted to complete my doctorate. I looked into various programs and determined the most practical thing for me to do was to resume my studies at Portland State University. To do this, I requested a nine-month leave of absence. I found Ad's response to my request odd. I thought he would have been overjoyed at the prospect of being rid of me for a while, and maybe he was. But he just couldn't seem to resist a chance to harass me. He chastised me for not coming to him first with my request. I'd followed the faculty guidelines as outlined in the *Faculty Handbook*, but that didn't seem to matter to Ad. I'd followed school procedures, but not Ad's procedures, and he expressed his displeasure about my recommendations for how and by whom my various job responsibilities should be filled in my absence.

Ad insisted that I give him a full report detailing duties that needed to be performed in regard to aquatics. It didn't matter that he was asking for information without any right to do so: in aquatics, as in academics, I didn't report to Ad. It didn't matter that what he was asking for would take considerable time and energy to produce, by an unreasonably short deadline. It didn't matter that I was in the middle of the championship portion of the swim season. What mattered was that I comply. I met his deadline and delivered the comprehensive report.

Over the course of the next month, I asked Ad repeatedly if he had read the report and wanted to go over the information with me. Each time he responded that he hadn't gotten to it yet. It seemed that the greater the hassle for me, the more pleased Ad became. In frustration I went to the dean of faculty, Ken Goodrich, and expressed my concerns about changing policies and practices and unreasonable assignment demands. Ken listened and, on February 10, 1993, told me to do the best I could to comply with Ad's requests. He went on to say that he hoped I wouldn't consider prior commitments made by the college to me legally binding. He was specifically referring to a memo he had sent me responding affirmatively to my recommendations for filling my job responsibilities during my leave of absence. In essence, although he expressed concern for me and the situation I was in, he left me to fend for myself and to try to deal with Ad as well as I could. He clearly wasn't willing to disagree with or confront the almighty Ad Rutschman.

About this time I had yet another unpleasant Linfield experience. It was mid-April 1993, and I was up for faculty evaluation. The review committee consisted of the dean of faculty (Ken Goodrich), a faculty representative from the Rank, Tenure, Sabbatical (RTS) Committee (Vince Jacobs, an old fishing buddy of Ad's), and the acting department chair (football coach Jay Locey). Given the makeup of the committee, I shouldn't have been surprised at the meeting's tone or outcome. But of course, being ever optimistic and naive, I was.

The meeting started with Ken asking why I'd put my file together using the same format that would later be required for my tenure review. It seemed to make sense to me to begin this process and then work to build the file with the tenure review format in place. However, for some reason, Ken didn't see it that way and wanted to make clear that I wasn't up for tenure, which I was quite aware of. Various comments were made, mostly suggestions for strengthening my file, which I actually found quite constructive and useful.

Then, Vince began to question why I wanted to pursue my doctorate in educational leadership when I would be reviewed for tenure as a "coach and teacher." Vince went on to question the faculty support I had received by being granted a leave of absence. He couldn't understand and didn't agree with the faculty minigrant funding I had been awarded to help with tuition costs. He concluded by questioning my academic career "center," as he put it.

I had met with Vince earlier, seeking his counsel as a senior faculty and RTS member. In that meeting he had been supportive of my desire to resume doctoral study and felt confident the RTS Committee would look favorably on such efforts. He had said he felt my tenure clock (the number of years a faculty member has prior to coming up for tenure review) should continue to "tick" during my leave (as opposed to being stopped for the year of my leave and thereby delaying my tenure review).

In this meeting, however, he was a different Vince Jacobs, with very different input. In fact, not only was Vince questioning my academic center, but he went so far as to recommend I voluntarily remove myself from a tenure track position (a considerable demotion in academic terms). He further stated he had concerns about my collegiality given the strength and tone of my self-evaluation statement, and referred to Jay Locey's comments in my file (Jay had written that he was upset with the way I raised Title IX issues). At this point the meeting deteriorated into a diatribe concerning issues of collegiality and my apparent lack of it, particularly where Title IX was concerned.

As the meeting progressed there was no mention of my teaching effectiveness, other than to report that in five of the eight courses I taught, I had received perfect ratings on my student evaluations. There was no mention of the progress and success of the swim program, a program I had developed into a veritable small-college national powerhouse, and, as Vince pointed out, one of the key components of my tenure review. There was no mention of the progress and success of women's athletics; the women's athletic teams had risen from "cellar-dwellers" in the conference to highly competitive teams, even out-performing Linfield's men's programs in many sports. There was no mention about the safe, clean, and efficient functioning of the aquatics facility. Basically, my job performance was not addressed.

I stayed in the dean's office for a while after the meeting. I was extremely upset, which is putting it mildly. I cried. Saying I was disappointed would be a gross understatement. I was confused and deeply hurt. I spoke at length with the dean about the treatment I had been subject to since raising Title IX issues, the RTS meeting being only the most recent example. I relayed numerous situations and incidents, some of which he was already aware of and even party to. He responded that he could probably play devil's advocate and argue against any one example, but that perhaps the point was these examples represented a pattern of behavior. In fairness to Ken, he said he was willing to talk with Ad if I was okay with his doing so, although he was worried that I might experience even greater backlash if he did.

After the meeting Jay came to visit with me in my office. He wanted to assure me that he felt I was an excellent coach and an asset to the department (things he certainly hadn't said in the meeting), but again echoed concerns regarding collegiality. I didn't much feel like talking with Jay; I wasn't feeling very collegial at that particular moment. I shut him out and would not engage the conversation, more evidence, he would later say, that I had some real problems as far as collegiality was concerned.

In early May 1993, President Bull called me to tell me that Pam Jacklin, the attorney retained by Linfield, would be conducting a Title IX audit for us. She asked me to forward various Title IX resources I had collected to Pam and indicated that we were finally on track. Our gender-equity review was under way.

Soon after, Ad called a last-minute department meeting to inform all the coaches we would be undergoing a Title IX review in response to the fact that "Cindy [had] raised concerns regarding Title IX compliance at Linfield." Ad described his December meetings with the president and dean and his request for legal advice on the matter. He indicated he would be engaged in various meetings focusing on Title IX and would need all our help in supplying information for the Title IX review, often on short notice. He asked for our cooperation and support.

During this meeting some of the football coaches acted quite surprised and concerned. Ed Langsdorf (the offensive head coach) asked me about the "nature of my concerns." I responded with a brief account: I detailed learning about the law and thereupon drawing the conclusion that we needed to take a look at our programs in relation to compliance issues.

Although Ad had made clear to all that I was the reason we would be addressing Title IX, I felt a glimmer of hope. Maybe we would finally move beyond the personal and begin to address gender equity in athletics. As it would turn out, that glimmer was premature.

4

The Only Person Who Could Help

As the school year wound to a close, Ad continued his almost daily harassment, and I finally began to realize that there wasn't anyone inside Linfield who was willing or able to help. Over the course of the winter, I'd gone to the department chair, the dean, and the president. All had at various times acknowledged my plight and the problem of trying to confront Ad, and each offered sympathy and concern. But that was as far as it went. No one was willing to simply and directly tell Ad to knock it off. It took a while, but I finally realized the only person who could help me was me.

In late May and early June I began to fight back. I contacted Carol Bernick (a Portland-area attorney who typically specialized in the employer side of employment discrimination). We met and I supplied her with extensive documentation regarding my treatment at Linfield since raising Title IX concerns. I retained her as my attorney, and on June 9, 1993, we sent a letter to President Bull.

The letter outlined the history of my Title IX involvement at Linfield and described specific examples of the negative treatment I had endured since raising Title IX concerns. The letter stated that "contacting an attorney [was] not intended as a hostile act; rather a last effort to work cooperatively with the school to both ensure Title IX compliance and guarantee against any retaliation."

The letter concluded with suggestions for resolution of the mounting conflict. The suggestions focused on attempting to get me out of the direct line of fire by (1) splitting men's and women's athletics, or (2) reassigning my direct reporting responsibility to someone other than Ad, and (3) stating and enforcing a "no retaliation policy."

After the letter was sent, I felt that I was living and working inside a live bomb. I'd go to school each day expecting some eruption and then nothing would happen. Time went by and the letter received no response. After about a week I had a brief phone conversation with Carol and sent a follow-up letter with a documentation chronology detailing more recent incidents.

The letter chronicled date-by-date documentation, diary-type entries for the month of June 1993. The documentation included Ad's apparent paranoia about making sure all fund-raising money went across his desk and changes he wanted made in the accounting procedures for women's athletics. I had assured Ad that except in cases in which people made donations directly through College Relations, in which case I wasn't aware of them until they showed up on account reports, all fund-raising money for women's athletics was directed for deposit through him. As to the accounting changes, what Ad wanted was to open individual sport accounts, as opposed to keeping line-item records for each sport in one central account. This was a change neither I nor accounting was keen on, and quite a fuss resulted.

Not only were the changes annoying to me, but they would result in considerable added work for the college accounting office. In response, the individual who would have to implement the changes called, asking me why practices that had been working well were being altered. The result was a "kick the dog" effect. A letter from accounting expressing concerns about the changes was sent to the accounting supervisor, who then passed the letter along to his supervisor, who contacted the dean of faculty, who contacted Ad, who accused me of instigating the whole thing. One of the interesting fallouts of the mess was a conversation I had with Dennis Klaus (the accounting supervisor), during which he told me how at one time when the former president of the college had instructed accounting to consolidate some small endowment funds, Ad had responded by demanding that the funds from the athletic account be put back into their original state. Dennis said that the administration complied with Ad's demands. The whole thing was a ridiculous nightmare born of what appeared to me to be Ad's power-hungry paranoia—power he apparently possessed.

My letter to Carol concluded by documenting Ad's and my discussions in regard to my upcoming leave of absence, and what would turn out to be a telling piece of secondhand information about President Bull. A person in Linfield's Development Office shared with me that there was a sexual harassment case under way in her office. According to her, the person filing the complaint had written to President Bull in the fall about the situation. When she didn't receive a response or acknowledgment, she went to an attorney and filed a complaint. My source's feeling was that the situation would never have become a legal issue if President Bull had responded to the initial letter.

Summer progressed and despite Carol's efforts to contact President Bull and Pam Jacklin, she had great difficulty getting a response to the letter we'd sent. What she had been able to glean was that Ad felt I had gone about raising Title IX concerns in an "aggressive" fashion, and that I had personally attacked him, his judgment, and his integrity. As far as Linfield was concerned, Title IX issues aside, this was a personality conflict, and I had wronged Ad. This would come up again and again over the following years. It was, I thought, the wrong focus, and served only to deflect attention from the real issues: gender equity and Title IX compliance.

On July 6, 1993, after almost a month of no real response, I got a memo from Dean Goodrich informing me that the college would like Ad and me to engage in what he called mediation and conciliation meetings. Carol thought that mediation might not be a bad idea, although I felt suggesting mediation was a further attempt by Linfield to deflect attention away from the issue into a personality conflict instead of facing issues of Title IX compliance and whistleblower retaliation.

The suggestion of mediation caught me off guard, and, among other things, I thought the timing was weird. I would be beginning my leave of absence that fall, focusing full-time on my doctoral study. I wasn't excited about engaging in any meetings with Ad during my leave. I told both Carol and the dean I'd think about the idea.

July 1993 was a busy month. During this time I met with Pam Jacklin in Portland to review the history of my Title IX activism at Linfield, my Title IX reports, and various questions and information requests related to the department budget history and practices, scholarship awards, and so on. I also indicated to Pam that I had been keeping a detailed documentation log and could support with dates, quotes, and memos the incidents I claimed occurred.

I'd been keeping a detailed log for some time at this point. Tim Cheney, at that time my friend (and now my husband), suggested I keep track of what was going on at Linfield and carefully document the various incidents. Tim grew up in Portland, did his undergraduate work at Stanford, and went to law school at Santa Clara. Following law school he'd been a lawyer for a number of years in the San Francisco area. After five years of practicing law, he'd decided to make a life change and move back to Oregon where he began teaching classes in business law at Linfield. I immediately liked Tim. He's an attractive man, quiet yet personable, highly intelligent without being overly academic; he possesses a clever wit and an enjoyable sense of humor. He is a sports enthusiast, and we struck up an easy friendship shortly after my arrival at Linfield. Over time, as my Title

IX ordeal evolved, his friendship, advice, and support would become anchors in my life.

Pam asked for and received (with names blacked out—as per her instruction) a partial copy of that log. Following this meeting, other women's sport coaches (and I presume Ad and the men's sport coaches) were interviewed by Pam.

The end of July rolled around and the dean returned from vacation wondering why things weren't resolved and mediation set up. The dean told me he thought I had already agreed to mediation. I informed him that his memo was the first I had heard about it, that I had not agreed to it, and that I had not finished considering the request.

Final arrangements for filling my position during my leave were worked out. I won some and I lost some. Aquatics and coaching were combined, which was too much responsibility and work for one person with relatively limited experience (especially when my recommendations, backed by program growth and sport comparison data, for assistant coaching support had been shortchanged); the assistant athletic director was retained as a distinct position and assigned to Mary Kincaid (the women's basketball coach). Apparently, according to the dean, Ad reconsidered his position on the assistant athletic director interim appointment after learning of the letter from Carol Bernick. The dean quoted Ad as saying it was "too risky to disagree with Cindy. . . . I don't want to get into a fight with Cindy over it." The dean asked me to rethink my position regarding women's athletics and Ad's proposed assumption of those duties for the next year. He felt Ad was sincere in his interest and quoted Ad as wanting to "use this opportunity to get to know the women's programs and coaches." He thought Ad would accept the position change if I agreed not to oppose it. Much to his disappointment, I didn't agree with his appraisal of Ad's intent and stood by my original recommendation that Mary Kincaid be appointed assistant athletic director during my leave.

As I look back, I am amazed that so much time and energy revolved around decisions about how to fill my job responsibilities during my leave. Ad just didn't want to buy in to my recommendations. Maybe it was because they were my recommendations, and he simply couldn't agree with me. Maybe it was because he saw my absence as an opportunity to seize total control. Maybe he wanted to see the programs I had built weakened and crumble in my absence. Maybe it was for all or none of those reasons.

As August wound to a close I met again with President Bull to discuss what Linfield called my "allegations of retaliation," my request that upon my return women's and men's athletics be separated, at least for the duration of our Title IX work, and a request for reimbursement for the expenses I incurred by retaining Carol Bernick's legal representation (I knew this latter request was a long shot). Unfortunately, this meeting did not bear fruit. Although I followed a written outline during the meeting, the president would later be represented by Linfield's attorney as not being clearly informed and aware of the retaliation I experienced, as I claimed. Linfield would deny that I actually told President Bull what was happening with respect to the retaliatory harassment and abuse I continued to experience. However, in regard to my request for legal fee reimbursement, memories were quite clear; after a series of memos and letters between me and President Bull (September, October, November, and December), she informed me that "[i]t was not Linfield's policy to reimburse such expenditures."

That was where my first contracted association with a lawyer ended. For all intents and purposes, the letter Carol Bernick sent had little impact, and the associated legal expenses were mine to bear.

Part II

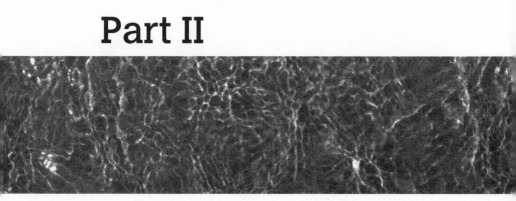

5

Making Progress?

During the fall of 1993 I began my leave of absence. In many ways it was wonderful timing. Things at Linfield were unpleasant, and between my responsibilities as assistant athletic director, aquatics director, teacher, and coach, I was tired. I've always been a "type A," workaholic person, and, given the nature of my job, there was always something more to be done.

My leave was also a special time for me personally. It was the first time since I was thirteen that I'd been able to go to school without also going to work. I was living with my mother so I had minimal expenses, which was a big part of what made taking a nine-month unpaid leave possible. And, I'll give Linfield this, it supported my efforts by awarding me a series of small grants to help with tuition costs, holding my job for me, and continuing to cover my health insurance benefits. Between lowered living expenses, Linfield's support, a student loan, and my savings, I was set to attend school full-time. It was a luxury I am appreciative of to this day.

Other than wrangling over how my Linfield job responsibilities would be covered during my absence, one of the things I wondered

most about was how I would react to not coaching. I'd been involved in competitive swimming since I was ten years old, and I'd
coached at one level or another since I was fifteen. My life had revolved around the sport of swimming. For the first time in a very
long time that would not be the case, and to my surprise I didn't
miss it.

I think I'd known for some time that I was ready to quit coaching. That really was the motive for resuming my doctoral study in
the first place. I knew if I didn't go back and finish my degree, I'd
be forever trapped as a coach. Taking a leave of absence didn't have
anything to do with Title IX, contrary to what most people believed. I'd simply decided that I didn't want to be forty years old
and still working fifteen-plus hours a day, with weekend swim
meets and road trips denying any possibility of a normal life.

I've loved my life in swimming. I was a very successful youth
league, high school, and collegiate swimmer. As a coach my club
teams had been very successful, as had my masters, high school,
and collegiate teams. At Linfield I'd had numerous All-Americas, Academic All-Americas, national champions, and national record
holders, as well as a winning team record. I was one of the few female coaches in the country, in any sport, to coach collegiate men,
let alone do it successfully. I'd been named coach of the year at the
conference, district, and national levels. At one point the men's
team had a forty-plus consecutive meet winning streak. To this day,
I may be one of the most successful female collegiate men's sport
coaches in the history of the NAIA. It was fun and exciting, but I'd
decided in 1992 that it wouldn't be my life forever, and in order to
move beyond coaching I needed to complete my doctorate.

In September 1993 I was thirty-four years old. I established a
personal goal and time line, giving myself five years to complete my
degree and move on with my life. My leave would have been just
about perfect if I'd been able to divorce myself from Linfield completely during that time. But that wasn't to be. Having raised Title
IX concerns, although I could and did leave teaching and coaching,

I continued to be engaged in Linfield's ongoing Title IX controversy.

As I mentioned, Linfield had contracted an attorney, Pam Jacklin, to conduct a Title IX compliance audit of the athletic program, and Pam had agreed to do so pro bono. Originally, the administration had hoped that a report from Pam would come sometime near the start of the 1993 school year. That hope was overly optimistic. It took longer than expected to gather information and to schedule and conduct interviews, and, understandably, Pam's volunteer time and effort on Linfield's behalf would have to be integrated with her paying clients' needs.

In November 1993 the school newspaper, the *Linfield Review*, ran the following Title IX story: "College Examines Athletics for Title IX Violations." I was interviewed at home by telephone and was quoted as follows: "The reason for the audit was increased awareness of issues that would impact the students, faculty and athletes. There was not any one thing that happened [to spur the audit]"; "you would have to look at both sides of the issue"; and "I think Linfield has become more sensitive and responsive to women's sport participation." Despite carefully worded comments such as these, Linfield refused to see me as anything other than a Title IX lunatic.

Then, just after the new year, we began to make progress—or so I thought. On January 17, 1994, a meeting was called involving all athletic department faculty and staff, as well as various Linfield administrators and the newly appointed Title IX officer, Bill Apel (the college chaplain and a professor of religious studies). Bill is a quiet, thoughtful man; at that time he was well regarded among Linfield faculty, staff, and administrators. As the college chaplain, he seemed a calming choice for the role of Title IX compliance officer.

Legally, all schools are required to have a Title IX officer. Prior to Bill Apel's appointment, Linfield skirted this issue by including in Ad's and my job descriptions responsibility for ensuring that

"federal and other regulations on nondiscrimination and equal opportunity are complied with." With Ad at the helm, it was like having the fox guard the hen house: ineffective if the goal was change
in the long-standing status quo.

Bill opened the meeting by introducing himself and outlining
his role as Title IX officer. According to Bill, the purpose of the
meeting was "to begin a planning process which will reflect our
commitment to gender equity in Linfield's athletic programs as we
move into the future." President Bull followed with some introduc-
tory comments, thanking people for attending and indicating that
I had been helpful in "bringing issues forward and identifying complications." She went on to announce that Pam Jacklin would be
working on Linfield's behalf as a Title IX consultant. I remember
wondering if being our consultant was different from or in addition
to conducting the audit. Vivian emphasized that we were now dealing with Title IX not because it was a legal issue, but because it was
"consistent with the history of the college," and that pursuing issues of equity was something we wanted to do and were not being
forced to do. According to Vivian, we had been advised by Pam that
we "needed to get our house in order." She went on to say that we
had "chosen not to receive a legal opinion . . . [and that] our
response to Pam Jacklin's feedback [was] the initiation of this
process."

I was pleased and excited that we were going to begin doing
something, but I was skeptical and very disappointed that Linfield
had chosen not to receive a legal opinion. My guess is that through
her interviews and documentation collection, Pam discovered we
had some relatively serious Title IX compliance problems. Had Linfield received that assessment from an attorney, I think the college
would have been more immediately bound to correct the situation.
By not receiving a legal opinion, Linfield would be free to set its
own pace in the compliance process.

In defense of Linfield, although I was frustrated by this tactic, it
was sound. Almost any leadership theory advises building internal

consensus among stakeholders, especially when the projected out-come is uncomfortable change. I do believe that Linfield was at-tempting to work within its own systems, with its own personnel, and trying to build consensus for the process of engaging a proac-tive Title IX compliance initiative. The problems were that the ath-letic department was fragmented over the issue and the leadership was dysfunctional. The athletic department was incapable of partic-ipating in a leadership initiative that essentially called into question much of what Ad believed in and had built over the past quarter century. It just wasn't going to happen.

The meeting proceeded with Bill Apel identifying both long- and short-term goals. According to Bill, we were to develop "long-term goals which [would] be part of the planning process for Lin-field College." Bill went on to say that "those closely involved in the athletic programs (athletic department and coaches) [would] need to provide leadership in discussions and planning," and that our short-term goals would include "(a) Assuring common written policies and practices govern men's and women's athletics and that female and male students receive substantially equal treatment; and (b) Expanding women's participation in athletics as opportunities become available based both on interest and readiness of female student-athletes and availability of financial and other resources for program development."

It all sounded pretty great except for the second short-term goal. Presumed lack of interest and resources is an excuse used by schools across the country to justify shortchanging women's school sport programs. If these were indeed our goals, then Linfield had a built-in mechanism to justify maintenance of a disparate status quo. In addition, I believed, from my reading and study, that we were assuming a position that was not legally defensible.

I voiced my concerns about short-term goal number two, and the administration indicated it would take my comments under ad-visement and run them by Pam. Various coaches asked questions and expressed concerns. For the most part, the women's sport coaches queried the process and urged openness. Most of the men's sport coaches feigned confusion and concern about why we were even raising these issues. Ed Langsdorf, Ad's successor as head football coach, just couldn't believe that the way we'd been operating was a problem. He asked if we'd "been in the dark for the past twenty-one years?" The president replied, "We [weren't] the only ones who've been in the dark." That's another typical counter used by many schools, the "everybody does it" defense, which really isn't a defense at all. It seemed that many just didn't think we had an equity problem, or perhaps it was beginning to dawn on them that with limited resources, equity would mean a redistribution of the pie, and their slice might become a bit smaller, an outcome they were highly motivated to avoid.

At one point in the discussion, after considerable debate about the merits of the law, interpreting the law, and its apparent flaws and needlessness, I pointed out that it really didn't matter whether we liked it, it was in fact the law. At that, Ed lost it. He turned red in the face and angrily addressed me: "Don't hammer us over the head with the law!" He went on to say that he just didn't believe there was adequate participation interest to justify developing our women's sports programs, regardless of funding availability. According to Ad, at the high school level nationally, athletic participation was 64 percent male and 36 percent female. His point was that there weren't enough female sport participants at the high school level to recruit from. In reality there are many more high school female sport participants than available collegiate opportunities. Statistics from the National Federation of State High School Associations indicate that during the 1999–2000 year, there were 2,675,874 girls participating in high school sports. Recent collegiate participation numbers indicate that the total number of female sport participation opportunities has yet to exceed 200,000.

Ultimately, Ad agreed to begin work on the first short-term goal, writing down operating policies and practices. Jay Locey (the defensive football coach) suggested we simply drop men's minor sports and be done with the equity issue. Ad offered that if we just dropped football we'd be fine in regard to the proportionality aspects of gender equity. It was amazing; they thought they were making completely unrealistic, ridiculous suggestions to show how absurd the idea of gender equity was. In reality, I thought Ad's suggestion was pretty good. Eliminating football would take care of the problem while maintaining the widest possible scope of alternative men's sports for male athletes to participate in. Further, the myth that football financially supports not only itself but entire athletic departments is just that, a myth. The NCAA's own evidence shows that most often all sports lose money, especially at the NAIA and NCAA Division III levels.

Football programs rarely support themselves, let alone entire athletic departments, and in most cases there isn't any financial reason for football to be viewed as sport's sacred cow. I did not say all this, although maybe I should have, but they already suspected I was a half-crazy "feminazi," and support for eliminating football would only have confirmed their suspicions. The president responded that all viable options would be considered as part of the planning process. The meeting ended, and our internal Title IX process was officially launched—or so I thought.

6

Internal Efforts

Although I was on leave and fully involved in my doctoral studies, I willingly agreed to be involved in Linfield's gender-equity process. I forwarded to Bill and Ad the times I could meet, as well as background information regarding Linfield policy issues, potential areas of inquiry, and topics for discussion regarding Title IX compliance. Even now I wonder if the scheduling of Linfield's Title IX process during a time my availability would be limited was accidental or purposeful. It really doesn't matter. But at the time it seemed one more example of ongoing efforts to limit my ability to have an impact on our compliance efforts and punish me through inconvenience for bringing gender-equity issues up in the first place.

Around the time that we were working out scheduling details, the February 25 issue of the student newspaper, the *Linfield Review*, printed an article titled: "Title IX Audit Data Inconclusive." I guess it shouldn't have surprised me.

The main text of the article began "The result of a voluntary Title IX audit last year seems to be good news for Linfield. Portland attorney Pam Jacklin implied the college complies with Title IX. . . . Jacklin began Linfield's voluntary Title IX audit last spring at the request of President Vivian Bull and revealed her findings late last fall." The article went on to quote Bill Apel: "[Jacklin] did not in any way indicate that we are out of compliance with Title IX, but she did indicate it is important for Linfield to keep its house in order in relation to gender equity issues." Ad was quoted: "I wanted to have an expert come in and find out if there were any areas that we needed to be concerned with. So far there really hasn't been anything pointed out."

Here we were scheduling meetings to begin the process of reviewing our Title IX compliance status in response to Pam's direction to "get our house in order," and the school paper was saying we didn't have a problem. The reality was we weren't complying with Title IX. The article went on quoting Ad: "we've got common policies on all sports . . . [and] we have been trying to do things like expand women's basketball." I'd recently been berated by Ad for stating that we'd played some JV women's basketball games, and here he was using that as an example of the equity progress we were making. The image Linfield portrayed for public consumption was, at the very least, inconsistent with reality.

Toward the end of February, Bill called me at home to let me know a copy of the Athletic Department policy manual Ad had drafted would be coming via Federal Express, and that our second Title IX meeting—scheduled specifically to begin review of the manual—would be February 28. I dutifully reviewed the manual and before the meeting spoke with Bill about it. He agreed that the document "need[ed] more work" but went on to say that working on the document would need to be handled delicately because Ad thought it was good to go.

On February 28 I went to campus to attend the meeting and later met separately with President Bull. Bill opened the meeting by thanking everyone for the information he had received. He clarified the meeting parameters, time line, and goals, and indicated that after we reviewed Ad's draft of the manual, a small group would be appointed to revise and finalize it.

The meeting was not well received by Ad. All the coaches had questions and comments about the manual draft, which Ad responded to angrily. At one point he exploded, heatedly asking Bill and the president exactly what his role as athletic director was if it wasn't to establish policies and practices. Ad fumed that it bothered the "heck" out of him to have "all the responsibility with no authority!" Ad concluded by informing all present that he wanted the manual accepted as he had put it together—period. The reality was, however, that the department was united and didn't agree with Ad. Ad's draft did not reflect department policies and practices. It reflected Ad's ideas about how he wanted to control the department, not what we had been doing or would agree to do.

During my later meeting with President Bull, I again requested that women's and men's athletics be separated, at least for the duration of our Title IX process. When I had first come to Linfield, the women's and men's sport programs were separate and the athletic directors for each, at least in theory, were considered equal. After the women's athletic director resigned, the position I assumed was a lesser position as assistant athletic director, reporting to Ad as the athletic director. Sadly, this is typical at many colleges. One of the negative consequences of Title IX has been the loss of women's sport administrative leadership and autonomy. Although not required by Title IX, in the aftermath of its passage many schools combined their women's and men's athletic departments. Almost without exception the women's sport leadership was lost, with female athletic directors assigned secondary and tertiary positions under existing male athletic directors.

According to a twenty-three-year study by Vivian Acosta and Linda Carpenter (*Women in Intercollegiate Sport*), in 1972 more than 90 percent of women's programs were administered and directed by women. By 1994, less than 21 percent of those same programs were administered and directed by women, and by 2000 the number of women who were head athletic administrators had dropped to just over 17 percent. Given Linfield's relatively recent sport leadership history, there was precedent to separate women's and men's athletics. I felt it was impossible to move forward under a combined leadership structure with Ad at the helm, but my request fell on deaf ears.

About a month later, Bill called me at home to inform me that the small group to review the manual had been selected and would include Garry Killgore, Laura Kenow, Bill, and me. There was, however, a problem: the entire committee (with the exception of Bill) was composed of untenured, junior faculty. This meant that we had everything to lose—including our jobs—by bucking the status quo and almost no ability to proactively support change.

Bill outlined the manual development process, and we ended the conversation with my query regarding the legal defensibility of the language in the second short-term goal. Bill responded that he had followed up with Pam Jacklin about the language and she hadn't gotten back to him. However, he had looked into the matter himself and agreed that I was correct. A lack of funds was not a defensible argument when an institution was under Title IX compliance scrutiny. Bill readily admitted this error to me, but never clarified the correction more broadly.

Spring concluded and the school year drew to a close. There were various dust-ups and inquiries led by Ad attacking women's sport coaches—even in my absence—myself included. Ad continued to question preapproved budget expenditures, especially when it came to swimming. The softball coach's athlete meal expenditures were scrutinized, and Mary Kincaid was confronted by Ad about various women's sports actions and inactions. Life in the Linfield athletic department trudged on.

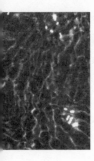

7

Coming Together and Falling Apart

That spring (April 1994) the dean called me at home and asked that I meet with him to discuss the school's mediation proposal. I'd always liked Ken Goodrich. He is a quiet, thoughtful man, slight in stature, with a craggy face clearly aged by the pressures of his position. Ken was uncomfortable with conflict and personnel issues and seemed overwhelmed by the situation he currently faced.

Ken described to me the mediation format: the first meeting would involve Ad and me separately talking with Kenton Hill (a Portland-based professional mediator and leadership coach) to hear what he had to offer via mediation and "leadership coaching." It would be an exploratory meeting, in which the parameters of the issue would be delineated. These might include school issues, personality conflict issues, management problems, gender-equity problems, and legal problems. After this first meeting, Kenton would assess our situation, get back to Linfield with his perception of the problem(s) and possible benefits of mediation and leadership coaching, and then we would consider where we would go from there.

I wasn't keen on the idea of mediation; I still believed it deflected attention away from Title IX compliance and gender equity and diminished the focus to an "Ad-Cindy thing." I also didn't like the idea of spending time during what remained of my leave engaged in it. (My leave would end with the academic year and I would be back at Linfield full-time starting in June 1994.) I made clear to the dean that should I agree, I wanted a female on the mediation team; although he assured me that it would be arranged, it never was. In the end I agreed to the mediation and leadership coaching process. It would turn out to be one of the best decisions I've ever made.

My first meeting with Kenton Hill occurred April 21, 1994. I would be lying if I said I felt anything other than skeptical and guarded. I didn't trust the people at Linfield or anyone associated with or hired by them.

Kenton Hill is an attractive, middle-aged man and a thoughtful, perceptive, and attentive listener. He had an ease about him, and, despite myself, I soon felt comfortable, trusting, and willing to engage the process. During that first meeting we talked about the problems as I viewed them. I told him about my job description and contract, which included express instructions to monitor and ensure compliance with nondiscrimination laws. I also told him about the retaliatory treatment I'd been subjected to upon attempting to do my job. I gave examples of what I perceived as slanderous behavior by members of the athletics department, as well as Ad's negative behavior toward me—his hostility, inconsistency, and capricious decision making. I shared my concerns about Linfield's legal standing in regard to Title IX, and the absolute frustration and near hopelessness I felt about the lack of trust within the athletic department and the college administration.

That first meeting was exhausting and at times tearful, but with that first meeting, I surrendered myself to the process. I wanted Title IX compliance. I was tired of constantly having to be on guard, always looking over my shoulder for the next attack. I was tired of the day-to-day little torments inflicted by Ad and, as time wore on,

Scott Carnahan. I was tired of being the constant object of suspicion and doubt, having my motives questioned and second-guessed. I wanted once again to enjoy my job and look forward to resuming work with something other than dread.

The next step in the mediation process involved completing a series of personality inventories. I was nervous about doing this. I have what I consider to be a healthy skepticism about standardized tests of any kind. But, true to my decision to engage the process fully, I completed the tests in an honest and timely manner.

In most cases, the test results didn't tell me anything I didn't know. They indicated my strongest career interests involved leadership and inquiry, that I was extroverted, intuitive, and thoughtful, and preferred living an organized and well-planned life. The results labeled me as logical, decisive, organized, tough, strategic, critical, controlled, challenging, straightforward, objective, fair, and theoretical. No real surprises there.

In theory, Ad and I were supposed to be engaging parallel processes. In reality, Ad didn't follow through as expeditiously as I did, and, as a result, I benefited more from the process. During that spring and summer Kenton became my leadership coach. I practiced the various strategies and tactics we worked on, and under his guidance and with his input and support, I resumed my work at Linfield, which included meeting regularly with Ad. Typically, my meetings with Ad included Scott Carnahan and resulted in a closed-door, two-on-one attack. Even so, my resolve was strong, and I was determined to put to use the leadership coaching Kenton and I had been working on.

On June 16 Ad called a meeting with Scott, George, and me, and I decided to employ Kenton Hill's strategies. My first tactical attempt was to ask that the meeting be moved from Ad's office to the department conference room—neutral ground. Ad nixed the idea and was emphatic that the meeting would be held in his office. The athletic director (Ad) technically reported to the department chair (George), but theory and reality were very different things at Linfield.

Ad opened the meeting informing me of the things he said I hadn't done. He was angry, accusatory, and reprimanding—not a good start. We then discussed full-time faculty load credit allocations for coaching. At Linfield, load credit was the way coaching was factored into each faculty and staff person's overall job responsibilities. The men's sport coaches had for a number of years received more load credit than the women's sport coaches for doing basically the same job. For example, the men's basketball coach received ten load credits for coaching while the women's coach received eight. What that ended up meaning was that the women's sport coaches were required to do more teaching in addition to coaching. Translation: unequal pay for substantially equal work. In response to my raising this issue, Ken and George had been looking into the matter, and the result was that the men's sport coaches' load credit was lowered to the women's sport coaching level. It was a small victory, although largely cosmetic, as what constituted a full load was adjusted to range from twenty-three to twenty-five credits a year, as opposed to being set at twenty-five.

Other Title IX issues were discussed. Ad and I were in disagreement about our current compliance status, but we did not argue about disagreeing. Ad again instructed me, as he had many times before, to identify specifically where I thought we were out of compliance. I replied, as I had in the past, that I was very willing to respond to his request, but that I needed budget and roster information on the men's sport programs to do so. Ad replied that I could not have that information, but that I was to do the best I could without it. Still the ever-willing participant, as the meeting progressed, I was able to agree with some of his comments and frustrations, and I took those opportunities to affirm his feelings and perspectives. I told Ad I truly believed we were on the same team. He replied that he "didn't know about that," but that he did want equity, and had never made a decision he didn't think was right.

And that was the crux of the problem. How could Ad have always made right decisions if we were indeed not in compliance with the law? This was a paradox he was incapable of resolving.

Later during that meeting I attempted another Kenton Hill tactic and moved beside Ad (as opposed to across from him) in order to review some information he was referring to on his desk. Ad responded uncomfortably and heatedly directed me back to my seat, which was opposite his.

The meeting concluded with Ad informing me that he'd reduced by a third the student work-study support budget allocated to women's athletics and me specifically. He stated his rationale as wanting to be sure to keep things equal between Scott and me. Funny how Ad willingly jumped on the equity bandwagon when he thought it would negatively affect me. The reality was that Scott served as facility director, baseball coach, and professor. I served as assistant athletic director, aquatics director, swimming coach, and professor. Scott had three hats to wear and I had four. But in Ad's mind, making the support help we received equal addressed equity, and as a result I had to do more work with less help.

It was an emotional and trying meeting. The hostility was palpable, and again the scenario evolved into a two-on-one confrontation. George was in the room, but he just sat there. In private, almost without exception, the women's sport coaches and even some of the men's sport coaches agreed with my position and often expressed sympathy for what I was going through. It was obvious to people inside and outside the department that I was the object of Ad's wrath. In public, however, and especially in the presence of Ad, no one in the department confronted him or disagreed with his position. I was very much alone.

By June 19 I had fulfilled Ad's request for a specific compliance analysis and carefully worded a brief report that identified my "best estimate of where we need to look regarding possible Title IX violations." I followed this report ten days later with an addendum that identified additional Title IX compliance concerns regarding financial aid counts and statistical tests to measure compliance. I later relayed to Kenton my efforts during this meeting and others, as well as my attempts to comply with Ad's requests. I told him I would keep trying, but that as yet I did not feel my efforts had been successful. No matter what I tried, when it came to working with Ad, nothing short of absolute submission and agreement was effective.

Toward the end of June, Kenton called to tell me he had finally met with Ad to go over his test results (a part of the process I'd completed weeks before). Kenton expressed concern that the process hadn't moved as far ahead as he'd expected, and said he'd try to get the new dean of faculty, Marv Henberg, involved to expedite the process.

Ken Goodrich had resigned his position as dean of faculty by this point and was spending his final year at Linfield doing institutional research for the college. I was sad to see Ken relegated to crunching numbers. He was a good person and a relatively effective dean of faculty. I thought he never received the respect and thanks he deserved for his years of Linfield service.

During this time, I communicated with President Bull on two occasions. The first was in a June 1 memo in which I again suggested that women's and men's athletics be separated. The second communication occurred at a meeting a couple of weeks later. I talked with the president about Title IX compliance and our internal Linfield process. I shared with her Ad's statement that he would not make any changes until someone told him to, and suggested that perhaps we should look to outside help.

I suggested the Office of Civil Rights (OCR), which angered Vivian. She became red-faced, her body tensed, and she heatedly asked, "Was [that] some kind of a threat?" I was taken aback, but I guess as I consider it now I shouldn't have been. The overall climate at Linfield was just too threatening. I responded, "No, it wasn't a threat." If I'd wanted to go to the OCR and force compliance, I'd have done so already. I went on to say that my suggestion that we seek impetus from the OCR was based on Ad's unwillingness to take my, Pam Jacklin's, or Kenton Hill's word with respect to Title IX compliance violations; and maybe, if the OCR indicated we needed to make changes, he'd be willing to consider the idea. Vivian apologized for jumping on me, and that was the end of that.

Another few weeks went by, and on July 7, during an administrators' meeting, Vivian told me to work directly through Bill to gain access to the information I needed to do a thorough Title IX compliance assessment. She stressed that we needed to have open books, and that she would instruct Bill to provide the information I needed. I replied that I was uncomfortable with her direction. I felt following her instructions would put me in direct violation of Ad's chain of command. It was a Catch-22 to be sure—do what Vivian instructed and go against Ad, or ignore the president's directive and obey Ad. Without doubt this was a no-win situation, especially when, regardless of who held what title, Ad was clearly the Linfield power broker. Despite knowing either way would be trouble, I complied with President Bull's instruction and sent a memo to Bill Apel requesting the information I needed.

Shortly after, in a phone conversation with Kenton, I expressed my concerns about being instructed by the president to go around Ad. I told him I was very concerned about Ad's reaction to what he would probably perceive as a circumvention of his chain of command; by following the president's directive, I would be renewing my conflict with Ad. Kenton agreed that the situation was a difficult one.

About a week later I met with Kenton in Portland. I took him copies of some of the budget calculations Ad was having me redo, as well as evidence of other assignment annoyances. Kenton was ever the professional. Sometimes he'd look sad for a moment, and I know I saw compassion and concern in his eyes. He knew I was quickly losing ground. Yet during that meeting we focused on what he called DESC strategy, something I have found useful to this day.

DESC means Describe the situation in a nonjudgmental way

(what are the facts?); Explain your reaction to the situation (how do you feel? what effect does it have on you?); State what you would like to have happen (what do you want?); and point out what the Consequences will be if you get what you ask for (what will be the positive results?). Kenton asked me to consider what I needed from Ad to work as a partner and to function as an effective assistant athletic director. I remember telling Kenton that I would think carefully about this question, but that Ad really didn't have partners.

Then, during a July 19 meeting with Ad and Scott, a new twist emerged. Ad informed me that he was "working with an outfit in Illinois" that did Title IX compliance work, and that he planned to take a proposal to the president to have them come and do a review for us. Ad said it would cost between 10,000 and 20,000 dollars, but that he believed the president would be receptive. The name of the organization was Sports Services Incorporated. Ad concluded the conversation by stating that he would continue Title IX discussions then and not before.

The meeting proceeded with Ad instructing me to redo the budget calculations for a variety of women's sports, this time with his numbers. At this point I was frustrated and angry. I'd already redone the calculations a few times and had repeatedly asked Ad for base numbers to complete the budget assignment with. It was a lot of work to keep redoing, and other than an intentional effort to irritate me, I couldn't think of a legitimate reason why he hadn't given me his numbers in the first place.

The best way I can describe the situation is to liken it to water torture. No one single incident was ever all that bad. It was the accumulation of little things that just kept on happening. Changing assignments, redoing assignments, reducing my support help, instructing me to do things I couldn't do without information he wouldn't supply, and then criticizing and discrediting the work I produced.

That's why harassment often goes unacknowledged. There

doesn't have to be a single "big" event, although that makes it easier to recognize. In many cases harassment occurs day-to-day, with small acts. That's what makes it so insidious, and ultimately so debilitating.

On July 28 Kenton sent a letter to President Bull informing her that his "work with Ad Rutschman and Cindy Pemberton [had progressed] to the point of our first joint sessions." The agenda for those joint sessions was to clarify expectations of roles and responsibilities, resolve key issues—particularly Title IX concerns—and establish guidelines for our ongoing working relationship (in regard to communication, decision making, and resolution of future conflicts). Kenton, much like me, was ever the optimist.

There were many other things going on during this time. I was continuing my work with Bill, Garry, and Laura on the athletic manual revision process. I was supposed to be working on Title IX compliance specifics (although I never would receive the information I needed to actually do this assignment). And I was responding to Bill's request to look into potential interest and ability surveys regarding Title IX compliance and the expansion of women's sport opportunities. With regard to the last, I called the OCR, the National Women's Law Center, and the NCAA for possible survey models. In each case, I received good information about the pros and cons of developing and using survey instruments and passed that information along to Bill. I dutifully continued to support our gender-equity efforts, comply with information requests, and research various aspects of compliance. As I look at it now, that too makes me angry. The Linfield administration never took my suggestions or Title IX compliance input seriously, and I don't believe they ever intended to. To repeatedly require me to engage in the effort seems now to have been nothing more than an ongoing attack on my energy, expertise, and work potential.

It seems all I did that summer of 1994 was meet with Ad and

Scott, or Bill; work on the athletic department manual; and meet with Kenton Hill. In early August, Ad, Scott, and I met yet again, and as usual Ad was angry. As I look on it now, it seems comical. Ad was upset about the spring 1994 softball end-of-season awards banquet. According to Ad, the softball coach hadn't followed policy, and he wanted to know why. He was agitated and accusatory. I didn't have an answer for him and reminded him that the alleged misdeed had occurred during my leave of absence. It was hard not to laugh. Ad was upset about something he was sure he could blame me for, and I couldn't have committed the crime. Ad mumbled past his faux pas and said he'd address the issue of following policy with all the coaches during the coming fall.

The next day, August 3, Ad and I met jointly for the first time with Kenton Hill. During this meeting Kenton asked me to tell Ad what I needed from him to do my job. I responded and gave examples. What I needed was for Ad to allow me to do what he asked me to do, and to give me the information and time I needed to comply with his requests. I offered various examples and asked that he work with me and not go around me. When it was Ad's turn, he in effect told me that what he needed was my absolute compliance with his dictates without question. There wasn't much room to maneuver there, but we pressed on.

Our second meeting was held the next day. During this meeting Ad and I talked about the past, present, and future, and it didn't go well. Ad's basic points were that the Title IX memos and reports I wrote a year ago hurt his reputation, that I hadn't followed the chain of command, and that he simply could not trust me. He went on to say that he was not opposed to gender equity and never had been. What he was opposed to was "the way I went about it." Realistically, I couldn't be attacked for what I'd said about Linfield's Title IX compliance status—I was, after all, right. That left only repeated personal attacks on the way I'd done things, a classic "shoot the messenger" scenario.

I remember responding carefully to Ad. I apologized for any

hurt my actions may have caused. I told him that it was never my intent to hurt his reputation, and that I had tried to the best of my ability to follow not only the chain of command, but his directives. I gave examples of my efforts and how I saw them as very different from the way he saw them. I expressed my frustrations with the slow pace of our Title IX progress, the diminished capacity of my position as assistant athletic director, and the ongoing retaliation and harassment I had been experiencing.

Throughout the meeting Kenton repeatedly tried to refocus our attention on the agenda and lay the groundwork for what he called a "mutual success agreement." After we had vented our frustrations, he asked each of us to state what we needed to work well together.

Ad went first and, to his credit, opened with a positive. He said he needed me to continue to work hard, that I was a good worker and an excellent swim coach. But it went downhill from there. Ad went on to say he needed me to be thorough, exact, and accurate, to go through channels, to solve problems and not create them, and to accept and support his decisions. He was quite clear that compliance with his decisions was not enough. What he needed was absolute, unconditional obedience. He accused me of bad-mouthing him, his program, and his decisions. He told me not to go to the dean or president and really didn't have an answer for how I was to respond when they initiated meetings or gave me direct instructions to do something.

Then it was my turn. I told Ad I needed him to share information so that I could be thorough, exact, and accurate. I told him I needed less micromanagement. I needed to have my voice heard and occasionally receive positive feedback for my good work. I needed Ad to be consistent in his assignments and expectations. I needed more advance notice and more freedom. I needed to feel he trusted me and asked that he stop going behind my back to check up on me. I told him I worked best when I was given freedom and independence, as I was during our first three years working together, when I was left to simply do my job and occasionally report to him on the status of my work.

Kenton concluded the meeting by attempting to draw together and summarize what we each said. And, although we really weren't ready, Kenton moved us forward to develop a "mutual success agreement." The gist of it was that we were to agree to work together in a mutually supportive and respectful manner. We were both to sign the agreement, which was followed by a "commitment to equity" statement—again to be signed by both of us. Following these meetings we were to move forward by editing the agreement document and then meet with the president and dean to solidify the work we had done and share the commitments we'd agreed to. What happened instead was that Ad further tightened my choke chain.

During the days between our joint meetings, work continued on the department manual. I met with Bill on August 10, to talk about Ad's version of the athletic department manual and its impact on my position as assistant athletic director. Ad had written my position out of the loop. I also expressed my opinion that the manual should be gender neutral in language, and that our athletic department philosophy should include a more participatory sport model. During that meeting Bill informed me that the administrators had decided to support Ad's recommendation to hire Sports Services Incorporated. I think they felt that this might be the trigger needed to get Ad onboard. In theory it was a good leadership tactic and seemed likely to increase Ad's receptivity to Title IX compliance issues.

Sports Services was led by Lynn Snyder, a man I think Ad felt he could relate to. I suspect Ad thought he'd finally hear what he wanted; Lynn was a "guy" and an ex–athletic director (he'd been the athletic director at Oregon State University in the recent past).

The Sports Services consulting team included Lynn Snyder as lead consultant and Cheryl Levick as his assistant. At the time,

Cheryl was the associate athletic director at Stanford University. According to Bill, the president would meet with them first, and the focus of their work would be Title IX compliance assessment and departmental management. In many ways this was good news to me. Yet I continued to be skeptical that it was just another stall tactic. Linfield hadn't implemented the advice they'd received from past consultants, and the focus on departmental management seemed one more diversion. Perhaps by this time I was just paranoid.

During the now-dreaded Ad, Scott, and Cindy attack meetings, Ad continued to bombard me with various assignments relating to women's athletics, denied budget requests for the swim team, and finalized reductions in my work-study support. In frustration, I sent Kenton a letter on August 18 detailing what had been going on since our last meeting. I told him that I didn't "honestly believe that things [would] get better regardless of agreements signed, and I doubt[ed] that agreement signatures [would] really give me much of a leg to stand on given Ad's and my very different interpretations of the 'reality' any agreement would imply." I went on to say that I appreciated the opportunity I had had to work with him and that I knew I was a better person, aspiring scholar, and leader as a result, but that I felt the option we were currently pursuing would "do little more than hang me out to dry." I asked if there were any other options we could pursue.

Kenton called after receiving the letter. He expressed concern and recognized that clearly Ad was "tightening the screws" on me in response to our work together. Kenton stated that he probably needed to meet with President Bull and be frank with her about how he saw things working—or not working—between Ad and me, and that perhaps the best solution would be to separate women's and men's athletics.

At the end of August I had another conversation with Kenton. In this conversation he related to me that he had talked with President Bull, and that he felt that "Vivian [had] a pretty good understanding of Ad's strengths and weaknesses." He told me he had assured Vivian that I had fully cooperated and participated in the process of mediation and leadership coaching. He stated that my participation had been "exemplary," and that I had been respectful and proactive with Ad. He went on to tell her that he did not feel my ego was involved with the Title IX issues, and that the perception held by some in the athletic department and Linfield's administration, that I was a "Title IX crusader," was, in his view, simply not accurate.

At that point Kenton advised me to step back and give the president and dean, the committee, and the consultant group the benefit of the doubt and let the Title IX process be carried forward by them. He advised me to keep a journal of what happened, how it happened, and who said what and when. He concluded this advice by saying, "Who knows for what reasons . . ." He advised me to be careful, to be a good listener and negotiator, and that time was on my side. He told me he again raised the idea of reassignment, removing me from Ad's direct supervision; he thought it was not fair to continue to have me report to Ad. And that was the last of my official Linfield work with Kenton Hill.

Ultimately, I think the Kenton Hill bill totaled about 10,000 dollars, which was a lot of money to spend, especially when the process was left unfinished. As the 1994–95 school year began, Linfield moved on to yet another attempt to either stall Title IX compliance efforts or build internal consensus; I guess it depended on the way one looked at it or maybe to whom one talked.

Part III

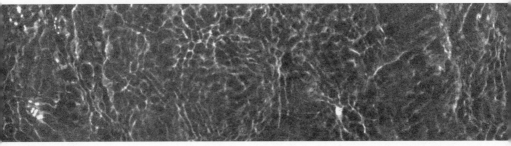

8

Same Place—Different Day

I believe the reason Linfield decided to stop the mediation process without reaching any real conclusion was that the administrators didn't hear what they wanted. Starting, stopping, and then moving on—like deciding not to receive a legal opinion from Pam Jacklin, embarking on an internal Title IX assessment process that didn't go anywhere, and formulating an athletic department manual committee unable to do any real work—appeared to be another diversion in a never-ending series of stall tactics. Enter Sports Services and Lynn Snyder.

Sports Services was contracted to conduct a Title IX compliance review as well as to consult on departmental leadership. Over time, that contract would be expanded to include help with our athletic department manual, which even up until the summer of 1998 had never been fully completed. The Sports Services price tag was hefty, running in excess of 10,000 dollars.

In late August 1994, I received a questionnaire from Sports Services that seemed to target information about position descriptions and departmental staff effectiveness. This mildly annoyed me. The Sports Services questionnaire asked about leadership style and management, and given the fact that Ad had pretty much eliminated my leadership role and taken control of women's athletics, I felt it important to ask the women's sport coaches to differentiate between Ad and me in their survey responses. With that purpose in mind, I sent a memo to the women's sport coaches on August 30, suggesting that in their survey responses they make clear whose leadership they were referring to.

I thought the memo was appropriate and necessary to allow the consultants an opportunity to effectively review our current athletic department leadership organization. I took pains to carefully word the memo and openly distributed it to the women's sport coaches.

On September 1, the department received a memo from the dean and Ad indicating that the consulting team would be on campus to begin its work and would conduct in-person interviews with coaches and administrators. The visit was scheduled for September 8 and 9. Coincidental or intentional timing? Ad and the dean knew that I would be out of town those dates for the national coaches' convention I attended annually. Not only was the convention part of the approved budget, but my travel advance funds required Ad's and the dean's signatures. Both the dean and Ad had to have known I would be gone on those days. Being absent during the consultant visit was a concern to me.

I raised this issue, along with ongoing concerns regarding our lack of Title IX compliance, to President Bull during a conversation that same day. She assured me that I would have an opportunity to give input and detailed how that would occur. According to her I would have a two-hour conference call from the consultants prior to my departure, followed by another conference call later, and a visit from Lynn Snyder when he returned to campus. She also asked that I call Cheryl Levick and gave me her number.

On September 2 I talked with Cheryl on the phone. We talked about Title IX and the memos and reports I'd prepared for the department. She indicated that she'd read some of the documentation

I wrote. Her response was that I'd done an "incredible job of depart-mental self-analysis and that the reports [I] wrote were accurate re-garding their analysis of Title IX." I thanked her and thought to myself that she wouldn't be part of the consulting team long. I had little doubt that once the Linfield administrators heard that her as-sessment supported my Title IX findings, they'd find a way to ig-nore or eliminate her input.

Less than a week later, I got a call from President Bull and Bill requiring an immediate meeting. They wouldn't tell me the reason for the meeting, just that I had to meet with them right away. It was urgent!

When I arrived in the president's office, the meeting was intro-duced to me as a "serious matter" and dealt with the August 30 memo I'd sent to the women's sport coaches regarding the consul-tants' survey. Bill and Vivian asked with solemn looks and dark tones if indeed I had sent the memo. I responded openly that of course I had. My name was on the memo as its source, and I'd made no attempt to conceal authoring or distributing it. They asked omi-nously why I'd sent it. I responded that the surveys asked for infor-mation about immediate supervisors, and as Ad, George, and I could all be considered immediate supervisors, depending on the context, it made sense to ask that people make clear whom they were referring to when they filled it out. It seemed obvious that the only way the survey information could be useful was if it was clear whose leadership was being referred to. At this point, I remember thinking that the meeting and conversation were very weird. I wasn't at all sure why they were behaving so seriously and acting so upset. I thought it was obvious I'd written the memo and why. I didn't see what the big deal was; in fact, I thought it was a glaring flaw to have overlooked the complicated nature of our athletic de-partment leadership in the first place.

Vivian and Bill informed me that in their opinion, my memo may have jeopardized the entire survey process, and that they con-sidered this a very serious matter. I pointed out that the results would be uninterpretable and meaningless if immediate supervisors were confused. They told me that they would need to ask Lynn if he thought the survey was "compromised." They indicated that they accepted my answers, but that I should not have sent the memo and that "some women's sport coaches thought it was an attempt [by me] to influence their responses." Apparently I was in serious trouble. I'm not sure, but I suspect in their minds I had committed a nearly fireable offense.

To me the whole thing was ridiculous, and frankly I was beyond being scared. In the end, the immediate supervisor results were lumped together, and because of that the survey results were not useful, and no analysis of the department leadership and supervision was completed. This seemed consistent with Linfield's mode of operation and perhaps was the intent all along.

I departed for the coaches' convention in Washington, D.C., and used the opportunity to track down the National Women's Law Center. I had the good fortune to meet briefly with Deborah Brake, an attorney for, and later director of, the center. Deborah Brake is a very intelligent, thoughtful, and effective Title IX advocate. I was pleased to be able to meet her and have since heard her speak on numerous occasions regarding Title IX. She is always an impressive speaker and a compelling advocate of equity. Later I would turn to the law center to seek help with Title IX issues at Linfield, and, disappointingly, they would decline my request. In fairness, during my brief visit, it was obvious they were overworked and understaffed; my later request for aid was probably one of many they were unable to accommodate.

With the start of the school year, my full-time work routine resumed. This included coaching swimming, teaching classes, running the aquatics facility, and doing countless secretarial chores assigned by Ad. By this point, although I'd completed a year of full-time doctoral study and program residency, I still had a few years to go before I would complete my doctorate. This meant full-time work and nearly full-time school at the same time. Throughout my course of study, I'd taken every opportunity to expand my knowledge and understanding of Title IX. I explored its legislative and legal history and its ongoing evolution and application. I reviewed past and present court cases. I reflected on Linfield's Title IX processes and events as case studies in education administration, management, power, and politics. I became absorbed in Title IX as an academic object of study and worked to achieve a removed perspective. As I look back, that grounding and removed perspective probably were contributing factors to my ability to stay relatively sane throughout Linfield's frustratingly slow and ineffective Title IX efforts. My Linfield work with Title IX also provided wonderfully relevant material for numerous papers and projects.

It was in regard to my doctoral work that I contacted the Office for Civil Rights (OCR) to ask how to gain access to information using the Freedom of Information Act. The OCR responded, and I put in a request to get copies of recent Title IX compliance complaints filed in Region X (the region that covers the Pacific Northwest). I did this out of curiosity, not knowing what information I'd receive. It was through these efforts that I discovered Oregon State University had undergone a Title IX compliance review during Lynn Snyder's tenure as athletic director, a contextual element I found mildly amusing, and something Lynn hadn't mentioned.

As to Linfield's work with Sports Services, contrary to what the president indicated, there never was a two-hour conference call with the consultants. As a result, whatever information they gathered during their September visit about women's athletics and swimming was gathered without input from me. I called Bill about this on September 15, and he replied that he didn't know why I hadn't had more contact with the consultants, and wasn't sure where they got the swim program information without interviewing me. However, he assured me that the consultants would be in touch and that they would conduct exit interviews after they were done with information gathering. Talking with me after they were done gathering preliminary information didn't make sense. Bill closed the conversation assuring me that the consultants were addressing the Title IX issues I had raised.

Coincidentally, the next day I got a call from Lynn Snyder updating me on their progress and asking for information about the swim program. Lynn told me the thrust of their efforts was to develop a three- to five-year compliance plan that would increase women's sports numbers while "protecting football." According to Lynn, he was in the process of drafting a preliminary report, would send it to President Bull and Ad for input, and then come back to campus to gather further information before completing a final report.

Toward the end of the month Bill called to inform me that he, Ad, and the president had the preliminary report. I told him that I was aware of this, that Ad had been sharing the report with select men's sport coaches, but not with me or the women's sport coaches. Bill didn't know how to respond, but assured me that the preliminary report identified gender-equity issues and offered recommendations that he was confident would help us move forward. I wanted to believe him.

In frustration, and needing to touch base with sanity, I decided to contact Kenton Hill. Kenton had made clear to me that it was okay for me to call him, even though his role as a contracted leadership coach and mediator had for the most part ended. I called Kenton the day after my conversation with Bill and updated him on the consultant's process, our ongoing athletic department meetings, and my frustrations about the lack of information being shared with me and the women's sport coaches. Kenton told me he had talked with Vivian, and that she had told him she and Ad would see the preliminary report. Kenton had stated that I too should have access to this information. According to Kenton, Vivian replied that she thought I'd see the report as part of Linfield's Title IX committee, and that she was surprised that had not happened. She then brushed the issue aside by telling Kenton that the consultants would be back in October, and she expected Lynn Snyder would talk with me then. That was one of Vivian's frequent tactics: feign surprise, then convincingly brush the issue aside.

According to Kenton, Vivian indicated that we (meaning Kenton, Ad, and me) would meet again to conclude our work. That never happened. Kenton's tone in the conversation then turned serious and concerned. He cautioned me to "be careful" and advised me to operate as if I thought the consultant work was a good process and strongly urged me to cooperate with it. I'm not sure how he could have gotten the impression I wasn't cooperating with the consultant work. I'd been trying to cooperate throughout. It was clear he was afraid for me.

On September 30 I received a phone call from Lynn. He told me that he'd sent a draft of the preliminary report to the college and that once Ad and Vivian replied with their input, he'd update the report and send a more formal preliminary report to all the coaches. Clearly any delusions I still maintained about being part of the athletic department leadership team were quickly dissolving. I was, as Lynn so aptly put it, just one of "all the coaches."

Throughout the fall, Ad, Scott, and I continued to meet weekly. During those meetings, Ad would list things he wanted me to do or things he thought he could accuse me of not doing, and then coordinate with Scott on various aspects of the facility or departmental administration. Mostly he assigned me miscellaneous to-dos, and then without my knowledge would ask his secretary and wife, Joan, to do the same things, or follow up by doing them himself.

In mid-October Lynn phoned to say he'd sent the final preliminary report to the president and that she would distribute the report to the staff. Lynn also indicated that he would be in town to meet with the staff the following Friday. I wasn't sure if it was better to be one of the coaches or staff. Either way, I was fast losing any remaining fragments of leadership status.

On October 14 the final preliminary report was put in my mailbox. It was a conservatively worded document, clearly attempting to protect football and soften the blow of Title IX compliance. However, it was also a document that identified numerous "Title IX deficiencies, the most significant being participation levels and financial aid." In many ways it mirrored the original 1992 reports I had produced and identified areas of Title IX "deficiencies" in almost every Title IX compliance area. I jumped for joy. Not only was I not crazy (something even I had begun to wonder) but someone else, a team of expert consultants, handpicked by Ad, had said what I'd been saying since 1992. I was happy. I was relieved. I couldn't help it: I wanted to shout "I told you so!"

9

Moving beyond Paper

On October 21 Lynn met with the athletic department to review the preliminary report. During this meeting Lynn assured us that the compliance plan numbers detailed in the report were flexible and should be considered guidelines for achieving proportionality over time.

After introducing the report, Lynn invited comments and questions. Scott expressed concerns about proportionality as it related to Title IX. In his opinion proportionality smacked of quotas, and he just wasn't in support of quotas. Lynn responded that we would be okay in regard to Title IX compliance if we had a plan in place that targeted the growth of women's sports, what he called a "working proportionality plan." What Lynn was saying was that all we needed to do was exhibit the appearance of making progress over time and we'd be in a Title IX "safe zone."

The sad truth is that most often Title IX compliance input, and institutional equity efforts, focus on staying out of trouble as opposed to doing what's right. The law establishes the legal minimum—how bad we can be before we get into trouble—but it

doesn't dictate how good we should be. Wonderfulness is considerably higher than the legal minimum.

Various coaches also took issue with the report. Ed thought that
there were compliance issues particular to small schools that should
be differentiated from those at larger schools—an interesting perspective, but not relevant regarding the law. George (who was still
coaching cross-country at that time) was opposed to the idea of creating a JV cross-country team for women to boost numbers, saying
that we'd be the only school in the conference with such a program
if we added it (a full spectrum of JV women's sport additions was
one of the major participation suggestions outlined in the report—
something that is legally viewed as a Title IX gray area in regard to
addressing compliance through proportionality). Ad responded to
George, stating that it would be the responsibility of the coaches to
recruit athletes for JV squads; women's sport coaches would be held
responsible for attaining and maintaining the participation numbers outlined in the report: a not-so-subtle threat. George took issue
with Ad's stance and was concerned about the pressure such participation goals would create and potential conflicts in regard to faculty
and coaching responsibilities and tenure and promotion issues.

Ed chimed in that whatever was needed or done, "Football
needs to be protected!" That is always such an interesting stance in
gender-equity discussions. Typically people can agree that equity is
a good thing; the rub comes when it begins to dawn on the "haves"
that in a reality of limited resources, they may have to give up a
little for the "have nots." This never sits well with those who have
become accustomed to a steady diet of affluence reinforced through
long-standing traditions.

More conversation ensued and concerns about fund-raising
were raised. Scott repeatedly came back to the proportionality issue,
and Jay suggested we eliminate the problem by simply cutting the
men's minor sports. His position was that if we'd just cut men's
golf, tennis, and swimming, we'd reach proportionality and be
done with it. This too is a response I've observed many times. Pit-

ting the "have nots" against the "have nots" deflects attention away from the real problem: a bloated standard of living enjoyed by a few men's majors sports (football chief among them).

The meeting was deteriorating fast. Lynn stepped in and addressed issues of cost and fund-raising. According to Lynn, potential donors needed to be approached from an equity standpoint. Lynn believed over time, given the opportunity, women's sport participation numbers would increase. Lynn also thought that the coaches should have fund-raising as part of their contractual responsibilities. This idea and the problems inherent in such responsibilities with respect to tenure and promotion showed that although Lynn was trying to be helpful, he didn't seem to fully understand, coming from an NCAA Division I background, the position complexities that characterized our department.

At this point in the meeting things became almost humorous. I expressed unease about placing the burden of participation numbers and recruiting on the coaching and teaching faculty, relating it to victim blaming, and that's when Bob MeWhinny (another assistant football coach) became upset. He launched into a spiel about almost going to law school, and that based on his experience, "not all laws were good laws." The example Bob gave was *Brown v. The Board of Education, Topeka Kansas,* and the overturn of *Plessy v. Ferguson*. What Bob appeared to be saying was that *Plessy v. Ferguson*, the Supreme Court decision that supported segregation based on race, was an example of a good decision. Desegregation, in contrast, as per *Brown v. Board of Education*, was a bad decision. The absurdness of it all would have been funny if it wasn't so sad and offensive. At this, Lynn stood up at the end of the table gripping its edge, and in a carefully controlled tone informed the room that "The bottom line is it's the law and it is being enforced, and the level of enforcement is being increased—you have no choice!" I couldn't help it; I giggled.

The conversation continued. Scott voiced the opinion that it would be unfair for the men's sport programs to have to share fund-raising or booster money with the women's sport programs. His solution was to have the women's coaches work harder at raising their own money or, better yet, tap into the husbands of female athlete alumnae to seek financial support.

Frequently in Title IX discussions, the question of allocating fund-raising money comes up, and it is often one of the more difficult issues to get a handle on. The notion that if one works hard, one gets what one deserves is deeply embedded in the American psyche. The reality, however, is that reaping what one sows is in large measure dependent on who is doing the sowing and reaping, who is privileged. The playing field isn't level, and we don't all have an even start. As a result, working hard yields different results depending on who you are and where you are. Given the different sport histories of women and men and the broader sociocultural realities women and men face, it isn't possible for there to be as many affluent female ex-athletes able to donate to women's sports. With this in mind, Scott's suggestion to tap into the husbands of ex-athletes, sadly, wasn't far off the mark.

Ed asked questions about load equalization. He didn't like the idea that things might be equalized. The football head coach had traditionally been assigned eighteen load credits for coaching (out of a flexible maximum load of twenty-three to twenty-five credits) and the various full-time assistants about nine load credits. The most that any women's sport head coach got was between eight and nine load credits. It wasn't tough to figure out that, given that courses needed to be taught and facilities run, it wasn't likely that load credits were all going to be elevated to eighteen for head coaches. To this day, although like sport load credits have been equalized, Linfield's allocation for the head football coach far exceeds that of any other sport.

Ed was also concerned about the squad caps suggested in the report that would limit men's sport participation. This just didn't seem right to him. The fact that women's sport athletes had been denied opportunities for generations didn't seem to matter. What mattered was that the 120th football player might not be able to sit on the bench. The meeting ended with an exasperated Lynn inviting individuals to schedule time to talk with him privately.

A few days later, Lynn called to ask how I was holding up. During his visit it had become clear that I continued to be the target of considerable hostility. I told Lynn that I remained committed to the issue of gender equity and to Linfield. I broke down a bit in this conversation and said I couldn't help becoming emotional at times, given the situation I was in. Lynn replied that my reaction was understandable. We talked about the OCR report information on Oregon State University. He thanked me for forwarding the information and for my ongoing input and support of gender equity and Title IX.

My tearful responses were really beginning to annoy me. Throughout my life I'd been able to maintain my composure even in the toughest of situations. But increasingly that was no longer the case. When it came to Linfield and Title IX, the frustration was beginning to be more than I could tolerate.

Lynn's final consulting report arrived November 16, 1994. It began with general observations about how impressed the consulting team was with the professionalism and dedication of the Linfield athletic department staff; it noted that Linfield was not "alone" among colleges needing to address Title IX deficiencies, and that the report had been designed to achieve proportionality.

The next section of the report addressed "points of emphasis" and outlined recommendations intended to serve as "guidelines." This section went on to identify Linfield's complete failure to meet the interest and abilities area of Title IX compliance. Based on this, the consultants recommended a goal of increasing women's sport participation numbers over a five-year period. This section concluded by emphasizing the need for implementation flexibility to be responsive to changing circumstances and budget flexibility to meet needs that might change as the five-year plan progressed.

The third area of the report addressed "equity issues," targeted specific areas of gender equity, and included a recommended time-table for completing a reallocation of resources. Interest and abilities was again reviewed with sport-by-sport participation goals identified; the result was a recommendation for caps on men's sports, and growth targets for women's varsity and JV programs.

Financial aid in regard to "bump money" (that is, money provided to athletics and allocated to various sports by Ad to allow coaches to increase student-athlete scholarship awards—within the bounds of financial need) was also addressed. The lion's share of this money had historically been allocated to men's sports, specifically to football. According to the report, we were "not in Title IX compliance and [would] not be until participation levels [were] adjusted and financial aid support . . . adjusted accordingly." This would become a moot point as the institution moved from the NAIA into the NCAA Division III, a collegiate division that doesn't allow athletics-related financial aid, but the recommendation was in contrast to Ad's earlier proclamation that we were "close enough" regarding these allocations.

Coaching, teaching, and administrative loads were next addressed. The report recommended a thorough review of existing loads as well as some specific reallocations. Travel was addressed by recommending standardizing practice through the development and application of written policies regarding per diem allocations, and recommended "bus travel be explored for 'large' squads . . . taking long trips" and not be limited to football.

The report recommended funding for equipment and supplies be reviewed annually and allocations in like sports be similar. Additional money for women's sport recruiting was recommended, a review of policy and practice regarding athletic trainer travel was advised, and completion of the facility development of the softball field was strongly urged. The report noted that it was not okay for only men's sports to benefit from their own sport media guides. Work-study support was reviewed, and the recommendation was that allocations needed to be annually considered relative to growth needs. In particular, the report indicated that the women's sport programs needed additional support. There was minor concern regarding scheduling, and the report recommended that the issue of like sport scheduling be addressed at the conference level.

The next section outlined a specific five-year plan and included a timetable and funding suggestions. In this portion of the report, recommendations were made to address the Title IX deficiencies noted in each of the earlier sections. The report concluded with a section on departmental management, which focused on the "need for clearer lines of authority and responsibility" and "written policies and procedures."

For me, the report was a huge relief. Someone outside the institution again confirmed what I had been saying all along. Yes, Linfield had Title IX problems, and yes, they needed to be addressed. The Linfield administrators' response to the report findings and recommendations was completely in line with their past pattern of behavior, and we embarked on a long, tedious, and flawed internal process they titled "Linfieldizing" the five-year plan. In essence, Linfield stalled for another series of months.

10

Linfieldizing the Plan

A lthough it had been over two years since my original reports, and Linfield had gone through soliciting and then rejecting legal feedback and mediation feedback, and now seemed committed to mutating the Title IX consultant feedback, Ad maintained that I was the problem. In late November I received a call from Linfield's director of college computing. One of his coworkers, Ted Henry (a former assistant football coach under Ad), claimed that the whole Title IX ordeal was about me wanting women to get as much money as men. According to Ted, if that happened, football would be ruined. I responded to the director's questions about Title IX, what it meant and didn't mean, and clarified the misinformation he'd heard.

Often myths about Title IX include misinformation about equal funding. In 1974 Congress passed the Javits Amendment, which allows reasonable provisions considering the nature of particular sports. What this amendment means is that it's okay to spend different amounts of money on different sports, as long as the overall benefits provided are equivalent. If it costs more to outfit a football player than a volleyball player, differential spending is fine, as long as both are outfitted in equivalent ways, given the particular needs of each sport.

Toward the end of the conversation, the director was so impressed he urged me to consider giving a faculty lecture on the topic. I almost laughed. I told him I'd been trying since my leave to gain access to that forum, but as yet my requests had been denied. He was shocked. He couldn't imagine that I'd been denied the opportunity to share my expertise and knowledge on this subject. I thanked him for his efforts to follow up on suspect information.

Typically, faculty members give lectures after sabbatical leaves or other significant academic pursuits or accomplishments. My original proposal to give a faculty lecture had been denied by the former dean, Ken Goodrich. Later, under Dean Marv Henberg, I investigated the possibility of giving a lecture on Title IX in the Faculty Perspectives lecture series. This was a secondary faculty forum instituted by Marv.

Marv and I bantered this request back and forth for some time. Marv wanted Bill Apel to present with me. He cited the need to reach resistant audiences, the authority of Bill's position as Title IX officer, and his long-standing tenure as "guardian of the institution" as rationale. I saw copresenting with Bill as an infringement on my academic freedom and an attempt to limit, monitor, and censor my ability to share information about Title IX. We had an interesting concluding e-mail exchange on December 6, the full text of which appears in the appendix. The outcome was that I declined to participate in what Marv termed a "shotgun wedding."

Marv responded that he was "happy with the result and [would], indeed, ask Bill Apel to make a presentation on his own." He went on about respecting the integrity of my decision, and, for the time at least, once again my voice at Linfield was silenced.

November 28, 1994, Marv and I met to discuss various personnel issues. At the end of the meeting he informed me that he was dedicated to Title IX, that it was "more than the law, it [was] the right thing to do." He acknowledged that I'd been carrying much of the weight of this issue, and "rightly so as women's athletic director." He assured me that he, Vivian, and Bill would be there to help me carry that weight as we moved forward. Marv went on to tell me that he believed that Ad was from the "old school" and was using Title IX defensively. He said that Ad would not be here forever and that he hoped Ad would come to see that he could "go out on top" regarding this issue if he wanted to.

Despite my skepticism, conversations such as this were cause for hope. Even though publicly I continued to be the scapegoat, privately there seemed to be a growing clarity and acknowledgment that I wasn't the problem.

Fall moved into winter and in early December, while at a multiday swim meet, I again heard rumors that Ad had been working to undermine me and the swim program. According to the Pacific Lutheran University swim coach, Ad had been telling the other conference athletic directors that anyone could achieve swimming All-America status, that it wasn't a significant achievement at all. At the time Linfield swimming had more All-America athletes each year than all other Linfield sports combined. The coaches around the conference didn't appreciate Ad's deriding comments any more than I did, and some were annoyed, assuming I must have said or done something to give Ad that impression. In a way they were right. I had done something: I'd generated success.

I also learned that Ad had been working with the University of Puget Sound's athletic director to threaten the NAIA with withdrawal from the national swimming championships if it didn't move the meet to a geographical location better suited to our conference. Ad never told me about any of this, nor did I receive copies of the correspondence he sent to the NAIA. In the end the NAIA did not give in to the threats, and the conference schools sent their qualified athletes to the national meet.

Other minor irritations continued to present themselves. For example, Ed was in charge of the department video equipment and claimed that football camp money had been used to help purchase the equipment, so he assumed it was reasonable for football coaches to commandeer it for their exclusive use. The reality was that the original video equipment purchase had been from a joint allocation between women's and men's athletics and academics. Football's contribution had been later purchases of lesser-quality video equipment. The incident proved to be nothing more than an irritating annoyance that I was able to clear up by showing Ed the original purchase documentation. However, at the broader level, it served to illustrate an ongoing lack of understanding in regard to Title IX compliance. According to Title IX, the funding source doesn't matter. What matters is what the money buys and whether a disparate accommodation results. Even if the video equipment had been purchased entirely with football money, it would not have been okay for the football coaches to have exclusive use, unless other similarly suitable equipment was available for women's sport use.

Another irritation surfaced during a December 8 meeting with Ad. I felt it was unfair and unsafe for the swim team to drive home from Tacoma, Washington (after a multisession invitational swim meet), departing at 10:00 P.M., in order to have the vans back in time to pick up the men's basketball team from the airport the next morning. Ad didn't see any inconsistencies in allowing the football team to travel by bus, or the men's basketball team by plane, while insisting that the swim team travel by van.

I then asked him about the comments I'd heard regarding All-America achievements and the NAIA national championship threat. Ad didn't deny making the comments and elaborated on his belief that it was easy to achieve swimming All-America honors. I tried unsuccessfully to convince him otherwise. He did, however, begrudgingly apologize for not telling me about the NAIA threat and correspondence.

During that same meeting I questioned Ad about his new policy requiring the women's athletics work-study time cards be submitted to him instead of passed on directly to payroll. I asked if there had been any problems with my accuracy in accounting and queried whether Scott too was to send his facility work-study time cards through Ad. Ad responded that there hadn't been any problems with my accuracy or accounting, and that no, Scott was not required to go through this extra step. Inconsistency apparently didn't bother Ad, or maybe he just didn't see it that way.

By mid-December tensions within the department were considerable, and according to Marv they were beginning to affect students. In response he called a meeting to "clear the air." Marv opened the meeting by informing us that athletics was about educational opportunity and that we needed a balanced athletic-academic philosophy. He said that Title IX was federal law, but that it was not "our main issue." According to Marv, Title IX was about "opportunity for everybody, and frankly opportunities had been denied to women." Marv continued by stating his and the administration's unflagging commitment to Title IX and to preserving Linfield's inherent athletic strengths. He next discussed issues of departmental "climate." Marv instructed us that we were to use "political correctness" if we criticized each other, and that he would listen only to issues of policy, not questions regarding personal motives. Marv told the department that he would be meeting regularly with Ad; he said that he planned to be actively involved with the department, but stressed that we were to adhere to the chain of command within the department. He told the department that the Linfieldization of the consultant's report would be conducted by Bill, Ad, Scott, and me. Our charge was to modify the recommendations to better fit Linfield and then make recommendations to him. This was the first I had heard of this special assignment, and I openly asked Marv if there could be another female on the committee. There was some discussion about this request. For the most part the men in the department didn't like the idea. Marv deflected the discussion by saying he would "receive e-mail correspondence"

from the department on the issue and then decide based on majority input. Not surprisingly, with the overwhelming dominance of
men's sport coaches in the department, the majority was not in
favor of adding another female, and I was left to fend for myself. So
much for Marv's earlier assurance that he and Vivian would share
the weight.

On December 21 Marv followed up with a memo outlining the
framework for Linfieldizing the Sports Services report. The memo
formally denied my request for another female committee member,
designated the president's conference room as the site for our meetings, and identified the target outcomes of the committee's work.
These outcomes were to take seriously the consultant's recommendations and proactively work to increase women's sport opportunities, yet maintain bus transport for football only and address load
credit inequities. The memo concluded by instructing the committee to direct points of disagreement to the dean or president, and
informing us that Lynn Snyder had been further retained to advise
our work. With that, our official Linfieldizing process was launched.

11

Working Hard and Going Nowhere

In January 1995 our committee began to Linfieldize the Sports Services report. Although Linfield had been hearing the same things about Title IX since my first reports in the fall of 1992 from a variety of sources, for the most part the mentality and sentiment of the men's coaching staff remained unchanged. This became especially clear in a memo Ed sent to the dean titled "Responding to Title IX."

Ed remained committed to the position that proportionality "smack[ed] of a quota mentality," and believed if we were going to address proportionality in athletics, we needed to do so also in areas such as elementary education and physics, where he claimed there were great gender inequities in male and female student numbers. He couldn't seem to understand that gender imbalances in programs where participation was limited based on sex were not the same thing, legally, as those where disparities exist based on socio-cultural norms, values, expectations, and perceptions of choice. Both are issues of concern, but only the first has legal implications in regard to to Title IX.

Ed continued by saying, "If the disproportion that presently exists between male and female athletic participation figures is the

100

result of funding inequities for men's programs at the expense of women's programs and if that disproportion could be rectified by putting caps on men's participation levels thereby freeing up monies to be applied to women's programs, then I would be very supportive of such action." Ed didn't believe that money really was the problem or that capping men's sports would free up money. Certainly money wasn't the only factor, but when resources are limited and disproportionally allocated for generations, money is a significant factor in existing inequities. Ed wrapped things up by saying that he thought Linfield should just "forget this proportionality nonsense." Ed's memo summed up what most of the men's sport coaches thought, Ad included. It was against this backdrop that we began our Linfieldizing discussions.

Initially, I think there was a good-faith effort, at least on Bill's part, to establish a focused, goal-directed meeting agenda with specific target outcomes. Our discussions were to start with efforts to establish a safe and fair van transportation policy and appropriate squad size limitations for men's sports. Bill's January 6 agenda memo stated: "My judgment as Title IX Officer is that our continued efforts to insure substantial proportionality must include limitations on squad sizes for men's sports as we increase opportunities for growth in women's sports based upon the accommodation of interest and abilities." With those directives in mind, we met for the first time on January 11, 1995.

The meeting was uneventful. Ad still didn't appear ready to face up to the reality of squad limits and instead wanted to focus on increasing women's sport numbers, which in an ideal world of unlimited resources is the best approach. Unfortunately, we don't live in an ideal world, and encouraging women's sport growth without at least temporarily capping men's sport growth typically isn't an option. Still, Ad persisted. He proposed men's sport roster limits in line with existing squad sizes and then projected unrealistic women's sport participation growth numbers—with the onus on women's sport coaches to meet projected participation goals.

The meeting ended with agreement on the need to encourage women's sports growth, disagreement about cutting or capping men's sports, and the decision to move forward by talking to the sport coaches about reasonable sport squad numbers.

The next meeting took place about a week later and opened with Ad stating that he "[did] not see that we, as an institution, must go to proportionality to be in compliance." According to Ad there were "three ways to meet compliance." Ad was correct: we could try to show a history and continuing practice of program expansion—something that, given our sport history, was unlikely—or we could encourage the growth of women's sports in a manner responsive to expressed interest and abilities. Actually, this latter choice was what Linfield was trying to do, while temporarily capping men's sports during the growth process.

Ad was frustrated at this meeting and made clear that he wanted the record to show that he did not favor proportionality. Ad wanted his stand stated to the board of trustees. Scott supported Ad's position and said that the use of arbitrary numbers to set squad limits did not make sense to him and represented a quota system, which he opposed on educational and philosophical grounds. My position was that although proportionality was not the only way to look at compliance, it played a central role. We simply could not go on without considering it as an ultimate outcome. At that point, Bill decided that he needed to take our disagreement to Marv and Vivian for clarification before proceeding. Disagreement was an interesting way of perceiving our impasse. There was no disagreement, just an apparent inability to reconcile ideal desires with limited realities.

The meeting resumed with discussions about squad sizes, limitations, and goals for men's and women's sports. At its conclusion, once Ad and Scott were gone, Bill complimented me on my conduct. He told me he thought I did a "good job of remaining positive yet holding [my] ground." I asked him if he was willing to state this for my tenure and promotion file. He hedged and requested that I ask him again at the completion of the process. He never agreed to publicly comment positively on my behalf, although he was willing to do so privately. Frequently, as time and meetings wore on, Bill expressed sympathy for me in response to the harsh and inappropriate treatment I endured from Ad and Scott.

Vivian and Marv responded to Bill's disagreement query with the following memo: "In addressing the report of the Title IX consultants, Linfield College will focus on increasing opportunities for women to participate in intercollegiate athletics. We do so in the belief that increasing such opportunity is the primary means of improving the proportion of women who actually do participate so as progressively to reduce the current disproportionality."

During the next meeting we discussed this response and its meaning. All were able to agree with the basic tenets of this statement. However, I questioned how we were to increase women's sport opportunities and still meet the five-year target of basic proportionality without also limiting men's sport growth, unless we had a significant influx of new funding. I thought what Ad and Scott wanted was to burden the women's sport coaches with unreasonable work expectations and participation numbers, without allocating the resources needed to facilitate the demanded growth. The meeting proceeded with Ad's introduction of a squad size proposal—a proposal he didn't give out in advance. True to form, he'd spring things on people without prior notice and then demand immediate agreement. The only men's sport that Ad recommended squad cuts for was swimming. His no-cut and no-cap philosophy extended to every men's sport but the one I coached.

We continued to meet in February, and, for the most part, the meetings were frustrating, with Ad and Scott seemingly bent on taking every opportunity to lash out at me and swimming while protecting football. Bill was ineffective, always seeming to ride the fence and look for a rational way to proceed.

Back in the department, during one of our regular athletic meetings, Ad introduced what was to be his final bump money proposal. The only sport to experience a net loss in bump money from the previous year was swimming. Ad looked me in the eye and said with a straight face that swimming was doing fine and therefore didn't need the money. That was the end of that. Swimming took another hit. I responded protectively. It was one thing to attack and harass me; it was another to do it to the athletes I coached.

On February 21, 1995, while I was away at the conference swim meet, Bill gave his Faculty Perspectives talk on Title IX. At my request his presentation was taped so I could hear what he had to say.

Bill's talk had two foci. First, he introduced the law itself, what it meant, and its importance to higher education. Then he talked about Title IX at Linfield, the findings and recommendations of Sports Services, and our efforts to Linfieldize the recommended compliance plan. It was a fairly informative talk, brief and to the point. In general, having the Title IX officer give a faculty talk on Title IX was probably a good thing and did inform at least some people about where Linfield had been, and where the administration said it was trying to go.

At that point our Title IX Linfieldizing meetings came to an end, and Bill was charged with writing up our version of a compliance plan. We had reached some points of agreement, but there remained many gaps.

Along with the special Linfieldizing committee, over the past year I'd been working with a small committee on the athletic department manual. We'd been meeting sporadically, using Ad's version of the manual as our starting point. This work, like most of the work that dealt with the Linfield athletic department during this time, was going nowhere. In response the college decided to stop our internal process, and Lynn Snyder was contracted to write the manual for us. In early March 1995 Lynn submitted a revised draft and distributed it to Ad, Scott, Bill, and me.

Lynn's draft addressed basic athletic department policies and procedures, while still maintaining the original tone of Ad's document. The good news was that it codified usable polices and procedures for the administration and management of the athletic department. This may seem a small thing, but for us it was huge. Prior to this the only athletic manual that existed was one I had put together for the women coaches shortly after my arrival. The men's programs and later, with Ad's takeover of women's athletics, the department as a whole had been run by Ad, as he saw fit. The bad news was that it clearly reflected an emphasis on men's sports, even down to word choices and phrasing. The manual also minimized, and in some cases eliminated, the role of the assistant athletic director for women's athletics. Despite this we worked, exchanging drafts, comments, and feedback with Lynn through the spring, summer, and fall of 1995.

At one point the exchanges were fairly humorous. I wanted the wording to switch evenly between women and men, instead of always listing men first and having their sports always precede the women's. It may seem a small thing, and I announced I was ready to concede it as such if people were willing to admit they would be just as comfortable switching it. That is, making it so the women always preceded the men. Unsurprisingly, people weren't as comfortable and couldn't articulate why. In the end the text alternated, which was a small victory, I suppose.

On the positive side, my working relationship with Lynn became quite pleasant. He was complimentary and supportive of my editing suggestions and mainly agreed with the policy questions I raised. At one point he asked again how things were going. I responded that things were not well, and he replied with encouragement to "give it a little time." He was genuinely optimistic that things would begin to happen. During this conversation I asked him if he'd be willing to write a letter of support for my tenure and promotion file. He responded quite willingly that he would be happy to do so, but he never wrote the letter.

Ultimately, the drafting process never was brought to closure. What we would end up with in January 1996 was a memorandum from the dean declaring the draft manual "in force." Barbara Seidman, who would later replace Bill as Title IX officer, would be given the task of completing the revisions.

On March 8, 1995, Kenton called to let me know that he had approached President Bull requesting we bring closure to the mediation and leadership coaching work. According to Kenton, Vivian indicated she would consider his request, although Kenton didn't think anything would come of it. This was a nice gesture on his part. It's crazy, as I look back on those times. So many different people independently came to the same conclusions about Linfield, the athletic department, the administration, Ad, and Title IX. Still, with Vivian, Marv, and Ad at the helm, no one seemed to make a difference.

During this time I had been working on another one of Ad's annoying assignments. Since we'd started Linfieldizing the consultant report, Ad had repeatedly pushed for coaches' responsibility for recruiting outcomes—a sort of "or else" mentality.

To a degree, this was an okay idea. However, the reality at Linfield was that all the women's sport coaches were either teachers who coached (that's what they were supposed to be anyway—as opposed to coaches who taught) or part-time coaches with outside full-time jobs. With that in mind, along with the fact that attending Linfield included a price-tag exceeding 20,000 dollars a year, it was a difficult place to recruit for. Additionally, efforts to increase women's sport participation numbers were not being supported by increased staffing, coaching load credit, or release time, or other resource support. The women's sport coaches were just supposed to get the job done. Ad's expectations were unrealistic and seemed to be an attempt to pressure and harass the women's sport coaches, letting the burden of blame, if participation goals were not met, fall on the victims themselves.

In an effort to deflect this, I suggested that we survey all coaches about their recruitment strategies and plans. By doing this, we would be able to develop department-wide guidelines and strategies that could be of use to everyone. Ad wanted just the women's sport coaches' recruitment information, and I was to collect it. By mid-March I had finished, compiled the results, and forwarded a copy of the report to Ad and the women's sport coaches. Actually, it could have been a useful document, but like most things Ad asked me to do, once the report went to him, there it sat, just one more pile of papers.

Also during this time, the public dialogue about Title IX heated up. I was invited to make a presentation on Title IX to the local American Association of University Women (AAUW) group, which I did on March 27 in McMinnville. It was a fairly innocuous presentation, educational and informational in focus, and worded so as not to accuse Linfield of any wrong. A few days later I gave a similar presentation on campus for women's history month. The main difference between the two sessions was pointed questioning about Linfield's Title IX compliance status from Linfield faculty and staff members and the dean of students, Dave Hansen, during the on-campus presentation. I responded carefully but openly that Linfield did have some specific Title IX compliance problems; yes, we were in violation of the law.

After that presentation, Dave Hansen sent me a follow-up e-mail. His message focused on three points. First, he reasoned that if there were twice as many male high school athletes as female high school athletes, then wasn't it okay for there to be twice as many college opportunities for males? And, if this disparity wasn't maintained, would that mean the male athletes were somehow underrepresented? Second, he wondered what sport I might recommend adding for women at Linfield, assuming we were not providing sufficient opportunities. Third he asked, "Can you name a woman athlete at Linfield that doesn't have sufficient opportunity now because of their sex? Who? In what sport? How?"

Aside from Dave's confusion, other feedback was fairly supportive. The director of Linfield's international programs sent an e-mail saying, "I thought you did a splendid job today. Thanks very much for helping clarify what Title IX is all about, and keep up the good work!" One Linfield faculty member, despite advice from her immediate supervisor to steer clear of me and not be seen in my company, also sent words of encouragement and support and complimented me on my presentation.

Later that day, Ken Wheeler from the *Oregonian* called to ask my opinion on the recently released Brown University decision (which said Brown was in violation of Title IX). I responded to his questions regarding possible meanings, interpretations, and applications of the decision, but declined to make Linfield-specific comments. Over time, in response to repeated appeals by Brown University, the case worked its way through the court system to the Supreme Court. In September 1997, the Supreme Court declined to hear the case, which meant that the lower court ruling would stand. That ruling, as described earlier, found Brown in violation of Title IX and sharpened the focus of Title IX compliance in regard to interest and abilities in achieving substantial proportionality.

On March 31 the school newspaper printed an editorial entitled "Who's Afraid of Title IX Talks?" The editorial began "A nationally recognized scholar spoke at a casual noon-time meeting on Tuesday. She is preparing a dissertation and speaking before a powerful national conference this summer. And, she is one of Linfield's very own. . . . Despite these credentials . . . Cindy Pemberton . . . gave her first scholarly lecture at her home institution on the invitation of a student club, not the administration." The article queried why Linfield was unable to schedule me to speak on Title IX during the faculty lecture series: "Perhaps there was a sudden rush of faculty eager to speak this year. Perhaps it was an innocent oversight. Or, perhaps someone has a lot to lose by letting her speak." The article went on for a few more paragraphs, casting Linfield in a poor light. I didn't have anything to do with the article and didn't even know it was coming out until I too read it in the school paper, but I'm sure Linfield believed I was behind it.

On April 4, I responded via e-mail to Dave Hansen's earlier query. I tried to address each of his questions, drawing on the underlying legal premise of Title IX, information from the Brown decision, and of course my own background and expertise with Linfield's particular gender-equity issues. To his third question, asking specifically who at Linfield had been denied opportunities, I responded as follows:

> Regarding naming students who have been and/or are presently experiencing discrimination, i.e., not receiving equitable opportunities, well here goes . . .
>
> (1) I'd refer you to the entire sport rosters of most of our women's sports programs. Under the law there are 13 different compliance categories, and we are not currently in compliance in all of them. Some glaring areas of concern include: coaching load allocations for both full and part-time personnel, recruiting resources, mode of transportation, publicity and support services. This is not an exhaustive list, but I assume you get the point.
>
> (2) Other discriminated women include all the women who have over the years been denied an opportunity to compete because JV programs were not available. Examples include: softball (Joanne English's [Linfield's prior women's athletic director] request for JV softball was turned down as you recall), volleyball (almost every year athletes are cut, i.e., they don't make the varsity team).
>
> (3) "[N]ameless" others . . . i.e., women who didn't come to Linfield because of lack of opportunity, and those women on

campus who don't go out for sports due to lack of opportunity
. . . i.e., people don't sign up for classes that are not offered.

I concluded that e-mail with the following commentary:

> I did not go into these specifics during my presentation in-
> tentionally. My intent was to be somewhat non-specific, in-
> formational and general. . . . I opted for this route in another
> of many attempts to be supportive of Linfield's efforts to ad-
> dress Title IX compliance. Perhaps questions, such as the ones
> you have asked, might have been better addressed had I cho-
> sen to speak in specifics about Linfield.
>
> Dave, I fully recognize that change is often difficult and
> painful. I have, and continue to suffer retaliation and harass-
> ment for having raised these issues. I have absolutely no con-
> fidence in Linfield's ability to prevent ongoing retaliation and
> harassment, but remain committed to gender equity and Title
> IX compliance. This federal law is 23 years old. That is older
> than most of our Linfield students have been alive. I am sim-
> ply unwilling to wait any more "lifetimes."

I didn't hear back from Dave again. Sadly, it was during this time
that what had been a strong and supportive personal and professional relationship, a friendship between Tim and Dave that included sports broadcasting and shared holiday time, not to mention
academic camaraderie, came to an abrupt end. For me, another particularly difficult aspect of all that transpired was that those close to
me suffered because of me. Battle lines were drawn and, for those
who stood beside me, even decade-old friendships ended.

In April Bill revealed our Linfieldized Title IX report. His April 5
draft covered the basic areas of Title IX compliance we'd been working through and, in my view, not only left the college legally vulnerable, but inaccurately represented me and my views in many

areas. The drafting process went back and forth, with Bill making some adjustments and changes, but in the end, the final report fell short of Title IX compliance.

Throughout our Title IX gender-equity work, I was repeatedly accused of not being a team player. In one respect I resented that remark. From 1992 through the early summer of 1995, I fully engaged in every one of Linfield's failed efforts to address gender-equity problems. In another respect that label was accurate. If being a team player meant playing on a team that violated federal law, not to mention discriminated against women, I didn't want any part of that team.

On April 24 I submitted a "Title IX Consultant Report Response Clarification" to Bill and placed it on reserve in the library alongside his version of the Linfieldized Title IX plan. My response addressed the issues of proportionality, coaching and teaching load credit, travel, equipment and supplies, recruiting, facilities, publicity, and work-study support, and included an organizational chart and closing comments. I identified where I felt the college had left itself legally vulnerable, as well as places where the report misrepresented my position and understanding of Title IX. I closed with the following: "I REMAIN (as I have for the past two and two-thirds years), dedicated to Title IX compliance and issues of gender equity in athletics. My focus has been, and continues to be, to pursue these issues relative to the best interests of the College and its student athletes." I announced the availability of this report to the campus community via a campuswide e-mail message: "Although I gave written and verbal feedback to the Title IX Officer during the drafting phase of the final Title IX consultant report response, I do not believe my input was adequately and/or in some instances accurately included in that report. Therefore I will have on reserve in the Library beginning Monday April 24th a response clarification that addresses my input."

On April 25, Bill sent a private apology for misrepresenting me in the report. As I look back now, the contents of my response clari-fication weren't all that earthshaking, even though at the time I was furious. What was earthshaking, although I wasn't as aware of it as I should have been, was that I was beginning to publicly break ranks.

12

Breaking Ranks

During this time (spring 1995) Marv queried whether I was planning to go through the tenure and promotion process during the coming year. In a way, it was an odd question. Of course I was planning to apply for tenure and promotion; that's what having a tenure track faculty position is all about. The dean was concerned and informed me he was preparing for it to be an "ordeal." It would later become obvious that I should have been more concerned than I was.

Increasingly throughout that spring, public attention focused on gender-equity issues at Linfield. For me it was an odd time. I was both relieved and scared. I'd been so closed about everything for so long, I didn't know how, and didn't trust myself, to begin to speak openly.

On April 21 I got an interesting call from a mother of a female Linfield athlete. She called to let me know that she was considering a class action against Linfield. She knew that we had been violating Title IX and that, as a result, her daughter had been cheated out of financial aid. Although I sympathized with her and thought she was probably right, throughout the call I calmly worked to correct her misinformation and encouraged her to have faith in our internal work toward Title IX compliance. I told her that every day someone puts on her armor and goes into battle for equity.

On April 25 I gave my first Title IX interview to the school newspaper. I insisted that the interview be taped, and we talked for more than three hours. The reporter, Jennifer Jones, appreciated my concerns about accuracy and the sensitivity surrounding Title IX issues at Linfield. As a result, she transcribed quotes from the tape and sent them to me to be okayed prior to publication.

The feature article came out on April 28 and was titled "TITLE IX: Understanding the Controversy." The article included quotes from many Linfield faculty members and coaches and did a good job of framing the issue. It was a fairly innocuous article, well written and accurate. I remember thinking how good it felt, yet how scary, that finally the issue was becoming public.

During this time Ad gave me his 1995–96 part-time coaching salary schedule recommendations. Although swimming had the third largest participant roster, the worst coach to athlete ratio of any sport on campus, and the longest season duration and practice requirements, he allocated only one assistant coaching position for swimming, and the salary category he assigned it resulted in a drop in pay. I argued that Ad's proposed salary schedule was further evidence of retaliation against me and did not adequately support our Title IX compliance efforts. My objections were ignored, but I persisted, and finally, after conducting a salary survey of the conference swimming programs, which supported my contention that swimming at Linfield was undersupported and underfunded, I drafted a formal internal Title IX complaint on May 24, 1995.

My internal Title IX complaint asserted that (1) Ad's assistant coaching salary schedule further exacerbated Linfield's lack of Title IX compliance in regard to coaching; (2) the administration's refusal to meet with me about it was not in keeping with our policies regarding proactive attention to Title IX compliance; and (3) it violated whistle-blower protections, as it represented further retaliation against me and the sport of swimming. The memo also addressed Ad's edict targeting only women's sport coaches and programs for recruitment tracking. That little memo generated a series of responses that lasted ten months.

The first response came from Bill in a matter of days. He noted that the coaching salary issue should be addressed by the dean, but iterated that if we were going to require the women's coaches to track recruitment, then we would also require it of the men's coaches. This went against what Ad wanted, and I'm sure added more fuel to his already smoldering fire. Marv talked with Ad, then wrote a memo to me. Ad fed him his version of the story—much of which was untrue—and I was put in the position of having to refute and correct Ad's misinformation. I wondered if Ad too had to document his version of events.

In the end, the dean issued a memo supporting Ad's salary schedule, despite the fact that he relied to a substantial degree on input from Lynn Snyder, who indicated that the "original recommendation for a higher pay scale for the assistant swimming coach was based on the fact that at that time, the head women's swimming coach had additional administrative duties." I was astounded. The head women's swimming coach was also the head men's swimming coach, and unless I'd missed something, my other duties (assistant athletic director, aquatics director, and assistant professor) hadn't changed. How Lynn's comments supported Ad's decision to cut assistant coach support for swimming was a mystery.

That was one of the baffling aspects of the whole Title IX ordeal. There seemed to be an endless stream of half-truths, misinformation, and misrepresentations, all accepted at face value despite clear evidence to the contrary.

In May Vivian brought to campus an attorney and editor of a legal newsletter named Ken Weeks. He gave a talk about the legal climate of litigation in higher education and specifically addressed Title IX and the Brown University decision. Mr. Weeks supported Brown's appeal, which basically meant he was antiproportionality. Interestingly enough, during one of his presentations, Mr. Weeks made a mistake regarding the legal status of the Brown University case. Although I pointed this out to him, who was going to believe I was right and he was wrong? The funny thing was that ten days later, Vivian issued a campus e-mail at Mr. Weeks's request clarifying the issue and admitting that he had misstated Brown's legal status.

Throughout that spring, we were also dealing with women's lacrosse issues (we had a women's lacrosse club sport program and the team members wanted to achieve varsity status). Eventually, lacrosse was added as a varsity women's sport, but not readily. There were also a series of letters to the editor and articles in the school newspaper about Title IX. Some of the catchier titles were "Football Earns Its High Status, so Should Other Sports," written by a Linfield football player; "Defending Competition and the Pigskin," written by a Linfield assistant professor of communications; and "Squad Size Caps on Football Positions Start Next Season," written by Bill. Also, during this time, my name was mysteriously removed from the Linfield Women's Caucus mailing list—the female faculty group I had snubbed upon my arrival at Linfield and later apologized to. No one seemed to know how, when, or by whose hand this deletion had occurred.

13

All Hell Breaks Loose

I should have known something was up, but I didn't. On May 23, 1995, I left a phone message for Ad asking about the status of various projects and queries that had been left unresolved. That day I got a call from Paul Daquilante, sports reporter for the *News-Register* (the local McMinnville paper) requesting an interview about Title IX. I was suspicious and asked why he wanted to do an interview now. He responded that he really couldn't answer that, but that he wanted to gather some educational Title IX information. I agreed to an interview as long as it was taped. Paul came to my office and interviewed me for about an hour. It would soon appear that I'd been set up.

The next day Ad returned my call with responses to the questions I'd asked. Of course, the answers he gave me were less than satisfactory, but really weren't any different from what I'd come to expect. The conversation was brief and directive, but nothing out of the ordinary.

The morning of May 25 I woke up to the *News-Register* and an article announcing Ad's retirement. There was a part of me that had wanted Ad to retire for some time, but I'd never expected it to really happen. I'd had no idea it was coming, and I remember feeling both excited and relieved, as well as sad. Despite all that had gone on, I knew that Ad probably didn't want to retire, and that it no doubt hurt him deeply. He'd been a pillar of Linfield athletics for a quarter century. He'd done a lot of good and had a lot to be proud of. He didn't deserve to be forced out, and that's exactly what I suspected had happened.

That same morning the dean's secretary called to inform me Marv needed to meet with me prior to my departure for the day. I met with Marv at 9:15 A.M. He handed me a press release announcing Ad's retirement, effective at the end of the next academic year (June 30, 1996). I told the dean that I felt bad for Ad and acknowledged how hard this must be for him. The dean seemed annoyed and irritated. Apparently Ad was supposed to have held a department meeting to tell the coaching staff before the announcement appeared in the paper, but he had refused to do so. I later found out that he had told most of the men's sport coaches. It was just the women's coaching staff and I who had been left in the dark.

I then told Marv that I wanted to be an applicant for the athletic director position when it opened. Marv nodded, told me not to say anything to anyone, and our meeting ended.

Later that day I got a phone message from Laura Kenow. She'd heard on the radio that Ad had announced his retirement and wanted to know what was happening. I didn't call her back. I was true to my promise to the dean and didn't talk to anyone about it. It wasn't my place to gossip or speculate about the announcement. This was Ad's moment, such as it was, and I tried to honor that.

I'd been completely uninformed about Ad's retirement, but even so, quite a few people at Linfield and in the larger community wanted to blame someone, and I was the target of choice. In reality, perhaps I should have been flattered. Crediting me with Ad's demise was crediting me with more power and influence than I had. It didn't take long for the announcement of Ad's retirement to generate controversy. On the bright side, on May 26 I received the following supportive e-mail from a Linfield colleague:

Cindy, hang on to your hat and stand tall!!! There are lots of people behind you who are pleased with the job you are doing here at Linfield. When I saw the message from the president I was horrified to see all that list of "stuff" regarding Ad all over again. When he retired from head coach it was disgusting and now I hope we don't have to go thru the same thing again. I may even call the *News-Register*. His behavior at the awards convocation was horrid! [Ad had been irritated about the president's decision to recognize Academic All-Americas, the bulk of whom were swimmers, and had walked out.] You were great to hold up under that kind of snubbing. I am so sorry you have to be around that kind of thing. Title 9 is important! Women in sports is important! You are a good person and worthy of positive acclaim. Know there are people around who do regard you with great respect!

Like most things from that time—good and bad—I saved that e-mail. It wasn't often that someone went out of her way to be supportive, and, as I would soon find out, it would be an increasingly rare occurrence. I cherished those pieces of support. I am not sure if I would have been able to endure the firestorm that followed without them.

That day Marv and I had two phone conversations about my upcoming contract renewal. I wanted to have my contract revised to allow some time off during the summers. Previously (with the exception of my leave of absence) I had functioned with both faculty and administrative designations. Overall, my appointment had been considered full-time tenure track faculty, but my various job responsibilities and salary calculations had been based on both faculty and administrative guidelines and schedules, something that was confusing at times. I was willing to take a cut in pay to have my summer aquatics duties subcontracted out for a month. The agreement we reached was that I would be relieved of my aquatics director duties during the summer (with a corresponding pay reduction), and my summer workload would be reduced to one-third time, limiting my responsibilities to those of an assistant athletic director.

It was a good compromise, and one I was very willing to accept. The only area of contention was that Marv wanted to move my entire salary calculation to the faculty salary schedule. His rationale was that it would be easier for him to calculate my salary, which was true. I, however, was skeptical and felt such a move would further reduce my salary. I calculated that over the previous five years Marv's plan would have cost me about 5,000 dollars. Marv didn't agree with my calculations and further thought I would gain from a more clearly defined faculty status. I pointed out to him that according to my existing contract, I already had tenure track faculty status and should have been receiving all associated benefits. Marv became irritated. He wanted things simplified. Finally, I verbally agreed to the change. It just seemed easier, and, frankly, I was tired of fighting. The money just wasn't that important to me. At that, Marv and I came to a verbal contract agreement, and he told me he would have all the appropriate paperwork drawn up.

A few days later, during the commencement activities, I had a brief conversation with an administrator in Linfield's College Development Office. She shared with me her frustrations trying to deal with Ad's retirement announcement. Apparently the announcement and Ad's handling of the situation had wreaked havoc with public relations. She also mentioned that Vivian no longer met with Ad alone, and she was confused as to why I was expected to continue to meet with Ad and Scott alone, when the president of the college was clearly aware that such meetings were not a good idea. To this day the incongruities amaze and bewilder me. One minute Marv and Vivian were commending my Title IX efforts and assuring me that I no longer had to stand alone. The next, their actions left me vulnerable, the target of department, college, and community hostility.

On June 3, 1995, the *News-Register* printed an article and editorial on Title IX, based in part on excerpts from my interview with Paul Daquilante. The sports section article, "At Linfield Gender Equity Rearing Its Head," featured pictures of Ad and me and was peppered with out-of-context quotes from my interview with Paul. The article began "Cindy Pemberton recognizes Title IX athletic compliance as a hot issue on the Linfield College campus. The embers burn bright. Linfield's assistant athletic director, in charge of women's athletics, doesn't shy away from stoking the Title IX fire. 'We've been wrestling with this issue for three years,' said Pemberton." The article explained how Title IX compliance is determined and then launched into a tirade, accusing me of "dumping gasoline" on already burning flames. Ad was quoted sounding reasonable and supportive, while my quotes came across as laden with hostility.

The article addressed the Sports Services consulting report, headlining Cheryl Levick as opposed to Lynn Snyder. I suppose it played better to the media to insinuate that a woman was leading the charge in Linfield's athletic demise. Ad was quoted as saying the report was helpful but lacking. I was quoted as saying, in response to the assertion that: "the study demonstrates how Linfield is not in compliance with Title IX. 'That is absolutely true,' she said. 'There is no doubt about that.' " Although I'd said the same thing on campus during the women's history month presentation, this statement, as quoted in the paper and taken out of context, was to be the basis upon which Linfield would levy its ultimate blow.

The article continued by addressing the specifics of Linfield's five-year plan. Ad and various football coaches were quoted as dismayed at having to cut the 120th player, although no one seemed concerned about the fifteenth volleyball player who had been cut annually for years. The article addressed various women's sport additions, in progress and planned, and placed me in conflict with

Ad: "the study recommended that women's lacrosse be added next spring, but Rutschman said the sport is not a part of Linfield's intercollegiate plans. Pemberton wonders why not. 'There is a flourishing women's lacrosse club program,' she said, 'but their interests are not being met.' . . . Pemberton said 'we haven't been meeting the needs and interests of our (female) students over the years. Legally, if there is a demonstrated interest, the institution can't deny a request for the addition of a program.' "

Much of what was quoted was true. The problem was that Linfield-specific quotes were mixed with general Title IX compliance information, and relevant facts were left out. As a result I was portrayed as a hostile, unsatisfied aggressor. The article concluded with Ad touting Linfield's recent women's sports additions, and Bill Apel stating, "Striving for equity is part of our value structure in the college where men and women are concerned." The article was less than desirable with its half-truths and mismatched quotes, but if anything fanned already burning flames, it was the editorial that accompanied it. It was titled "Title IX at Linfield: Do Men's Sports Need to Be Cut Back to Create Female 'Proportionality'?"

The article began innocently enough: "Times change. Society changes. Policies change. And change is difficult, especially when the process creates conflict among people who are used to working together toward common goals. That seems to be the case within the Linfield College Athletic Department." It continued, referring to the sports section story and Linfield's "journey toward equalizing opportunities for female athletes."

A couple of paragraphs into this seemingly benign beginning, the editorial launched into the following: "there's a telling quote in the second paragraph attributed to Linfield Assistant Athletic Director Cindy Pemberton: 'We've been wrestling with this issue for three years.' " It continued: "Whatever form that 'wrestling' has taken—and there are many tales about form versus substance—it apparently created substantial tension within the athletic department. It is that tension, not the Title IX issue itself, that convinced

Athletic Director Ad Rutschman to announce his resignation, effective at the end of next school year." I might as well have been painted with a red target saying "shoot me."

The article quoted Ad, and then followed with "Pemberton is impatient about changing what she sees as historic discrimination. 'Athletics have been a male-dominated part of institutions, historically and culturally,' she said. 'That's reality. Ad (Rutschman) is a wonderful example. He has been at Linfield more than 20 years. But when the mode of operation has gone unquestioned at an institution, how can it be that it might not be OK (to seek change).' "

The article then discussed Linfield's long-standing tradition of football excellence, the perceived arbitrariness of proportionality, what the article described as my "style of pushing the issue to the hilt," and the departmental conflict that it was supposed to have caused.

The article quoted Ad as saying: "I'm not sure how valued my opinions are anymore. . . . That hurts. Every decision I've ever made has been based on what I think is right. . . . I've tried to do things the right way." There it was again, the crux of the matter: if Ad had always done the right thing, how could Linfield be having trouble complying with federal law?

The article concluded: "From her point of view, Pemberton has federal law on her side and intends to continue pushing." It quoted me for a sentence or two and then wrapped up with "We would join Ad Rutschman and Cindy Pemberton in their support of expanding opportunities for women athletes. But collaboration is a better tool than conflict for continuing that expansion." Once again, if fault could not be found with the concept, as the messenger I was the target.

I remember feeling sick to my stomach when I read those two articles. They had twisted my position and efforts with respect to gender equity and Title IX to make me look like some crazed bitch run amok. I was hurt. I'd tried for so long, in so many ways, to be a supportive part of Linfield's Title IX efforts. I'd been abused, scorned, and harassed in my work setting. And now I was being publicly misquoted, misrepresented, and misjudged.

I cried because I was hurt. I cried because I was angry. I cried because I was frustrated and tired. And then I stopped crying and began to take action.

On June 5 I called Paul Daquilante and told him I wanted a copy of the interview tape. Initially he said, "No problem." Then he called back and told me he would need to check with Jeb Bladine, the co-owner of the *News-Register*. When I later talked with him to try to expedite the process, he replied that he didn't have the equipment to make me a copy but said he'd look into it and get back to me. He didn't get back to me. After many attempts to get a copy of the tape, Jeb finally informed me that he had decided not to release it. I remember specifically asking that he hang on to it and not let anything happen to it. Ultimately, Jeb and Paul claimed they lost the tape. As a result, I never had proof of being misquoted and misrepresented.

Frustrated by the poor and false light I'd been cast in, on June 5 I sent the following campus e-mail:

Dear Colleagues,

I am sending this message to clarify what I believe is a very important context issue regarding Saturday's *News-Register* articles on Title IX.

On Tuesday 5/23 Paul Daquilante from the *News-Register* called me to ask if he could interview me about Title IX. We set up an interview for Wednesday (5/24) at 2:00 P.M. I asked that the interview be taped, and it was. At the time of the interview I asked Paul why was now he doing a Title IX article, he replied that he didn't have an answer for me. We talked for about an hour focusing primarily on educational information regarding Title IX.

On Thursday morning (5/25), Dean Henberg informed me

of Ad's retirement announcement. Prior to that time I had no knowledge of such a decision or announcement.

I am long past having the energy to be upset about being quoted out of context and represented by partial truths. My comments in Saturday's *News-Register* are part of an educational informational interview about Title IX, and do not reflect comments made in response to the retirement announcement of Ad Rutschman. I had no knowledge of his retirement at the time of the interview. Given the difficulty with which we as an institution and department are struggling to come to terms with issues of gender equity and Title IX compliance, it was important to me to clarify to my Linfield colleagues the context of the recent articles and editorials.

Thank you for taking the time to read this message. I would be happy to respond to any questions you might have, and would welcome an opportunity to be fully and accurately represented.

Responses began pouring in. As has been the case up to this point, some names are omitted to protect those who may still be vulnerable at Linfield or in the McMinnville community.

From a faculty member: "I just wanted to send you a note to let you know that I think it is very unfair for the NR and the community to try and make you the scapegoat for Ad's discontent. I think Ad is behaving very poorly, his comments to the media have been inflammatory. . . . I am very sorry you have to be in the middle of this."

From a senior faculty member: "Knowing the medium in which your comments appeared, I'm sure no one on the staff will infer any ill will or frustration with Ad's coincidental retirement announcement. We know you and Ad far too well to be misled by what passes for reportage in the local paper. Your professional standards are much too high for us to imagine that you have been pulling power plays or exercising undue influence as the result of your job description. It's too easy for the simple-minded editorial staff of the paper to draw false conclusions and to champion the cause of business as usual when we really do have to be redressing some long-standing inequities. . . . there are lots of people on your side."

From a Linfield Portland campus faculty member: "I sympathize with your predicament. The timing really was unfortunate. I for one did not think you had said anything wrong or were in any way responsible for any misinterpretation of Ad Rutschman's retirement. You have my support."

From a staff member: "take a deep breath and hold on. Sorry about the newspaper and the way they have handled this issue. They are known for misleading their readers. . . . remember Anita Hill—sometimes a person is called on for difficult duty!"

From an administrator: "I was very pleased to receive your response to the *News-Register*, or shall we say News Resister or Snooze Register, article."

From Frank Bumpus, a senior faculty member who would later replace Ken Williams as faculty athletic representative and serve on the athletic director search committee: "I just want to thank you for your very helpful email message. Please know that I'm really supportive of you and what you've done. And I am very disappointed in the things that another person or some other people are doing. . . . hang in there kiddo and know that Frank Bumpus is a big fan of yours . . . was, is, and will be."

There were these and other supportive notes, e-mails, phone messages, and even letters to the editor. One letter to the editor in particular felt good to read. It was from a woman I never met. Her name was LuAnn Anderson, from Carlton. It began: "It is now almost 36 hours since I read the June 3 edition of the *News-Register* and I am still angered by the two articles covering the Title IX issue at Linfield College." She fumed about the lack of attention in the articles to the real issue, Title IX compliance, and then said: "Ms. Pemberton . . . is portrayed in the Viewpoints article as a whiny female who wants her own way. She's criticized (read between the lines) for questioning Athletic Director Ad Rutschman and one can infer, the athletic program at Linfield. Mr. Rutschman on the other hand, is portrayed as the wonderful, all knowing athletic director who has lead the program for 27 years making decisions on 'what I think is right.' " She ended by saying, "The only conclusion I've drawn from these two articles is that inflammatory headlines and sensationalism sell newspapers despite the merit of the story being told."

In that same issue there was a letter from Lance A. Lopes (administrative office of the Green Bay Packers). The letter praised Ad's greatness and bemoaned his loss. And finally, there was a letter from Bill. Despite the many glaring errors and misrepresentations throughout the two articles previously published, Bill addressed only a correction in football squad capping. That was it, along with some general comments about the goal of the five-year plan to minimize the impact on Linfield's men's sport programs while developing women's sport programs.

I guess it was silly of me to expect otherwise, but I was disappointed that all Bill could muster was a correction about the football squad cap. Instead of taking the opportunity to correct wrong and hurtful information, instead of standing up for what was right, Bill left me to take the fall. By not addressing misinformation beyond football, Bill validated what had been printed.

I called Bill on June 12 and told him I was dismayed by his lack of response to the many errors and misrepresentations in the June 3 *News-Register* articles. Bill replied that he thought I would write a reply and that was why he hadn't. I responded that it wasn't my place to reply, it was his as the Title IX compliance officer, and that by not correcting misinformation and, worse yet, by responding only to the football squad limit errors, he indirectly gave credence to the other erroneous information in the article. Bill told me that he didn't delve into matters further because he knew he would soon be giving a full interview to clarify information. He went on to say that, unlike me, he had informed Ad, Vivian, and Marv that he would be giving an interview. Was he implying, perhaps, that I'd done something wrong in granting Paul Daquilante's interview? I should have been paying better attention.

When I reflect on those times, Bill Apel is one of the biggest disappointments. He held himself up as a man of justice and as the college chaplain, a man of god. Yet he, like many others, stood by, participating by omission in my career's demise.

At this point I began to receive pointedly negative and openly hostile responses. *The Advertiser*, a local direct mail paper, printed the following: "It is clear that the wrong person has resigned at Linfield College!" Perhaps they meant me, perhaps Vivian. Given what was to follow, I couldn't help thinking I was the target. I also began receiving hate mail, which ranged from fairly innocuous to downright mean.

From Baldwin, Missouri: "Given the nature of your tenure at the College, and the turmoil it has caused, you will best serve the profession and the College if you were to tender your resignation." It was signed, "A Friend of the College and an Advocate of Affirmative Action."

From Portland, Oregon: "Please do Linfield's athletic department a big favor! RESIGN!"

From Rochester, New York: "Now that you have the athletic department in an uproar, you should move down the road and leave this institution in the position it's been for years, before you arrived, in *good* hands. LEAVE!"

One of my personal favorites came from Salem, Oregon, dated June 10, 1995:

> I am writing this short letter to you Cindy, in the hopes that you will be able to fathom the hard feelings and negative climate you have created in the athletic dept. What you and a few others have done in such a short period of time to degrade such a proud and tradition rich Linfield athletic history is

both appalling and unforgivable to myself and many other alumni in this state & region. You should be totally ashamed of yourself for the stress and strife you have caused the Rutschmans. Just who in the hell do you think you are anyway? The great female crusader ordained by god himself to rescue Linfield from the evil king? Go back to Willamette Cindy, and take your Title IX BS with you. The sooner you submit your resignation the better off the college and local community will be for it. Cut your losses and leave now before you take down the whole athletic department with you. If nothing else, do it for your peace of mind, because if you choose to stay on Linfield will lose not only financial support from many alumni it counts on, but its athletic soul. GET OUT!

And finally, from Portland, Oregon: "For the best for McMinnville, Linfield, Linfield Alums, Linfield Athletics, it would be best for all if you would get a road map to find your way out-of-town. There has been too much done by many besides myself to have a person as self centered as you to ruin or tear it down. Please resign immediately."

None of these letters were signed.

In late June I got a phone message from Marv. I'd been forwarding to both him and Vivian copies of the hate mail as I received it. Marv's message was as follows:

I simply wanted to leave a message of support for you in trying to deal with the emotions that such letters raise. Obviously it's beyond the institution or any individual's ability to control such letters, but I can only repeat what I said when we met earlier this month . . . that you can't let yourself be dictated to by people who are too cowardly to put their names to things . . . [you are] dealing with these matters professionally and with a sense of your own integrity . . . don't let them dictate to your agenda. That's all I can say about it, other than

to really pass along my sympathies about it . . . the actions
that you've undertaken . . . [have] been out of conviction and
I credit that and I see that, and they certainly haven't merited
that kind of response, so hang in there.

That last "hang in there" was particularly amazing given what
would soon follow.

All these events meshed together during the month of June. E-
mail messages bounced back and forth, letters to the editor were
written and published, and hate mail and even prank phone calls
to my home became regular occurrences.

On June 13, 1995, the dean requested a meeting to talk about
the *News-Register* articles. I was glad to have this meeting—or so I
thought. Marv asked me about the quotes in the articles and
whether I'd said them. I asked if he had received and read my June
5 campus e-mail, and he replied, yes. I then told him the quotes
were correct in word, but that the context was wrong. I explained
the context of the quotes, emphasizing that the focus of my responses had been educational and informational, and that I had
only occasionally referred to Linfield for the sake of example.

Marv asked me about the quotes concerning the lacrosse club
sport thriving, needs not being met, and my response that we were
violating Title IX. In response to his direct query, I gave him an
equally direct and honest answer. In my opinion we were violating
the law. Period. At this Marv became agitated. He disagreed and said
that "we [had] a plan" and so we were "in compliance." While it is
true that when an institution undertakes a compliance plan, it is in
a "safe zone" in regard to the law, but being en route to a place is
not the same as actually being there.

Marv told me he had prepared my contract for renewal as per
our prior verbal agreement. But once the June 3 articles came out,
he and Vivian met, "talked long," and decided the institution
needed to move on. He informed me that administrators (which by

my faculty contract I was not) served at the "pleasure of the president," and that he and Vivian had decided to reassign me out of the position of assistant athletic director. He had told Ad that morning, and made clear it was "not Ad's recommendation." He had asked Ad to give him a recommendation about who should be assigned to replace me in the capacity of assistant athletic director. Marv concluded by telling me that my athletic administration duties would end effective July 1, although I would be paid through the year for those duties because they were not giving me the required 120-day administrative notice. Essentially, they fired me as assistant athletic director.

I was speechless. I asked Marv if he was willing to put it all in writing. He responded yes, and handed me my new contract offer in duplicate. I walked out carrying the folder in a daze.

Things began to happen quickly. Bad news travels fast, and almost at the same time I knew of my "reassignment," others across campus knew too.

I got a call on June 15 from a Linfield associate dean who expressed her sympathy and concern. She'd heard from an administrator, who'd heard from the dean of enrollment services, that I'd been relieved of my administrative duties.

Less than twenty-four hours after the time the dean and I met, before I'd had time to look over and consider signing and returning the new contract, and well before the established contract deadline, Marv sent a memo to the athletic department informing the staff that I'd been relieved of my duties effective July 1, 1995. In the memo he cited leadership as the reason for the "reassignment." It didn't take long for news to travel from the department to the media.

Part IV

14

Taking Action and Taking a Beating

On June 15, 1995, I met with Liz McKanna, a Portland attorney, and began a legal process that would change my life. Typically, people perceive society as "sue-happy" and litigation as an easy path to fame and fortune. In my experience, nothing is further from the truth.

I met Liz through mutual acquaintances. Tim had described my situation to some of his attorney friends and asked whom in the Portland area they recommended. The reply was unanimous and instantaneous: Liz McKanna. Mine would be a case that, according to one attorney, she could "sink her teeth into."

Liz is an attractive woman, somewhat slight of build, with medium-length blonde hair. She immediately comes across as intelligent, direct, and purposeful. She is bright and capable, and clearly likes the challenges of her job. Liz has a somewhat rushed manner, as if she hasn't had quite enough time to tidy up loose ends before launching into the next case, and a disappointing tendency to appear to only half-listen.

When we met she was representing one of the parties in the U.S. Senator Bob Packwood sexual harassment issue and was rapidly gaining recognition and positive press. Her obvious interest in sex discrimination, as well as her reputation for being aggressive and effective, helped strengthen my resolve.

Our first contact was by phone and was followed by a meeting in her Portland office. During those initial conversations I introduced myself and my situation, and asked if she would be interested in representing me on a contingency basis. I knew enough about the legal system to know I did not have the financial resources to pursue a case against Linfield. A contingency agreement was essential.

Contingency agreements work like this: the lawyers agree to defer billing for their legal services fees until the case is resolved. Once the case is resolved, the lawyers' fees are paid either as a percentage of the settlement or in full for billable hours, depending on the terms of the agreement. This does not, however, mean that there are no out-of-pocket expenses for the client. There are, and lots of them.

In my case, I was responsible for paying the initial legal services fees, which would range from 110 to 150 dollars an hour, up to 6,500 dollars. Beyond that, the firm agreed to continue to provide services on a contingency basis. Additionally, I was responsible for out-of-pocket expenses, billed to me monthly. Those costs included, but were not limited to, court filing fees, service of process fees, copying costs, long-distance phone charges, postage fees, travel expenses, court reporter fees, transcript fees, and investigation costs. These costs alone would run in excess of 10,000 dollars. I was also responsible for all preretainer fees and costs (which amounted to just under 2,000 dollars). In the end, the expenses I was responsible for totaled almost 20,000 dollars, and the contingent attorney fees that were ultimately paid out were just under 100,000 dollars. That's a lot of money and one reason why too often important and valid suits don't get filed. Not only does a person have to be strong enough to endure the harassment and abuse that

accompany going against the grain, but she must have the where-
withal to do so.

During our first meeting I was introduced to Lory Kraut, the
junior attorney who would be assisting Liz. Lory is a tall, athletic
woman who wears little make-up and exudes a wholesome vitality.
She comes across as intelligent but somewhat cautious, with a good
ability to focus on the task at hand. I thought her temperament
was a good counter to Liz's. Lory seemed more methodical in her
reasoning and conveyed a kind but wholly competent manner. I
felt they were a good team.

Those first weeks after my "reassignment" were awful. I felt sick to
my stomach daily. I was humiliated, confused, and angry. I was also
terribly hurt. I suspected the administration, despite what the dean
told me about meeting with Vivian and deciding after he read the
June 3 News-Register articles, had been waiting for an opportunity
to fire me as assistant athletic director. Things simply happened too
fast and too efficiently for me to interpret Marv and Vivian's pre-
paredness any other way.

On June 20 the front-page headline of the News-Register sports
section read "Linfield Reassigns Its Women's AD: Head Swimming
Coach Cindy Pemberton Is Considering a New Contract Offer." The
article quoted the June 14 memo Marv had sent to the department,
a memo I didn't get until June 20, after having to specifically request a copy. The news article quoted the memo as follows: "We
deem this reassignment a necessary step in installing administrative
leaders who share our common vision and will work to implement
it." The article went on to quote the dean: "In surveying the needs
for future leadership of the department, President Bull accepted my
recommendation that we need to build on some opportunities for
new leadership, and this was the time to put together that team for
the future."

I was crushed. Even now as I read back over that article, I feel a
flush of ignominy and bewilderment. I was guilty only of participat-

ing fully, effectively, and honestly in all of Linfield's Title IX efforts. As a result, I was not only removed from my athletic administrative job, but held up to public ridicule. McMinnville is a small community, and my name and picture had been in the paper often enough that I was well known. Athletics in the Pacific Northwest is a small community. There too I was well known. There was no blending into the scenery or fading from view. I was branded, and my disgrace headlined.

That same day, a friend and fellow worker gave me a hug and with tears in her eyes told me she was so very, very sorry, but she couldn't get involved. She was, in her words, "too old to try and look for a new job."

A couple of days later I called the dean to request an extension on my contract signature deadline. The extension was granted. I had until July 6 to decide what to do. A huge part of me wanted to tell Linfield to "shove it" and quit; but another part of me realized that despite the indignity, it was better to have a job than not, and fight from a position of relative strength rather than one of complete weakness. In the end, I signed the contract.

With each new development, I informed my attorneys of what was going on. On June 24 Jeb Bladine printed another Title IX editorial: "The Real Story Isn't Title IX." I'm not sure even now what he thought the real story was. The article was written in response to a letter sent by my attorneys, asserting that the misquotes and misrepresentations that characterized the paper's June 3 articles served as triggers for my "reassignment" and were in fact defamatory. The *News-Register* article opened "It's no surprise to see unusual twists and turns involving the Title IX story at Linfield College. After all, it really isn't a Title IX story! The real story is more complex, more involved, more gray and fuzzy." It quoted various parts of the letter and concluded by saying: "We can only hope that Linfield did not remove Ms. Pemberton from her position based solely on the content of our June 3 article. . . . Chances are, Linfield soon will be wrapped up in legal action related to its decision on Pemberton's employment. The Title IX situation has begun to evolve into what many insiders have characterized as the real story."

Luckily, I was out of town when this choice literary piece came out. I was at the American Association of University Women national symposium in Florida, speaking on Title IX.

The *News-Register* never retracted any of its statements and went unpunished for what I considered defamation. The legal standard for defamation concerning public figures, of which I was one, is considerably higher than for average citizens. As a result, the level of literary abuse of public figures can rise pretty high before it is actionable. In my case, because the *News-Register* had the only tape that could prove what was said, I was at its mercy, and it was merciless.

Fortunately, during this time threads of support and encouragement wove their way into my life, sometimes from the least-expected places. One afternoon I found some sticky notes on my desk from two women I'd never met. One said . . . "stopped by to say HI. We are behind you—and wish you WELL. If you need $ let me know." Even now I become teary-eyed reading that kind note. Another was from a Linfield alum, class of 1953. She left her phone number and simply wrote, "Just a note to let you know you have my support. Hang in there."

There was also a complimentary, supportive, and brave letter to the editor from Linfield's head volleyball coach, Shane Kimura. Shane opened the letter by describing his long tenure with Linfield College athletics (which was probably second in duration only to Ad's). He relayed the many positive strides women's athletics generally, and volleyball specifically, had made under my leadership. I remember being surprised and touched. Shane was not the kind of person to shy away from adversity, but anyone who openly supported me was taking a risk. The fact that Shane was willing to put his quarter-century coaching career in jeopardy was a very special and much appreciated gesture.

On June 27 I received a short letter from a 1995 female Linfield graduate. It is a letter I cherish even today:

> I just wanted to thank you for your involvement in Title IX. I understand that you have received hate mail due to your quest for justice and I'm sure this letter won't balance that out but I thought you deserved some recognition for what you are doing and what you will, I hope, continue to do. Though ignorant of the detail, I know that equality in sports is a must as anywhere it should be. Unfortunately, not everyone feels the same. The task then is a daunting one as I'm sure you have by now realized. Nonetheless, I encourage you to endeavor to overcome an adversity and carry on the struggle for equality. Good luck in the months to come.

It is the only such letter I ever received from a Linfield athlete I did not coach. Mainly, the memory of what I worked to make possible for women in sport at Linfield has been distorted by those intent on making me the villain. One of my saddest moments occurred some time later when I overheard a group of softball players wondering why I'd created all the fuss. What once stood as a field shared by women's soccer and softball, with no dugouts, fencing, scoreboard, PA system, storage, batting cages, bleachers, electricity, or water (all of which the baseball field had) was undergoing a complete makeover. From the softball players' view, Linfield was doing the right thing: the softball field was being upgraded. What they didn't understand was that it took a loaded gun pointed at Linfield's head to make it happen. What they didn't understand was the price I was paying to hold that gun.

I received other supportive e-mails from various faculty members. For the most part people were appalled that I was receiving hate mail. Some of the comments, for a moment, dulled the pain and made me smile.

From a faculty friend: "I will do what I can quietly until I have tenure (my boss has . . . warned me to be careful)."

From an administrator I'd worked with extensively: "I just today received Marv's memo of July 15 about the hate mail. I HOPE we don't have lowly scum like the sender on campus! Whether off campus or on, I hope the perpetrator is caught and punished—preferably sentenced to five years in a dumpster."

Others sent good thoughts and supportive words and offered assistance; some touched my heart:

> Cindy, I was deeply saddened by Marv Henberg's memo regarding the hate mail that you have received, apparently even from members of the Linfield community. It is particularly distressing to learn that Linfield has not risen above the fear, greed, lust for power and general disrespect for others that is responsible for so much sorrow and ugliness in the world. But we shouldn't be surprised, for in matters of the heart and soul, Linfield has lost its way. On behalf of the responsible members of the community, I apologize. I appeal to you to not take any of it personally but to recognize that the problem lies with the perpetrators not with you. Knowing that you have been going through a very difficult time, I apologize also for not having gone out of my way to offer encouragement. As so often happens when one doesn't know what to do, one does nothing. . . . Let me know if I can help.

In July the *News-Register* published a story, "Office of Civil Rights Opens Inquiry at Linfield." I'm quite sure Linfield thought I was behind the Region X OCR inquiry, but I wasn't. I didn't even know about it until I read about it in the paper.

What happened was that the women's club sport lacrosse players had tired of waiting for varsity status and filed a complaint with

the OCR. Linfield responded by agreeing to set up mediation between the players and college. The mediation session was held in
the Portland law office of Stoel, Rives, Boley, Jones, and Grey, with
Linfield attorney Pam Jacklin, Tara Lepp (Linfield's newly appointed senior woman administrator), John Reed (Linfield's vice
president for enrollment services), Bill Apel and Barbara Seidman
(Linfield's outgoing and incoming Title IX compliance officers), and
some female lacrosse players, who didn't have any legal representation present.

Mediation by definition is supposed to be a process through
which two sides in dispute attempt to reach agreement. Certainly
there were two sides and clearly there was a dispute. But the scenario established by Linfield wasn't what I'd call fair. Linfield out-
gunned and outmaneuvered the players, and the outcome was that
on Linfield's time line and terms, women's lacrosse eventually became a varsity sport, which I guess means it came out well in the
end.

Throughout that summer there were many articles, editorials,
and letters to the editor in the *News-Register* about Linfield athletics,
Ad Rutschman, gender equity, Title IX, and me. They ranged from
editorial slams aimed at humiliating and defaming me to full-page
features on the football team decrying "Title IX quotas" and pleas
to reject Ad's retirement. All in all, I suppose it was an exciting time
for the *News-Register*. For my part, I stopped reading the paper.

On July 6, 1995, I signed my new contract under protest and
officially began the process of learning to live and work with my
diminished status and public humiliation.

The next day I met with Etta Martin, a Portland-area counselor
whom a friend had recommended. Etta would become a vital support to me throughout my ordeal and a dear and wonderful friend.

I've always been a person who has rejected the notion of counseling. Not that it isn't useful for some people, in some situations,
but I just assumed I could deal with my own issues and didn't need

help. Although I wouldn't characterize my life as excessively hard, I would say it has been complex and challenging. That complexity and those challenges are what's made me who I am. Overcoming adversity and dealing with difficulty have made me strong; throughout my life, I've taken pride in being able to achieve, especially when it hasn't been easy.

My parents divorced when I was thirteen, and things were difficult financially. We—my mother, brother, sister, and I—were dependent on food stamps for quite a while, and from the time I was thirteen I've almost always worked. Academically, as I mentioned earlier, I struggled, and not just because I was excessively energetic. There was more to it than that.

Thankfully, during the third grade, an insightful teacher pulled my parents aside and suggested that my difficulties in school weren't a result of lack of ability, that perhaps there was something medically wrong with me. She recommended neurological testing. I was so young at the time I don't remember much, other than that it became an issue between my parents. I remember my father saying that there was nothing wrong with "his little girl." For whatever reason, this good and loving man struggled with the idea that I needed medical help.

Despite their disagreement, my parents scheduled me for an EEG test. I was hooked up to what seemed like hundreds of little pins pushed into my head, and then told to sit quietly and to think of a name for a small green hand puppet the nurse had given me. The outcome was that I was diagnosed with a mild form of epilepsy, "erratic brainwaves," as it was explained to me. The condition apparently was a significant contributor to my inability to pay attention in school, and hence to my almost failing grades.

I spent many of the following years on medication, medication we didn't talk about. I remember being confused and feeling guilty, as if I'd done something wrong, that somehow it was my fault. I was ashamed that I had to take pills. Over time my prescription dosage was reduced and, when I entered college, eliminated. According to my doctor, I'd outgrown the condition and learned to control it myself. He deemed the medication no longer necessary. I was relieved.

My difficulties, however, didn't end there. It wasn't until I was working on my master's degree in the early 1980s that I found out I was also dyslexic. I'd always thought I had poor reading comprehension, was a bad speller, and did poorly on standardized tests. I thought I just needed to work a little harder to get the job done.

That's how it was for me. I was raised to simply get over my problems and get on with life. Excuses were a waste of time, and excellence was the only acceptable level of performance. No one was ever harder on me than me.

It was because of this that despite the ongoing Linfield trauma, and my increasingly frustrating tendency to cry under the stress, I resented the implication that I needed help. To me seeking help signaled weakness, and weakness was not an option; it wasn't who I was, or who I could afford to be.

Grudgingly, I acted on the advice of my attorneys and contacted Etta. I called and made an appointment, and Etta and I met for our first session in early July. I would end up seeing Etta, sometimes weekly and later biweekly to monthly, for more than two years.

Etta is a wonderful woman. She is strong, caring, competent, and compassionate. She is a healthy-sized woman, and, unlike so many of us, appears comfortable with herself. I remember early on she told me a story about going to a new doctor and making clear that she would not start off any visit with the customary weigh-in. She informed the doctor that if weigh-ins were required, she'd leave and find a new physician. Etta was like that: clear, decisive, and firm. She immediately filled me with a sense of ease and trust. We started slowly, and our relationship built over time. Our sessions became a safe and calm place in an otherwise raging storm. We'd talk about what went on at Linfield, my incomprehension at what was transpiring, and the way I'd been, and continued to be, treated. And sometimes we talked about the nightmares.

Over the course of all the turmoil, I had begun having reoccurring nightmares. I'd wake up sweaty, disoriented, and exhausted.

In one, I am near the ocean, on a cliff overlooking the sea. It is a warm and breezy day, a nice day. I think perhaps I'm picnicking. In my dream a man approaches me, and although I don't know him, I'm not afraid. He is quite large. He is mentally deficient and can't comprehend his own actions. Somehow I know this. He comes at me. I can't go anywhere because I am at the edge of the cliff. He pins me to the ground, straddling me, and then shocks me with some kind of electric wand, over and over again, until I know I am dying. I am helpless in this dream. I can't call out. My mouth opens and closes soundlessly. I can't get him off of me, and I can't make him understand he needs to stop. I had this dream again and again, each time waking in a damp sweat, my facial muscles exhausted and jaw aching from soundless screams.

Another dream that originated with Michelle Barber was especially horrifying. Michelle swam for me when I started at Linfield and was one of my first Academic All-Americas. After she graduated I convinced her to work with me as my assistant coach. Michelle is a wonderfully bright and capable woman, insightful, sensitive, and caring. We worked well together, our very different personalities and strengths resulting in a highly effective teaching and coaching team.

During one morning practice, Michelle looked particularly haggard. I was worried about her and asked if anything was wrong. She relayed the following dream. In her dream I am strapped to a bed at the end of a long corridor in a hangar-type building, on what seems to be some kind of army base. Michelle has been looking for me, and she finds me unable to move, hooked up to machines draining the blood from my body, emptying me of life. Michelle wants to help, but she can't. There are people around us, standing, staring, emotionless. We know I'm dying. There is nothing to be done.

I felt sick inside as Michelle described this horror to me. My living nightmare was perverting even the sleep of those closest to me.

My sleep became increasingly fitful and restless. Sometimes I'd wake in the night feeling my throat constricting, as if someone was squeezing it from the inside. By morning I was often more tired than when I'd gone to bed. I'd clench and grind my teeth so tightly through the night that by day my teeth ached and my jaw throbbed.

Over time, the realities of my wakeful experiences spilled beyond my dreams, and even the quiet moments I captured were violated. Even now I can picture the images from those dreams. I can feel the tightening of my throat and chest. They are real, vivid, and with me still.

I have always been a very healthy person. I eat well (only occasionally succumbing to my sweet tooth), exercise almost daily, and, overall, live a healthy life. Physical ailments, like anything else, have always been something to get over without excuses.

I've dealt with a variety of physical annoyances: skin cancer on my face, foot and knee surgery, and what I affectionately called my "alien" (an ovarian cyst that grew to about the size of a small cantaloupe). In each instance, I dealt with what was wrong, fixed it, and got on with my life. But this wasn't a condition I could fix or have fixed, and that helplessness infuriated me. It was a pervasive, relentless state of being. There wasn't any surgery to do or physical therapy to engage in, just a seemingly endless deterioration of my vitality.

Even so, despite the increasing severity of my symptoms, I resisted the idea of seeking medical help until I began to feel so lethargic I didn't even want to exercise. For me, that was the really powerful alarm. Physical activity has always been a focal point in my life. I can't remember a time when I haven't been physically active. Not feeling the desire to work out was so unlike me that finally, in response to the urging of my family, my attorneys, and Etta, I scheduled an appointment for a full physical.

The outcome of the exam was that aside from my sleeping disruptions, and what would evolve into considerable teeth and jaw problems, I was the picture of physically, mentally, and emotionally exhausted health. I was given a prescription of doxipine, a sort of antidepressant relaxant, that was supposed to help me sleep.

Throughout my life I've avoided taking medication, even aspirin, unless I feel really terrible. Besides my emotional and psychological baggage about being medicated, I know myself. I'm the kind of person who will keep on working, as opposed to resting, if I feel okay. So for me, it is often best not to take medications to mask symptoms. If I feel bad enough I'm more inclined to rest. Because of this, I was resistant to the idea of taking an antidepressant. Taking a semiserious drug to regulate my well-being was an unwelcome flashback, and it scared me.

I felt I should be strong enough to handle myself and my body. I didn't want to rely on medication. In the end, however, I began taking the drug. It took some time, but I have to admit that it made a positive difference. I began sleeping more restfully, and I dreamed less, which was a welcome relief.

At the time of this writing, although my nightmares are rare, I continue to suffer jaw problems. I've endured a nighttime mouth guard to keep me from grinding my teeth, a twenty-four-hour, seven-day-a-week oral splint, and two years of braces, to try to realign my bite. All are daily reminders of the price I continue to pay.

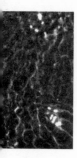

15

Living a Lawsuit

The Title IX controversy at Linfield and my role in it had fast become the centerpiece of my life. In addition to invading my sleep, it permeated all aspects of my wakefulness: my personal, professional, and academic life. One of the most frustrating academic invasions concerned my dissertation.

Since early in my doctoral study, I'd been working on my dissertation. Originally, I'd planned to conduct research, interviewing various college administrators, athletic directors, and coaches about perceived barriers to Title IX compliance, a follow-up study on an earlier work by Miller and associates (1978). As a result of my Linfield ordeal, that idea had to be abandoned. After I'd been fired as assistant athletic director and entered litigation, the odds were small that I'd have ready access to collegiate leadership in the Pacific Northwest. This was devastating. I'd been working for over a year reviewing related literature in preparation for my dissertation. Here it was, the summer of 1995, and I was having to start over.

Thankfully, Bob saved me. Bob Everhart was the dean of the College of Education at Portland State University and my doctoral advisor. He is an incredibly bright, patient, well-reasoned, and insightful academic with a calm, thoughtful demeanor. He helped me work through related dissertation ideas targeted to allow me to use the background work I'd already done, but with a new focus. What evolved was a work I am very proud of. Instead of researching barrier perceptions, I expanded my literature review to include adult learning and change theory and developed a proactive Title IX workshop for athletic personnel. The goal of the workshop was to deliver Title IX compliance information and to work through issues associated with the gender-specific value of sport in an attempt to understand the core of individual and organizational resistance to change.

For that reason, I contacted two female athletic directors, friends of mine, and asked them if they would be willing to have their departments serve as field test sites for my Title IX workshops. I set up dates in the fall of 1995 and winter of 1996 to conduct the workshop field tests. I was back on track.

In August, during a conversation with one of the athletic directors, I told her of my "reassignment." She was shocked. She told me that she had just returned from the national athletic director's meeting, and that one of the Title IX compliance recommendations from the national body was that women's and men's athletics be separated. At the national level, the "fox guarding the hen house" was increasingly being seen as an obstacle to gender equity. In contrast, Linfield had not separated women's and men's athletics and had in effect fired me as assistant athletic director, putting the men's athletic director completely in charge.

Another professional frustration was the infringement upon my academic freedom and teaching. In early August, just days before the start of school, the department chair asked if I'd teach an additional course, Foundations in Physical Education. I'd been teaching a course on gender issues in education and sport as an independent study (which translates to off-load and without compensation). My requests to teach this course as part of my regular teaching load had been denied repeatedly. George addressed this by telling me that he'd talked with the dean, and that they felt teaching the gender course might too narrowly stereotype me. However, if I was willing to teach the Foundations course, perhaps something could be worked out. On August 10 I met with the dean to discuss, among other things, my teaching assignment for the fall.

The dean welcomed me by asking how I was doing. I replied, "Not so good." I'm not sure what else he expected me to say. It was a silly question, really, and his feigned concern irritated me. We discussed various athletic issues, and my official Title IX complaint about coaching salaries and the recruitment project. We also talked about contract issues, and he handed me a letter of response from Linfield concerning the statement of protest I'd attached to my contract when I signed it. Next, we discussed teaching issues. The dean pressured me to teach the Foundations course and, in return, indicated he'd look into the status of my request to teach the gender issues course. The next day, after I agreed to teach the Foundations course, the gender course was approved. I was allowed to teach it for supplemental compensation during Linfield's one-month January term.

As August moved into early fall, Linfield shifted personnel so as to almost completely eliminate a female voice for women's athletics from all input avenues. Since June 1989, Linfield had moved from autonomous women's and men's athletic departments with semi-equivalent status to a leadership hierarchy and committee structure void of female input. It was a sad state of affairs for gender equity.

On September 14, 1995, weeks after I'd filed my lawsuit, the dean issued a campuswide e-mail announcing that fact. The e-mail briefly described the lawsuit as involving "allegations of Title IX violations, sex discrimination and retaliation" in connection with the college's decision to fire me as assistant athletic director, or, in their words, "reassign" me. It concluded with a reminder to all that the "focus on campus should be on our educational mission and maintaining collegial relations among faculty, students and staff."

There it was, a formal public announcement and acknowledgment that Linfield was being sued. It felt good. It felt scary. It was a relief. And of course, it was followed up by an article in the *News-Register*: "Swim Coach Files Suit: $1.5 Million."

The early aftermath of the lawsuit announcement varied. There were wonderful moments of support. An e-mail from a friend and colleague was particularly heartening:

> Cindy, this has been coming for a long time. KNOW you are not alone. There are lots of people in shock and caring for you very much. I don't know details but I hear and will be contacting whoever I know can help. . . . I know you cannot talk to anyone . . . but I can talk to lots of people and will begin doing so. I hope you can draw from the inner peace that comes from the center of the universe, knowing your personal integrity is in tact. Remember Anita Hill as that gracious lady said, "I have my integrity and it is my richest resource." Cindy you are a wonderful woman and worthy. My prayers are with you right now.

Her son, a past student and swimmer of mine, also responded. He wrote a letter to the editor that outlined the ways I had contributed positively to his education, growth, and development, as well as the growth, and development of Linfield athletics. It was a well-written and complimentary piece. I felt very good when I read it. I was proud of him for stating his position. I am proud of him now.

Beyond the effects it had on me, the controversy over Ad's retirement and the lawsuit announcement resulted in a backlash against the Linfield administration and Vivian Bull in particular. This backlash eventually escalated; the end result was a rethinking of Ad's retirement and a decision by the Board of Trustees to hold a closed-session vote to determine confidence in and support for President Bull. Ad's power base was impressive.

On September 22, the school newspaper reported on the growing unrest among Linfield alumni. A group of about four hundred Linfield alumni, calling themselves POLE (Protect Our Linfield Experience), had written a letter expressing dissatisfaction with the administration's leadership and concerns about the treatment of Ad Rutschman. The article stated that POLE planned to call for President Bull's resignation. I couldn't help feeling a bit of glee. I wanted to ask how she liked being in the hot seat. Ultimately, POLE's pressure prevailed, at least in part. On Friday, September 29, at 3:05 P.M., the president released a campuswide voice mail announcing that although Ad would retire as athletic director, he would continue to be employed by the college part-time. According to the voice mail: "This will allow our students and staff to benefit from the special gifts which Ad has in working with young people. Ad and I have worked together for the best interest of all of the Linfield community, including our alumni and current and future students. . . . In the true spirit of Linfield let us work together to be the best that we can be."

Although Ad's actual duties in his upcoming part-time capacity were yet to be detailed, President Bull asserted (as she was quoted in the school newspaper): "He wants to work. . . . He fits in well with the institution's needs and concerns. . . . He will definitely be beneficial." Ad would continue at Linfield in the newly created position of special assistant to college relations. There was no getting rid of Ad until Ad decided he was ready, and apparently, when Ad wasn't willing to "hew to the party line," he not only wasn't fired, he was unretired! I believe that the administrators had for some time been frustrated with Ad and his athletic leadership, but when it came time to try to do something about it, they were stuck. Ad was just too deeply entrenched in Linfield's past and present to follow through on what was really best for the department and the college. It was much easier to vilify me. Somebody needed to take the fall, and apparently Ad was just too deeply rooted to be felled.

The controversy surrounding President Bull, Ad, and POLE provided a short-lived diversion of attention away from me, very short-lived. On September 30, the *News-Register* printed another inflammatory editorial: "Diffusing a Storm Cloud: Linfield Leaders Forge Plan to End Controversy; Now, about That Lawsuit. . . ."

The article called for me to "drop [my] $1.5 million lawsuit against the school." The editorial labeled my advocacy of Title IX "militant" and asserted that "[t]ime will tell whether Pemberton cares about Linfield," after extolling Ad, the president, the administration, the faculty, and "hundreds" of alumni, who all cared deeply about the college. The *News-Register* once again reminded people who the real enemy was: me.

Despite the *News-Register's* efforts, another bright spot of support followed this article in the form of a letter to the editor written by a Linfield faculty member. Although the letter wasn't published, he forwarded a copy to me along with Jeb Bladine's response. The letter suggested that "at times the editorial staff of the *News-Register* has strayed from what should be its primary focus—objectively reporting the news, and has tended to unnecessarily raise the level of rhetoric beyond its primary task." It pointed out that characterizing my Title IX advocacy as "very militant" and questioning whether I cared about Linfield served only to maintain "an unnecessarily high level of rhetoric." The letter concluded: "it has been no secret on whose side the *News-Register* comes down. However, the time for taking sides is over and it is time for the entire community, including the *News-Register* to truly allow the 'storm cloud' to 'dissipate.' . . . Hey, *News-Register*, time to back off."

Jeb responded by clarifying that the primary focus of the editorial staff was not to objectively report local news, and stated that "[s]ometimes, opinions must take one side only." At least he didn't deny whose side he was on. Jeb further made clear that his rhetorical use of "very militant" was not, in his view, "unnecessarily high." He continued: "Had I wanted to reach an 'unnecessarily high level of rhetoric,' I would have drawn upon some extremely insulting rhetoric from others." It was scary to think Jeb's comments demonstrated an exercise in restraint. Jeb concluded the letter, "Cindy Pemberton is waging an ongoing legal battle against Linfield, and in our opinion, the time for taking sides on this is not over." Jeb would, as the months evolved, be true to his word. He didn't miss many opportunities to stoke the flames of animosity.

During the later part of September and throughout the fall, the department engaged in various meetings to discuss restructuring models. In theory this was a good thing. The administration, to its credit, kept trying to allow change to occur from within instead of imposing it from without. But theory and reality just couldn't mesh. Supporting anything but the status quo and total domination by men's athletics was seen as an affront to Ad, and that simply was not an option. Frankly, I can't blame the administration or athletic department. From what they saw happening to me, it wasn't in anyone's best interest to question the status quo.

Our September 26 meeting in particular exemplified the departmental leadership struggle. As was to become the norm at department meetings, I was isolated; no one was even willing to sit next to me, and the chair beside me was often vacant. People would actually walk around to the other side of the room or bring in a chair from outside. I'd try to make it easier by sitting at one end of the table or the other, creating only one open seat instead of two. This tactic of physical isolation, a sort of leper syndrome, served to sequester me and to create a visible barrier between me and any potential sources of departmental support.

At this meeting we were discussing various leadership models. For the most part, the men's coaches favored a "single-head" model, with the athletic director in the position of ultimate authority (the exact opposite of the model we had on paper, that is, the academic department chair as the pinnacle of the combined athletic and academic department leadership). The women's sport coaches and department chair favored either a single-head academic leadership model or a multiple-head model that would allow women's and men's athletics to have separate, equal leadership.

Although there was growing sentiment throughout NAIA and NCAA athletics that the best way to promote gender equity was to have independent and equal women's and men's athletic departments, the men's sport coaches (football in particular) dismissed the idea as being divisive. From their perspective, a unified leadership model, putting the men's athletic director at the helm, was the only coordinated way to proceed.

Interestingly, when the discussion shifted to the idea of whether there should be unified leadership with the academic department chair over academics and athletics, the reaction was different. Apparently, if the athletic director couldn't be lord and master of all, then independent and equal was their model of choice. Independent and equal was in the best interests of representational, proactive, interactive, communicative, and collaborative leadership when it came to athletics and academics, but not when it came to women's and men's athletics. To this day, I don't think the athletic department faculty and staff see the inconsistency in their position.

I sat quietly through much of this discussion, and spoke only at the end to ask why the arguments supporting a multi-head model of academics and athletics didn't apply to the multi-head model within the athletic leadership structure. There was dead silence. This same argument would be the central issue addressed by the department in a number of meetings throughout that fall and winter. The only real change as meetings progressed was that the female sport coaches became increasingly silent.

At one point, I kept comment tallies, noting who spoke and how often. After one of our meetings I shared my tally with the department chair. The tally showed almost a complete silencing of female voices in the department. George acknowledged this, but shrugged and said he didn't know what he could do. It was a pity. George was one of the few tenured full professors in the department, one of the few who could have acted otherwise without the threat of significant negative consequence. Ultimately, our attempts to reach consensus failed, and a vote was taken regarding which leadership model to adopt. There were more men's sport coaches and more men in the department, which didn't bode well for any vote. Unlike most of the men's sport coaches, about half of the women's coaches were part-time coaches, and so not included in the department meetings. Things heated up quite a bit, and at one point Ad angrily announced that if we didn't adopt the model he supported that we would be "making a mistake," and he just could not "support such a decision." That made things tough. Going against Ad was asking for trouble. George continued trying to build consensus around the idea of a single-head academic leadership model; as a result, any discussion of academic leadership over two independent, equal athletic leaders was abandoned. Finally, to my surprise and relief, the department did go against Ad and voted (by secret ballot) to support the single-head academic leadership model with one athletic director. This was exactly how the department had evolved on paper since 1989. It was amazing how much time and energy we spent to get to exactly where we were.

Once the administration approved the departmental leadership model, the next step involved advertising for the positions. I planned to apply for one if not both of the positions: a glutton for punishment, I guess.

Despite the departmental vote, the administrators did not approve the structure desired by the majority. Instead, they instituted a model that freed the athletic director from significant accountability to the department head and added a direct line of report to the president. They also slipped in a demotion of my position as aquatics director. No one ever mentioned anything to me; it just appeared in a chain of command hierarchy chart. In regard to aquatics, I was no longer to report directly to the athletic director for athletic matters and the department chair for physical education matters. Instead of aquatics director being in a position equal to the facilities director, I was to report to the assistant athletic director and facilities director, Scott Carnahan.

In all fairness, in another situation that chain of command might have made sense. But, given our situation—the realities of how I had been hired and contracted, the fact that I had been operating under a very different reporting structure since 1989—the change represented a demotion in my position and a reduction of my authority and autonomy. It was just one more example of Linfield's disregard for my contractual history and practice.

During this time I received a call from Jennie Lou Werlein, the dean's ex-secretary (she'd been let go or, in her words, fired by Marv). Jennie Lou had various things to say, mostly encouraging and supportive. She also told me that while she was at Linfield, she'd heard for years that there was just "no way" I'd be allowed to get tenure. This did not surprise me, especially at this point, although I had every intention of achieving tenure.

Fall also involved a transfer of files and records regarding women's athletics from me to Ad and Scott. It was a long and tedious process. I've always been a person who keeps copious notes and files. I made extra copies of materials I thought might be important to keep, records that could show my honest, accurate, and effective leadership in women's athletics. I feared the records and reports I forwarded to Ad and Scott would end up lost.

Since my taped interview with the *News-Register*, I'd begun to take precautions to make sure there was a way for me to refute accusations of impropriety. I even went so far as to have the designated senior woman administrator (SWA), Tara Lepp, sign off on the inventory I created detailing the files I forwarded to Ad and Scott. The SWA is a position assignment required by the NCAA (the athletic affiliation Linfield was moving into). It can be a name-only assignment or an active part of a school's athletic leadership. Although the position was originally created to ensure that schools include a female voice in their athletic administration, the NCAA does little to monitor whether this really happens. In fact, it is only recently that the NCAA agreed to designate an SWA within its own administrative leadership structure. With my removal from athletic leadership, Linfield had appointed Tara as SWA.

Thanks to the ever-vigilant efforts of the *News-Register*, I was the center of controversy not only within the athletic department and the college, but within the broader community as well. The local chapter of the American Association of University Women (AAUW) remained supportive, inviting me to talk on Title IX, and at times sending notes of encouragement. The chapter members were, however, confused. They just couldn't understand why there was a problem when Linfield had a female president. People frequently assume that just because someone is female, she supports other females and women's issues. In reality, that just isn't the case. Often women are their own worst enemies, particularly when they are seeking positions of leadership. Recall my own initial response to the Women's Caucus invitation.

In defense of this sometimes difficult-to-understand phenomenon, opportunities for advancement are limited, especially for suspect classes of people. Typically, instead of everyone vying for all positions, all the white males vie for most of the positions, and everyone else competes for a limited number of token positions. The result: if a person can't compete for all positions, and her opportunities are artificially limited because of sex, race, and class, then she needs to be fiercely competitive for those few opportunities that are available. In short, it doesn't necessarily behoove women to support other women. Therefore, just because one is female does not mean one is an advocate for women.

Even further removed than the general McMinnville community and alumni and booster support circuit, rumors of my situation at Linfield were circulating in the swimming community. I received calls from various coaches—collegiate, high school, and recreational—saying they'd heard I'd been fired and wanted to follow up. Needless to say, this irritated me, was a blemish on my professional career, and would prove to become a deterrent to my swim team recruiting efforts.

I was one of the few collegiate head coaches who coached both women and men. Early on it had been an amusing challenge for me. I'd call recruits and many times the men on the phone would ask when the head coach would be contacting them. They assumed that I, as a female, had to be the assistant coach. It was an uphill battle to develop what became one of the premier small-college swim programs in the country. Not only was I terribly understaffed, but the gender stereotypes that surround coaching made it difficult to recruit, particularly when it came to recruiting men. Those difficulties were compounded when rumors began to circulate that I'd been fired. Swimmers don't want to come, and coaches aren't keen on sending their athletes, to a program that appears to lack stability. I spent a fair amount of time and effort attempting to correct the false rumors. It was true I was no longer the assistant athletic director, but no, I had not been fired as head swim coach.

Some of the rumors were so far-fetched they were almost funny. In one instance, a Yamhill County school principal, whose children swam for the McMinnville Swim Team, and who had generously volunteered over the years to help officiate at our college meets, told me about a run-in he'd had with some community members who'd seen him talking to me. They accused him of holding "secret meetings" with me. What we'd done is say hello and exchange pleasantries for about five minutes on campus one afternoon. He told me he'd responded by saying that we hadn't had any secret meetings, that he'd known me for six years and I was a friend of his family, and that as far as he was concerned, I'd done a great job with the Linfield swim program. He told me he simply didn't believe the stories being fabricated about me. He stopped short of telling me what those stories were.

There were other rumors relayed by collegiate coaching colleagues: I'd lost my job as assistant athletic director because of a conflict with my doctoral dissertation; my boyfriend was my Title IX attorney; and, according to the Pacific Lutheran University "football guys," Ad was the one behind "it all." What exactly "it all" was, I never found out.

Oddly enough, that fall, in the midst of all the rumors and innuendo, I got a call from Ken Williams (Linfield's registrar and the faculty athletic representative). I had served since 1989 as the associate faculty athletic representative (FAR) for Linfield athletics, which meant attending athletic conference meetings with Ken and participating in decision making at that level. I had assumed that since I'd been removed from my position as assistant athletic director, I would also no longer be serving as FAR. According to Ken, no one had informed him that I was to be removed from that appointment. In his words, I had "served the college well in that capacity and [he] assumed I would continue as such." I halfheartedly replied that I'd pencil in the meeting date and try to attend.

In a way it was comical. Technically, the faculty athletic representatives are second only to the college presidents in decision-making power within the athletic conference. I'd been removed from all Linfield athletic leadership, but was still being asked to represent Linfield at the conference level in a position superior to that of the athletic director. It was weird, to say the least, and an oversight that the president would soon remedy. It wasn't long before I was removed from that position as well.

On October 23 the department began stage two of the leadership process, which involved developing a job description for the soon-to-be-available athletic director position. I attended that meeting and participated in the process, during which time it was made clear that Scott intended to apply for the position and so had removed himself from the deliberations. After the meeting I approached George and informed him that I too would be applying for the position, and queried whether I should remove myself from the department discussions. George responded that he didn't think Scott needed to remove himself, and that he didn't think I needed to either. In his view it was appropriate for both of us to attend the meetings. George felt the only person it wasn't appropriate to have there was Ad, and he wished Ad would excuse himself from the discussions.

Throughout the fall other little annoyances continued to crop up. Scott worked hard at schmoozing people to lay a foundation for his anticipated ascension to the position of athletic director. Our NCAA Division III transition continued, with most of the men's sport coaches grumbling about the added rules and restrictions. Joan Rutschman, Ad's wife and secretary, appeared to embark on a mission to catch me doing something wrong. She even called the administrative services director, Sherie Dulaney, to check on what account number I'd been charging copies and postage to.

Sherie is a woman with a keen sense of propriety and loyalty to her friends. She and I had become friends shortly after my arrival at Linfield. Sherie had worked at Linfield for many years, and if there was one person who was "in the know," it was Sherie Dulaney. She called to let me know Joan was checking up on me. It was a good thing my job performance record was squeaky clean.

Although my attempts to give a faculty lecture on Title IX had initially been stifled, I continued to pursue that forum. As far as I'm concerned, no doesn't necessarily mean no. It may mean I need to try again, ask in a different way, or be patient and wait. For whatever reason—maybe they felt the pressure of the lawsuit, maybe I finally wore them down—in response to my renewed requests, the dean agreed to let me give a faculty lecture. It was scheduled for November 8, 1995.

Shortly after being granted permission to speak, I was contacted by the student radio station (KSLC). The students wanted to tape the presentation. I agreed to allow the presentation to be taped as long as I got a copy. But when they found out I didn't anticipate addressing Linfield-specific Title IX issues, and instead would focus more generally on Title IX, they changed their minds. No one from the radio station showed up, which was another sign that what people wanted was to stir up more controversy. Minus that, there apparently wasn't any story to broadcast.

The day before the talk Vivian called and left me a message, telling me she was sorry she would be unable to attend, she'd be out of town. I would have liked to have had her there.

The presentation went well. The room was packed with students and faculty, so full in fact that people had to stand against the walls and sit on the floor. This was unusual. My experience had been that faculty lectures were typically significantly less well attended. My attorneys, Liz and Lory, also attended, which I appreciated. I wanted them to see me in action. I wanted the opportunity to speak publicly about a topic I was becoming an authority on, and to be seen as an intelligent, well-informed advocate for gender equity, not some raving lunatic bent on the destruction of Ad Rutschman and Linfield athletics.

16

Pick on Me—Not the Kids

On November 11 the *News-Register* again leveled a blow. The writers couldn't resist adding more fuel anytime it looked as if the heat was dying down. The article claimed that I was responsible for all the Title IX fuss; of course everyone wanted equity: these were all "good" people who wanted to do the "right" thing. I was the problem. I'd been overly aggressive, and I was overstepping the bounds of what Title IX intended. Apparently, the *News-Register* was better informed about the legal intent of the law than I, Linfield's attorneys, and the various leadership consultants Linfield had employed. The paper made it clear that Ad was not responsible for "creating" the situation; I was.

As it became apparent that the ongoing abuses against me were not having the desired effect, which I assume was to dissuade me from pursuing my lawsuit, verbal attacks were made on the swimmers. It was one thing to pick on me, but it was complete cowardice to attack my swimmers. Mainly, although I know it was hard on them, the swimmers handled it better than I did. I had a "mother hen" reaction. I wanted to protect them, to keep them out of it, but that wasn't possible anymore. Evidently some people at Linfield had no intention of letting me, or anyone associated with me, escape their wrath. One instance was particularly annoying and hurtful.

In one of her classes, the women's swim team captain, Stacy Michael, was put on the defensive about swimming All-Americas by a male cross-country athlete. Stacy had given a class presentation about the swim team. During the question-and-answer period the runner asked if it was true that it was easy to be All-America in swimming.

This had been Ad and Scott's party line for some time. In their minds, the only reason the swim team could have achieved such notable success had to be because it was easy. It couldn't be because we had worked very hard to achieve and sustain excellence.

Stacy came to me upset about the comment, and the fact that the athlete had been rather smug and demeaning in front of her whole class. I tried to convince her not to blame the athlete; he'd in all likelihood been misinformed. I explained to Stacy that championships based on qualifying standards were exclusionary by definition, and that therefore the number of national entrants was limited. That, however, did not mean it was easy to succeed. It was anything but easy just to qualify for the meet, let alone earn All-America honors. Stacy knew that from her own experience. If it was easy anyone could do it, and few qualified, despite hard work.

Another series of attacks concerned rumors of sexual impropriety. I should have expected as much, but once again I was caught off guard. The rumors being circulated were that I was sexually involved with my male swimmers, and that they earned places on relays by sleeping with me. At the same time, I was supposed to be having a lesbian affair with my assistant coach, Michelle. In the meantime I was living with Tim. As far as the rumor mill was concerned, I was one sexually active woman!

In general, the rumors became so ridiculous they were laughable. I was, however, concerned about how the swimmers and Michelle were handling them. To my great relief, the swimmers thought of them as quite a joke and weren't the least bit upset. The only discontent came from the women on the team, who wondered why they'd been left out. Michelle too was fine. She took the rumors with a grain of salt, and they never affected our relationship. Even so, for the sake of others, I became even more careful about anything with even the possibility of the appearance of impropriety.

I began leaving my office door wide open whenever anyone was with me, and I avoided physical contact. In athletics it is common for athletes and coaches to make physical contact. Sometimes it involves technique corrections and other times, overwhelmed in the moment of success, a hug. These became taboo for me. Sadly, I remember one instance when a swimmer who achieved a long-sought goal came up to me on the pool deck after his race and spontaneously hugged me. I stiffened, unable to return the celebratory contact.

17

Tenure and Promotion

In academics the concept of tenure is in place to support academic freedom. Tenure is a lifetime employment commitment and thereby helps ensure that professors are free to pursue both mainstream and controversial lines of academic inquiry. At Linfield tenure and promotion were based on three areas of performance: teaching, scholarship, and service. Teaching included classroom instruction and coaching, scholarship dealt with professional development, publications, and presentations, and service included department and college committee work and service to the broader community and profession.

I'd worked hard to ensure that my tenure and promotion file was of the highest quality and presented my candidacy in the best possible light. I'd gone to considerable effort to prepare a strong candidacy. I was very much aware that the odds were stacked against me. Linfield didn't relish the thought of having me around for another day, let alone sealing a potential lifetime commitment. I'd spent a lot of time over the preceding summer preparing my materials and had asked a senior faculty member, a tenured full professor, to review my file prior to submission. He did, and his response, "no weaknesses," was widely circulated among faculty and the Rank, Tenure, and Sabbatical Committee. I knew I had a strong file, and it was certainly stronger than anyone else's in my department. In fact, at that time I had more publications and professional presentations than all the other members of the department combined. I also knew I'd played a strong and important political card by having my file reviewed by a tenured senior faculty member prior to submission. I was learning at last the importance of playing the game. On November 2, 1995, I submitted my file, which amounted to three large black binders of documentation and information attesting to my academic accomplishments.

A few weeks later I went to the dean's office to look at my departmental colleagues' appraisals. The practice at Linfield was that each department member was to write an appraisal based on his or her assessment of the candidate's teaching, scholarship, and service. I shouldn't have been surprised, and I really wasn't, but it was still painful to read the comments made by some of my colleagues.

George and Mary were supportive and complimentary and recommended me for tenure and promotion. Laura was supportive and recommended tenure and promotion, but qualified her support relative to our "complex" times. This one in particular hurt. I knew Laura was afraid, and with good cause, but I didn't expect her to hedge. Sometimes I expected too much. Larry Doty (the men's basketball coach) sent his evaluation in late, but was supportive and recommended tenure and promotion.

Tara was supportive in her comments, but declined to make a recommendation about tenure and promotion. This would turn out to be an issue when Tara was required to explain her decision not to make a recommendation. Ad couldn't help being relatively complimentary in his comments, particularly with respect to my coaching, so he kept them brief. He did, however, manage to be critical in the area of service, stating that he had "become extremely concerned with the change in the climate and working environment within [the] department." Ad felt then, as he may even now, that I was single-handedly responsible for "tearing" down the department. He continued by dredging up a one-sided review of employee difficulties with a woman who served as Linfield's softball coach when I first arrived. She and I had not gotten along well, and there was no love lost on either side when she decided to leave Linfield. When it came time for Ad to check the "recommend or not" box at the bottom of the form, he did not recommend tenure or promotion.

Similarly, Ed, Scott, Jay, and Garry were not supportive and did not recommend tenure or promotion. They stated, among other things, that although I was clearly a good teacher and coach, had an outstanding record of scholarship, and had a strong service record, I'd created division within the department over Title IX and wasn't a "team player." Scott stated that "her advocacy of Title IX issues has not been a problem, but the delivery and collegiality by which she has presented materials related to her concerns have caused our department a great deal of distress that could have been avoided." I suppose Scott was right; a lot of distress could have been avoided if I'd never brought up Title IX.

The other interesting thing was that Scott, Ed, and Jay put in writing that they based their evaluations on reading student evaluations from my classes, and reading through my personnel file. At Linfield, tenure and promotion files were not open to everyone. The only people who were supposed to have access were select members of the campus administration and the department chair. Any other access would have to be granted, in writing, by the faculty member whose file was to be viewed. I'd never given Scott, Ed, or Jay permission to review my file, and none of them was on the RTS Committee at that time. None was serving as department chair, or as officer of the college. There was absolutely no way they should have had access to my file. The question then became, were they lying about reviewing my file, or had they violated college policy by reviewing my file without permission? Either way, they were wrong. As it would turn out, that wouldn't make any difference. Apparently, they could violate policy with impunity. I, on the other hand, drew attention to our violation of federal law and got "reassigned" for it.

I followed up over the next few days with calls to the dean and his secretary, Meridith Symons, trying to find out if and how Ed, Scott, and Jay had gained access to my file. I called Meridith and left a message, asking her to verify college policy about faculty access to tenure and promotion files. She returned my call and left a message, which I recorded. She was very specific: permission was required, and it needed to be in writing. There was no doubt. The person responsible for monitoring file access was aware of the policy. This issue would drag on for some months, sadly, without an acceptable resolution.

I had known for some time that I wouldn't have much departmental support when I applied for tenure and promotion, but seeing that lack of support in writing was still very hard. It was ugly and hurtful, and I felt surprisingly sad.

Outside my department, discussions about my tenure and promotion candidacy were heating up across campus. The chair of the Rank, Tenure, and Sabbatical Committee had been asking whether the committee's actions were covered by the college's liability insurance. Vivian and Marv responded to this query, informing the committee that it didn't need to worry about liability insurance because its role was limited to making recommendations, not decisions. The decision makers would be Marv, Vivian, and the Board of Trustees. Marv, according to Vivian, had his own liability policy.

On the bright side, the next day the swim coach from Pacific Lutheran University (PLU), Jim Johnson, called to tell me he'd nominated me for the position of athletic director and dean of their Physical Education and Athletics Department. Jim was a member of the search committee and thought highly enough of me to nominate me for the position of his boss. It was a bright spot in an otherwise dismal landscape. Jim also relayed a recent conversation he'd had with the PLU baseball coach. The baseball coach had announced during a department meeting that it was easy to be All-

America in swimming. The reoccurrence of this theme in so many different settings was really becoming an annoyance, not only to me, but to other coaches and swimmers in the athletic conference. It seemed silly to be so bent on trying to downgrade the accomplishments of athletes in one's own department. Jim's response was wonderful. He said that yes, he supposed it might be easy—for Linfield, because Linfield had such an excellent swim program. He said that he hadn't had a men's swimming All-America in five years!

That fall, Ed resigned as head football coach. The pressure of taking over the head coaching responsibilities (following Ad's quarter-century dynasty) was apparently too much for him; it wasn't fun anymore. On November 21 Ed and I had a conversation about his retirement. I approached him to tell him I was sad for him and knew his decision to resign as head coach must have been difficult. Ed asked that I sit down with him for a minute. He wanted to know if I'd read my colleague evaluations. I responded that I had. He told me he had struggled with a guilty conscience over not telling me eye-to-eye how he felt, although throughout the conversation he couldn't make eye contact. He said he felt he had to say what he did and hoped he'd done so professionally. He assured me that if I did get tenure and promotion, he could "move forward," and suggested that it would be best for us to "forgive and forget."

At that point I was in no mood to consider forgiving and forgetting. I asked Ed if he'd looked in my personnel file. He said he had. I reminded him of the college policy regarding file access without written consent. Ed replied that he "guessed" he was aware of that policy, that he knew the "files were closed," but that he went in and got access anyway. He told me it was very easy, no hassle at all; he didn't think it was a "big deal." I informed him that as far as I was concerned, it was a big deal, that I considered it a violation of college policy and an invasion of my privacy. Ed just sat there, and the conversation ended.

On November 27, 1995, I had my tenure and promotion meeting with the dean, the department chair, and the RTS faculty member, Kareen Sturgeon. Marv opened the meeting by identifying the purpose as an opportunity to clarify the record, answer queries and concerns, and give feedback to RTS members. He asked me to highlight my file in regard to teaching, scholarship, and service. I did so. He then asked that I elaborate on my teaching and my coaching as an aspect of teaching. He went on to say, "for the record," that all of my teaching evaluations were well above the college average. I remember feeling a glimmer of hope; maybe the meeting wouldn't be too bad. He wanted me to address this and implied that perhaps my "inflated" evaluations were the result of my teaching more favorable activity-type courses. Evidently, my evaluations couldn't reflect good teaching.

Kareen asked for some clarification about how the RTS Committee was to consider the administrative part of my work load. Marv responded that it should be considered a demand on my time and would therefore affect the three areas pertinent to tenure review (teaching, scholarship, and service). Kareen asked that I elaborate on some of my course philosophies and clarify professional development acronyms. She also suggested I comment more fully on my service record.

Marv then shifted the conversation, asking if I wanted to comment on the negative evaluations I'd received from some of my departmental colleagues. In reply, I asked that the RTS Committee look at those comments within the context of the difficult times we were having in regard to gender-equity issues. I further referred the committee to the many positive comments and letters from various outside sources (the conference athletic commissioner, Kenton Hill, and campus colleagues).

My tenure and promotion ordeal lasted for a number of months, well beyond the time when the fate of others up for review had been determined. Typically, faculty members submit their files for review in the fall, have tenure and promotion meetings in November, and then the RTS Committee meets to review files and forward recommendations near the Christmas holidays. Decisions are announced early in the spring semester. This, however, would not be the case for me.

In early January a memo from the dean appeared under my door. The memo was an invitation for me to respond to Tara's tenure and promotion clarification statement. Tara had been requested to explain why she had abstained from making a recommendation regarding my tenure and promotion. At this point, being embroiled in the lawsuit, I faxed the dean's memo and Tara's response to Liz and Lory. Working with Lory, I crafted my reply.

Tara's one-page response didn't say anything new. She complimented me on excelling in the areas of teaching and coaching and stated that she and I had "worked well together and [had] not had problems . . . personally or professionally." She then expressed concerns regarding collegiality, stating my interest in Title IX compliance had become a "personal crusade" and that in some "cases [I'd] lost sight of reality."

She addressed reports of anger and frustration expressed by members of the women's basketball team. The women's basketball team had enjoyed limited success, and player complaints had escalated beyond mere grumblings. The players had written a letter to the administration alleging that Mary's poor coaching was the reason the team hadn't done well. I hadn't been privy to the letter. Yet Ad and the administration were quick to assign me the task of dealing with the situation. The meeting agenda had been set by the dean, and my job had been to preside and make sure that the agenda was adhered to, and that it didn't deteriorate into a "coach-bashing" session. I should have seen it coming; in fact, sometimes I think my involvement in that ill-fated meeting was a setup.

The meeting had gone okay, with some issues being addressed and others just heard without a formal resolution. Mainly, the athletes were frustrated about successive losing seasons and were taking it out on Mary. I just got in the way. According to what Tara wrote, the athletes claimed their concerns hadn't been adequately heard or dealt with, and Linfield construed that as an example of my self-involvement and my disregard for women in sport. Nothing was further from the truth.

Despite my years as an effective administrator within women's athletics, Tara used my lack of connection with the previous women's softball coach and the basketball team's desire to engage in a crusade to oust its coach as examples of my lack of leadership effectiveness and personal self-centeredness when it came to women in sport.

I had to draft a response to Tara's "clarification of abstention." I pointed out that Tara had complimented my teaching and coaching, and that although she cited concerns of "collegiality," she also stated that she'd never had any trouble working with me. I replied to her comments about Title IX as a a personal crusade and my lack of touch with reality by stating that I disagreed with these characterizations and believed them to be unfair, misleading, and inaccurate. I concluded my response by stating again that the basketball player meeting agenda had been set by the dean. I'd simply adhered to it. As Tara had no firsthand knowledge of the meeting, it didn't seem appropriate for her to cast aspersion on me because of mere rumors about my conduct within it. All in all, it was an exhausting clarification process, and I was tired of having to defend myself against false and misleading accusations.

Finally, after all the folderol with file invasions and response clarifications, on January 11, 1996, I received a letter from the RTS Committee. The committee recommended I receive tenure and promotion. The recommendation was forwarded to the dean and president, and from there would go to the Board of Trustees for final consideration.

On February 27 I received a memo from the dean informing me that he and President Bull had chosen "not to forward a recommendation concerning [my] candidacy for tenure and promotion to the Board of Trustees at its February 24th meeting. [They planned] instead to forward a recommendation at the May meeting of the Board."

Later that month the *News-Register* simply could not pass up an opportunity to put me and the Title IX conflict in the paper again. On January 27 it ran an article rehashing information about the lawsuit and publicly announcing the RTS Committee's positive recommendation regarding my tenure and promotion. In reality this didn't upset me; but RTS recommendations were not generally made public, and the information had been leaked to the paper, probably by the same person who had been leaking information all along. The article also addressed my application for the athletic director position, striking a jab at the odds I would surface as the candidate of choice.

During the spring semester, instead of announcing tenure and promotion recipients at the spring faculty meeting (as had previously been done), a March 11 e-mail was sent out. My name was not on it. There were various avenues of publication about tenure and promotion. The weekly *Linfield Reports* were published with the information, and the school newspaper ran a story (in which the reporter repeatedly asked for my comment, and to which my lawyers instructed me to reply no comment). None of these publications mentioned me; my tenure and promotion decision had been deferred. It was just one more source of embarrassment and humiliation.

Also during this time, the Linfield attorneys had approached my attorneys inquiring about mediation avenues and possible settlement. I think that Linfield was trying to delay making a final determination regarding my tenure and promotion in the hope that a mediated settlement agreement could be reached, presumably one in which I would quietly leave Linfield.

Well, I didn't want to settle.

Finally, on May 18 I received a call from the dean. Marv informed me that the Board of Trustees had voted unanimously to grant me tenure and promotion. The inside scoop was that discussion about my tenure and promotion had gone to a closed session among the trustee Executive Committee and had been very contentious. Apparently, many people were unhappy about voting in support, but the board had been cautioned by its legal counsel that the decision had to be based on the tenure and promotion guidelines outlined in the *Faculty Handbook*; nothing else could be considered. I was advised to watch my back. Many people would be watching me very carefully.

The dean said: "Once a favorable decision has been reached, the dean owes the faculty member a congratulations." I didn't feel excited about the good news. Not only was the dean's congratulations less than celebratory, but it would have been better for my lawsuit had I been denied tenure, which Vivian, Marv, and the trustees probably figured out. On May 20, 1996, a campus e-mail was distributed announcing the decision.

Within days I received numerous congratulations from faculty across campus. In my department, however, only George, Mary, and Tara congratulated me. Everyone else was mute. At that point it wasn't an issue for me. I didn't expect any different. Their silence did, however, reflect the climate within the department.

Mary too had had her tenure and promotion decision delayed. Unfortunately, the decision was not favorable. She asked me what I thought she should do. Should she pursue the matter? She also asked George what he thought, as department chair. George responded that without a doubt the bar had been raised that year regarding review standards. According to George, there were quite a few members of the department who he didn't think would have tenure today if they'd been held to similar standards.

Part V

18

Calculated Injustice?

A lthough my tenure and promotion ordeal worked out, it was
just one more crisis I had to endure. In many ways, the entire
ordeal was like the constant drip of water from a leaking faucet. No
single incident was enough to put me over the edge, but the seeming endlessness of ongoing little things ate away at my well-being.

That's what makes it difficult to recognize and cope with discrimination: its subtlety. According to Title VII of the Civil Rights
Act of 1964, it is unlawful to discriminate on the basis of race, color,
religion, sex, or national origin, in regard to employment terms,
conditions, privileges, and compensation. Over the years, the courts
have determined that the congressional intent of this legislation
included a wide spectrum of disparate treatment, including subject-
ing employees to a discriminatorily hostile or abusive environment.
In 1993 the Supreme Court ruled on a Title VII case involving sexual
harassment. In this case, *Harris v. Forklift Systems*, the Court carved
a "middle path between making actionable any conduct that is
merely offensive, and requiring the conduct to cause a tangible psychological injury." In essence, the Court found that the harassing
conduct didn't have to lead to a nervous breakdown to be action-

able. Even so, there is no magic number of occurrences or gauge of incident magnitude required before something can be acknowledged as discriminatory. The reality is that the line is drawn in the shifting sands of social conscience, at a particular moment, in regard to a particular situation and the strength, stamina, and tolerance of the victim.

In addition to the time-consuming hassles and disruptions of the lawsuit, which required documenting every correspondence, conversation, and interaction, and numerous communications with my attorneys, I was attempting to function well at work. This meant coaching swimming in the early morning, doing a short workout afterward, teaching classes, tending to aquatics director duties, coaching afternoon swim practice, and then making recruitment calls in the evenings. In addition, I was responsible for the organization and execution of swim meets, home or away, almost every weekend. In a way, perhaps it was good that I was so busy. It left less time to dwell on the calamity my life had become.

My sessions with Etta Martin became increasingly important. I was surrounded by people telling me I was crazy, irrational, and wrong, and after a while it became hard not to question myself. With Etta, I had a chance to catch my breath and reground my thinking.

Etta would listen to my stories. Sometimes we'd cry together; sometimes she'd cry for me. We'd talk through concerns, at times delving into issues not related to Linfield or the lawsuit, just whatever seemed to need some air time and space. For me it was a healing time, a time of ongoing repair. During the week it was as if I was navigating a small raft with many tiny holes that was slowly leaking and sinking. Then I'd see Etta, we'd patch the holes, and I'd put to sea again, repaired but not made whole, not even now.

Linfield was awash in what appeared to be calculated injustice. One afternoon in late November I was in the department workroom and saw an e-mail to Scott in the printer rack from the dean of enrollment services, John Reed. John was being funded by the president to attend the NCAA convention on Linfield's behalf. Ad was not going, and so John recommended that Scott talk with Ad so that athletic funding could be secured to send him and Tara to the convention. Not that this was inappropriate, but the more time, energy, and money Linfield invested in Scott's athletic administration, the harder it would be for me to be seen as a viable candidate for the position of athletic director.

Early December brought our culminating midseason swim meet, the Pacific Lutheran Invitational. During the coaches' meeting one of the PLU swimming alums told me that his dad, a "diehard" Linfield and Ad Rutschman fan, had participated in conversations with Ad and his buddies literally plotting how to get rid of me. The PLU coach confirmed the gossip, telling me that a fellow swim coach had been accosted at a Linfield reunion event by people who were angry with him (by association with me) for raising all that "Title IX stuff."

These various second- and thirdhand revelations regarding alleged conversations meant little. But they did show how far rumors were spreading, and the general tone of their content. In a way I should have been flattered; again, people were crediting me with much more power and influence than I possessed.

I received word upon my return from an out-of-town swim meet that Ad and Scott had gone through all the women's athletics files (files that I'd forwarded to them, and that had been sitting available in the hallway cabinet for weeks). Again, not that it really mattered, but it was an annoyance to know they felt compelled to come in late one evening, rummage through the files, and then spirit them away. Sadly, although I tried on numerous occasions to track them down, the women's sport history scrapbooks and photo albums I gave to Ad disappeared once they left my possession.

Another annoying injustice occurred at this time. On December 11, 1995, I found another e-mail lying faceup in the communal printer tray. It was from Scott to Ad about the 1995–96 baseball coaching contracts and salaries. The memo detailed the assistant coaches to be hired and allocations of budgeted monies, supplemented by fund-raising, to be paid in salaries. There had been much fuss over Ad's proposed salary schedule and the limits it imposed. The information in this e-mail directly violated the approved salary schedule and Title IX compliance.

Scott was proposing that baseball be allowed to use fund-raising money to supplement assistant coaching salaries considerably beyond Ad's salary schedule. Apparently, the e-mail had been lying there for a while; Laura and Mary had seen it and were angry too. Both women's coaches verified that the assistant coach salary allocations they received coincided with the approved schedule. There were rules for public view, applied to women's sports and whomever else's feet Ad wanted to hold to the fire, but when it came to men's sports and his favorites, approved or not, policy didn't seem to apply.

It was at this time I suggested to my attorneys that we request all e-mail transmissions between Ad and Scott as part of our discovery process for the lawsuit. I was increasingly confident that we'd gain important information if we did. Unfortunately, I don't recall that they ever followed up on that lead.

Sometimes working with attorneys on a lawsuit is frustrating. To them it is just a job, a job with significant financial implications. And that's the extent of their involvement, no matter how wonderful they may be. In their defense, that distance probably serves them well in maintaining objectivity. But for the plaintiff, for me, it was my life. It was my present and my future. For me, the stakes were higher than just money.

On December 12 the department had yet another meeting with the dean to go over restructuring and job descriptions. Marv opened the meeting by stating he'd decided to amend the athletic director job description. Originally, even though the department had voted otherwise, the proposal suggested that the athletic director report directly to the college president as opposed to being under the department chair. Marv had reconsidered and decided that the chain of command would reflect the department vote, with the athletic director reporting to the department chair. Marv's rationale was that this reporting hierarchy would symbolically signal to the broader campus the academic focus of the department. He went on to say that he didn't feel the NCAA guidelines regarding the appointment of a senior woman administrator were anything more than guidelines. Therefore, he had decided that if the department chair was female, the designation of senior woman administrator could be assigned to that position and we'd be in compliance with NCAA requirements. Essentially this would further limit female voices among the Linfield College athletic leadership. We seemed to be moving even further away from any chance of a voice for women in sport.

The men's sport coaches, Ad and Scott particularly, expressed their dissent and concern. They felt that athletic advocacy would be compromised if the athletic director had to go through the department chair. Apparently, the lack of female voice to advocate for women in sports did not concern them. They argued that the athletic director, in their minds a male, and Scott the heir apparent, needed direct access to the upper-level administration. For my part, other than the lack of female voice, I was pleased with the modified chain of command. I felt it would prevent men's athletics from "running amok," although that safeguard hasn't worked out too well. According to a current Linfield faculty member, during the spring of 2000 Linfield had to produce an NCAA self-report for violations regarding football practice, admissions, and financial aid.

Marv went on to discuss "next steps." He favored the NCAA athletic leadership model, a single head over both men's and women's athletics. He then said that there would be an internal search for the athletic director position and that Lee Howard, the vice president for development, would chair the committee. He stated that there would be a national search for the department chair position, but that internal candidates would be considered. The dean also announced that he was confident the department would have an additional full-time position to allocate, because of the football position recently vacated.

In academics, when a position is vacated, it isn't a certainty that a department will retain that position. Sometimes positions are eaten up, so to speak, by the broader college staffing needs. In our case, however, we would retain our allocated positions. This was good news. It created an opportunity to address a staffing gap with our minor sports, such as soccer and tennis, instead of just assigning one more football coach to teach a few activity classes.

The idea did not, however, sit well with the football coaches. Ed stated that perhaps we needed to look as a department at eliminating some sports, that we simply didn't have the resources to "man" all our sports effectively. Ed thought that perhaps the department might be best served by cutting swimming.

Ad chimed in, stating no, we wouldn't look at cutting sports as an option; instead we needed to expand women's sport opportunities. At least he had that part right. And, according to Ad, we couldn't cut coed sports because we'd have problems at the "other end." Actually, he was wrong about that. We could, within the legal limits of Title IX, cut the men's half of a coed sport. Not that that would be desirable, but legally it was an option.

After the meeting I e-mailed Lee Howard with my intent to apply for the athletic director position. At this point as a department we entered into a phase of position madness. We had a search for athletic director and department chair and the determination of how to use the vacated faculty position all on our plate. Throughout the weeks to come the department discussed academic needs and possible options regarding the allocation of the vacated faculty position. The football coaches wanted another football coach. Evidently having four full-time people already coaching football wasn't enough (the most any other sport had was one full-time teacher-coach). It didn't seem to matter to them that there were actual unmet academic needs, and that many of our sports made do with part-time coaches and would greatly benefit from even one full-time shared position. All they could see was what football wanted. Another full-time football coach was more important, valued, and needed (along with the multiple part-timers) than the first shared-position, full-time soccer or tennis coach. It was the same with other program resources. Football's needs had to be met entirely, and anything left over could be meted out among the remaining sports.

What has always baffled me is that the other men's sports didn't and don't raise a fuss about this, at least not a public fuss. Instead of casting blame where it belongs, at an over-indulged football program, they too often blame and attack women's sports. Even now, in classes I teach, there is that phenomenon. Men's minor sports are often sacrificed in the name of gender equity, and the men end up feeling understandably angry. But they don't lash out at the real culprit. They lash out at the women, and the have-nots fight the have-nots. Attention is never directed where it should be, and football sits back, bloated and gloating, watching the little sports fight among themselves. It is a double bind. The difficulty for men involved in the minor sports lies in their casting aspersions on the very entity they are supposed to be, or at least supposed to want to be, a part of.

Later that day I got a call from Ken Wheeler, a reporter at the *Oregonian*. He was phoning to follow up on calls he'd been receiving from Linfield alums, claiming that football was being torn down. He said he'd phoned a variety of people at Linfield, including President Bull, and wanted to ask me some questions. I replied that I couldn't comment. He pressed, asking questions ranging from my feelings about Linfield football and its long history and tradition of success to Title IX generally, compliance at Linfield, and my lawsuit. Finally, he told me that "no comment" could sometimes make a person look bad in print—a threat, I suppose. Still, I replied, "No comment." I had strict instructions from my attorneys not to comment to the press about anything related to my lawsuit. It was frustrating not being able to say anything, not being able to defend myself or my position.

On December 15 I, along with all members of the HHPA Department, received a memo from Lee Howard with a copy of the athletic director position announcement attached. The required qualifications for the position were a master's degree in a health or physical education field and current employment at Linfield College. The desired qualifications included familiarity with Linfield College athletic programs; administrative experience, including budget, planning, and program development experience; familiarity with NAIA and NCAA regulations and compliance issues; understanding and commitment to Title IX; understanding of the place of athletics in the overall educational mission of Linfield College; and ability to lead in a collegial fashion. It asked for a letter of application, vitae, and four references. Application materials were due January 2, 1996.

I have reflected quite a bit on a reasonable explanation for my applying for the athletic director position. Part of me knew, given the circumstances, that I didn't stand a chance. Yet another part of me held fast to my naïveté. I had no doubt that between Scott and me, I was the better candidate. I'd been a coach and teacher, assistant athletic director, and aquatics director. I'd coached and taught at the NAIA and NCAA Division I levels. Not to apply would be to professionally stand still, and I've never been one to stand still. My life has been a series of preparatory stretches followed by advancement to the next level. I simply didn't know how to stay put.

As December wound to a close, I received a call from Liz. The opposing counsel was again asking about possibilities of a settlement, and she wanted my thoughts on "creative" settlement terms. I responded, as I would many times to follow, that what I wanted was for Linfield to right the wrongs that had been committed. I wanted them to say they were sorry. I wanted justice. I wanted fairness. Those things, however, are not what lawsuits are about. We pretend that they are. It feels better to believe they're about right and wrong. But the reality is that lawsuits are about winning. And winning typically involves money, nothing more and nothing less.

A creative settlement centered on rightness, justice, and fairness was asking for the moon. What they wanted to know was my price—the amount of money that would shut me up and buy me off. I didn't want money. And because money wasn't the objective, there wasn't a price. It was a fundamental dilemma that would haunt me and my lawsuit and frustrate attorneys on both sides. It was a dilemma that would never be resolved.

On January 4 I had a phone conversation with a swimming alum. I'd called to ask to her to substitute for me in my aquatics class. Her father was an attorney. She shared with me that he had recently been involved in a deposition during which a side conversation evolved with some insurance attorneys about Linfield and my lawsuit. According to that source, Linfield's insurance attorneys wanted to mediate and settle the case because they were worried that they "didn't have a case . . . [and] . . . didn't stand a chance." I'd share tidbits like this with Liz and Lory and be momentarily buoyed up. But in the long run, all that resulted was a moment of inconsequential levity.

By early January the athletic director search was in full swing. The committee included George, Tara, Frank Bumpus, Alan Hubka (a trustee I didn't know much about), Michelle Jones (a student and Jay Locey power-lifting protégée), and Bill Millar (the affirmative action officer and a good friend of Bill Apel's—it would have been almost impossible for him not to have had an earful about me and Title IX). Lee Howard served as the chair.

On January 12 the interview schedule for the athletic director search was worked out. There were three internal applicants for the position: Scott, Jeff MacKay (the student activities director), and me. I scheduled interviews with the department through George and the search committee, but all the times suggested by the committee, despite considerable schedule flexibility and availability on my part, conflicted with swim practice. That happened in so many instances, from department meetings to committee meetings that I believe it was either intentional or an illustration of how completely unvalued any sport but football was. It was probably both. When I wasn't at swim practice, providing my assistant Michelle could be there, my absence left the swim team with about a one-to-forty coach-athlete ratio, which is hardly ideal and certainly not safe. In contrast, schedules were always worked around football practice.

Finally, after various revisions, my interview was scheduled. I would present a Campus Community Forum on Friday January 26 from 2:00 to 3:00 P.M., and then participate in a series of interviews with President Bull, the HHPA faculty, Marv and the search committee the following Monday (January 29).

I received a candidate rating form along with confirmation of my interview schedule. The evaluation criteria, and my perception of my comparison with Scott, were as follows:

(1) Master's degree: I was within about a year of completing my doctorate; Scott had only a master's and no intention of working toward a doctorate.

(2) Administrative experience in higher education athletic programs: As assistant athletic director, I'd functioned, until I raised Title IX issues, with almost complete administrative autonomy. In contrast, Scott had functioned under Ad's decision making and had not had significant independent administrative experience in athletics.

(3) Commitment to a small, liberal arts environment: This one was innocuous and I suppose we were similar.

(4) Understanding of the place of athletics in the overall educational mission of Linfield College: I'd always been an advocate of the student-athlete model and considered myself a

teacher who coached, not the other way around. Scott's actions had demonstrated his focus was athletics. He was, in his own words, "just a coach for Christ's sake."

(5) Evidence of leadership and management skills: My background clearly depicted independent leadership and decision making in my roles as a coach, aquatics director, and athletic administrator. Scott's Linfield background reflected roles that were limited to coaching and facility direction.

(6) Participation in professional activities: I had served not only on the Conference Athletic Director Council alongside Ad, but also as the associate faculty athletic representative and attended NAIA national conventions on Linfield's behalf. Scott had only recently been involved at the broader professional level in athletic administration. His focus had been exclusively baseball.

(7) Ability to relate to external community: Prior to raising Title IX concerns, I'd been Linfield's "poster girl." I'd been featured frequently in the *News-Register*, the *Linfield Bulletin*, and the school newspaper, always in a positive light. All that had changed, however, and I'd since been blackballed. I'd give this one to Scott.

(8) Ability to relate to the internal community: Again, until raising Title IX concerns, I'd been viewed across campus as intelligent, effective, and capable, with solid connections among administrators, faculty, and staff. Since raising Title IX, how I was viewed would depend on who was asked. Scott was seen across campus for the coach he was.

(9) Understanding of intercollegiate athletics: Although our philosophies differed, we both had a good understanding of intercollegiate athletics.

(10) Familiarity with the Linfield athletic program: I was considerably more familiar with women's athletics than Scott. But Ad had always played his hand close to the chest, and I'm

not sure anyone, other than Ad, was very familiar with men's athletics.

(11) Familiarity with NAIA and NCAA regulations and compliance issues: My years of experience at Linfield with the NAIA and my prior experience at Nevada–Reno with NCAA Division I athletics put me ahead of Scott's one-time attendance at a NCAA convention.

(12) Understanding and commitment to Title IX: That goes without saying. After all, Scott was the one who said that his "wife gets that way once a month too."

(13) Ability to lead in a collegial fashion: This was interesting. In my view, Scott had engaged in pressure tactics attempting to convince the women's sport coaches I was wrong about Title IX. He'd violated college by policy by invading my personnel files; he'd violated department and college policy regarding the assistant coach salary schedule; and on more than one occasion, he'd demonstrated his less-than-sympathetic capacities with respect to women in sport. I, however, had been repeatedly labeled by select men's sport coaches as not a team player.

(14) Experience in budgeting, planning, program development, and supervision: Because of each of our coaching positions, we both had considerable experience here. In addition, I had been preparing and supervising the women's sport budget for years. Scott had no such experience with the men's budget.

Each of the criteria was weighted from .5 to 3. Interestingly, criteria I shined in, such as educational degree, experience, professional activities, familiarity with Linfield athletics and NAIA and NCAA regulations, were weighted low (.5 to 1.0). The big winner, with the only 3-point weighting, was the ability to lead in a collegial fashion. I'd served over the years on many search committees and had never seen a rating form like this one.

Between the time I submitted my application and the actual interviews, Linfield continued to downplay any positive work or success I was associated with, and repeatedly put Scott in a role of athletic leadership. Deep down I knew it was futile, but I was determined to force Linfield to publicly make the wrong choice.

On December 15 I approached the sports information director (SID), seeking some recognition for the swim team captains. The women's captain, Stacy Michael, had a 4.0 fall semester GPA and soon would be awarded status as a four-year varsity letterwoman in swimming. She had a cumulative GPA of over 3.5, held down a work-study job, was an exercise science major, and was applying to graduate school in sport psychology. The men's captain, Mike Westphal, had also earned a 4.0 fall semester GPA, had a cumulative GPA of over 3.5, was completing a major in elementary education in just four years, held down a work-study job, was national champion in 1994, and would soon be awarded academic All-America honors. These were two outstanding Linfield athletes.

Frequently the Sports Information office runs human interest stories on exceptional Linfield athletes. The publicity is good for the athletic program and the college. In this case, however, the word the SID received from his superiors was that there would be no special press release highlighting the accomplishments of these two swimmers. In the words of his boss, it just wasn't enough of a "hook." I'm not sure how much of a "hook" is needed if the accomplishments of these two weren't enough. Maybe the "hook" had to be in football, as when print and television media flocked around a Linfield football star who, during his last semester of eligibility, flunked almost all his classes. Frustrated and angry, I pushed the issue. I pressed the SID to name any other student-athlete who had a list of accomplishments that could match these two. He couldn't name one and became embarrassed and apologetic. These were the things that were really painful, the price those close to me paid because of me.

On January 19 we had a department meeting. The meeting had been called by Scott, I suppose in his capacity as assistant athletic director. The topics discussed were financial aid, admissions, and the NCAA convention. Although Ad was present, as was the dean of enrollment services and President Bull, Scott led the meeting. Another clue as to who would soon be holding the reins. Even so, I pressed on.

My athletic director interview began with a Campus Community Forum, during which I made a short presentation regarding my interest in the athletic director position and responded to questions. I received numerous positive comments and responses, and some people even e-mailed me copies of what they put in writing to the search committee. One e-mail in particular was very complimentary. After attending all three of the applicants' forums, an administrator forwarded a copy of what he'd sent to the committee. He began his response by citing the importance of the athletic director position and commenting on the academic preparation of each candidate:

> I believe based upon my looking at each candidate's background of degrees achieved that Cindy Pemberton definitely has chosen her field of studies to advance toward an administrative position. Furthermore based on my involvement with all three candidates when it comes to follow-through on projects, organization of planning and implementing, meeting deadlines and so on and so forth, that Cindy is the top of the list among these three candidates. I think one would have to check long and hard to find a person who has the ability to perform at a higher level as an athletic director than Cindy.

He continued, stating: "It would be hard to imagine how the other two candidates could be better prepared for Title IX issues than Cindy. Her doctoral study has allowed her to further expand her knowledge of these issues. Not only does she possess the most knowledge of Title IX of the three candidates but in my opinion, she would administer all aspects of Title IX fairly among all athletic programs." He also addressed the issue of continuing to coach while serving as athletic director. When the question had been posed to me, I said I believed it only appropriate, given the time demands and potential for bias, that I step down as swim coach were I selected. Jeff Mackay, the third candidate, also felt the position should not overlap with coaching. Scott, however, planned to continue as baseball coach. According to this administrator: "I think that it would be impossible to perform both as an athletic director and head coach without biases influencing one's decision when it came to a decision regarding one's own sport. . . . I've heard Linfield coaches complain in the past about how decisions seemed to always favor the program of the athletic director. . . . I think [Cindy and Jeff] realize the importance of the position more realistically than Scott."

The administrator concluded with personal comments about each of the candidates and stated that he did not believe Jeff MacKay had the experience needed for the position, that he had concerns about Scott, and that he "fully support[ed]" me.

Feedback such as this, as well as numerous personal comments, made clear that when Scott and I were compared, there seemed to be no comparison. During his Campus Community Forum, Scott's responses were poorly prepared and superficial. Scott came across as a coach whose stated reasons for wanting the job were that he was an alum, had talked to Ad about it, and thought it would be a new challenge.

The differences between Scott and me weren't just anecdotal or vague impressions. One of the interesting things about a lawsuit is that through the discovery process, one gets to see all kinds of documents and materials. One such batch of materials included the Athletic Director Search Committee documents. I was able to read the Campus Community Forum faculty feedback, and overwhelmingly, I was the lead applicant. For the most part the rankings put Jeff MacKay second and Scott a distant third. I suspect that even today, Scott believes he got the job because he was the best candidate. It depends on how best is defined. Frankly, I think the Campus Community Forums were a mistake on Linfield's part. They provided a public opportunity for people to see all three candidates in action and respond in writing.

On January 29 I had an innocuous interview with the president. The only interesting question was, could I work with the present administration? I was, after all, naming it in my lawsuit. I replied yes, and barely restrained myself from asking Vivian if she felt the present administration could work with me.

The HHPA Department interview was, in a word, an ordeal. Although the questions asked of all three candidates were similar, when asked of me, given my situation, they came across as hostile. For example, Ad wanted to know which five words I thought my colleagues would use to describe me. I responded, "Which colleagues?" believing that the response would differ significantly depending on who was asked. The chair of the search directed Ad to withdraw the question.

My interview with the dean lasted about thirty minutes and was also innocuous. I think he and the president were being careful. Finally, the day ended with an interview with the search committee, which lasted about an hour. The questions were standard and again my impression was that people were being very careful about the questions they would pursue.

At times the chair, Lee Howard, seemed to feed me questions. I had the feeling that he was surprised and impressed by how well I came across. In one sense this baffled me; I wasn't acting any differently from the way I always had. But then, Lee's interactions with me had been limited and I suspect the rumors he'd heard about me were in conflict with my "live" responses. Tara seemed somewhat uncomfortable, and George asked only a few basic questions. I think George knew that he was part of a sham, and he seemed visibly upset about it. Frank Bumpus, who'd claimed earlier to be a "big fan," was quiet; he asked little, and it seemed apparent to me that his cheerleading days on my behalf were over. Michelle Jones's questions were harmless. The biggest surprise was finding out more about Alan Hubka, the trustee representative. As it turned out, he had played football under Paul Durham (Ad's predecessor). He asked questions about Title IX and my past administrative experience. For the most part he frowned and looked stern. I definitely didn't win him over.

The whole search process was irritating. I shouldn't have expected anything different, but it disappointed and annoyed me nonetheless. My interview schedule was crowded into one marathon day; Scott's and Jeff's were spaced out over several days. My forum occurred before my interviews; Scott's and Jeff's forums occurred after their interviews. The deadline for Faculty Forum responses was Monday at noon for Scott and Jeff. My interviews were not even completed by that deadline. As a result, the deadline for faculty input regarding my forum presentation was 3:00 P.M. the same day. This meant that my colleagues would have only an hour to respond thoughtfully to my presentation, while having had days to respond to Scott's and Jeff's.

These timing issues, combined with the search committee makeup and position evaluation criteria, made it increasingly difficult to view the process as anything other than an obvious pretense. Still, I held on, despite my better judgment, to a glimmer of hope that people would do the right thing.

Once again, that hope was misplaced. On February 5, 1996, I got a call from the dean informing me that the committee had recommended Scott for the position of athletic director, and that he had accepted. My consolation prize was that, according to Marv, the committee wanted me to know that I had represented myself well during the interview process.

The next day, a campus e-mail was sent out: "I am happy to announce to the Linfield community that Scott Carnahan will be

Athletic Director, effective July 1, 1996." The follow-up media gushed with Scott's praise and was inflated and misleading regarding the extent of his accomplishments and abilities. The *News-Register* printed full-page articles, complete with pictures, extolling Scott's amazing baseball coaching accomplishments (to Scott's credit, I believe he is a good baseball coach), and leading the cheer supporting Scott's appointment as athletic director. The *Oregonian*, too, was provided a press release and photo in support of Scott's succession of the legendary Ad Rutschman, as was the student paper, the *Linfield Review*.

That was that. The committee chose Scott. Shortly thereafter I added discrimination based on sex, as exemplified by my denial of the athletic director position, to my lawsuit, which was how I came to see the search committee documents. My faith in human nature was eroding.

19

Repercussions

Throughout that academic year (1995–96), the sunshine in my work life came from my coaching. In a way that was interesting. I have always considered myself a teacher who coached, both in the pool and classroom. I believe good teaching is to a degree good coaching and vice versa. Even so, throughout my academic career coaching had been something that, despite my successes, I'd played down. To be a coach in an academic setting was to be considered less. Yet during this difficult time, coaching became my safe haven.

The swimmers were wonderful. They worked hard and performed well. It was almost as if we were a family, and mom was going through some tough stuff. Despite the frustration of being left in the dark, not knowing why increasingly I was distant, self-absorbed, and too often short-tempered, they trusted and supported me. For the most part we had great success in the pool and out. They swam fast, did well in classes, and demonstrated care and concern that touched my heart. They far exceeded my expectations. It seemed the worse things got, the more we pulled together, and the more we succeeded.

It was winter 1996 when Ad took actions to try again to limit our national swim meet attendance. Ad wanted to impose additional requirements, possibly preventing swimmers already qualified from attending the meet. Ad never seemed to understand that a qualifying time event was by definition exclusionary, and therefore already screened for excellence.

In mid-February Ad called to tell me that national travel would be limited to those qualified swimmers ranked in the top eight, based on last year's times or current NAIA rankings. This meant that I had to provide him with top times from the previous year's meet as well as current national rankings, which were not necessarily reliable indicators of future success. I did so, and I also provided him with the following rationale.

The current rankings would by definition be misleading and could exclude swimmers who might earn a top-sixteen place at the national meet. This was because the system allowed swimmers to be ranked in numerous events, while the national meet format allowed swimmers to compete in only three individual events. It was quite possible, therefore, and often happened, that some swimmers would be ranked in more than three events. I explained to Ad that there wasn't any way to know exactly which events which swimmers would compete in until the meet.

As for the past season's times, I suggested to Ad that these would be a good general guide, but might not be completely reliable indicators of potential for success, as swimmers graduate annually and teams move in and out of various national affiliations. Finally, I pointed out that Linfield's policy and practice—and a stipulation in my hiring agreement under the former president, Charles Walker—was that for swimmers to compete at the national meet, they were required to (1) qualify for the meet, (2) be academically eligible to compete, and (3) have, in the coaches' view, a reasonable expectation of being competitive. I also told Ad that I intentionally tried not to have swimmers reach their peak times prior to the national meet. The goal was to peak at nationals; therefore, their current times in all likelihood would not represent their best per-

formance potential. Eliminating swimmers from competition because of time rankings that were intentionally not their best would
be unfair. I reminded Ad that I had the best track record in the department when it came to decisions about which athletes should
attend national competitions and bringing home the gold.

What Ad wanted was a guarantee that the athletes who went
would place and score points. Of course, that was a ridiculous request, and one I could not comply with.

That afternoon, I had to tell the swimmers there could be some
problems with their national meet attendance. I urged them to
focus on the season plan and swim well. I assured them I would
continue to support them and fight for them. It was a difficult time
and a very big deal. Not only was the policy unfair to the swimmers,
but swimming was the only Linfield sport being subjected to such
scrutiny. When the football team made the play-offs, it wasn't just
the starters who attended the game. To top it all off, the policy was
being imposed just weeks before the championships and too close
to the conference meet to alter the overall training plan in regard
to peak performances.

Further, with sixteen places for both individual and relay
events, limiting meet attendance to swimmers ranked in the top
eight would have a negative impact on our ability to score team
points. Perhaps this was Ad's intent all along. The better we did, the
more annoyed he seemed to become, and I suspect any possibility
of dampening our success was, at least subconsciously, appealing to
Ad.

On February 20 I became aware of another annoying inconsistency. The conference championships for swimming and men's
basketball were being held on the same weekend at Whitworth College in Spokane, Washington. The swim team was traveling by van,
with coaches and swimmers driving. The basketball team was flying. I was furious. I tracked Ad down and asked him how this disparity could be acceptable. Ad responded that the swim team too could
travel by plane. We just had to raise the money to do so. I told Ad

that I thought this was an example of disparate sport accommodation. He just shrugged, smirked, and told me to fund-raise.

First, this was another example of Ad's and the school's misunderstanding of Title IX. Fund-raising money cannot be used as an excuse for differential treatment among sports (women's basketball wasn't flying anywhere). Second, it was another example of how Ad would lash out at the swim team any chance he could. The result of this disparate travel arrangement was that the swimmers would be at greater safety risk, miss more school time, be less comfortable, endure a less-than-ideal study environment, and without doubt enter their championship competition with greater fatigue.

The swim team did fund-raise during the school year, but the bottom line is that minor sports simply don't have the fund-raising potential in this society that major sports do. It isn't a matter of time or effort spent. It is an undeniable, inescapable part of our culture.

Later that evening one of my team captains called to tell me that two swimmers had been arrested. Just what I needed! Two male swimmers had gone on a joyride with two women; they trespassed and damaged private property when their four-wheel vehicle got stuck in a field of mud. Early on it was unclear what the charges might be. I called Ad at home and told him about the incident. We decided to meet the next morning to discuss it.

I've always been a stickler for rules and not one to support athletes' getting special treatment. The reality was that the athletes had blown it, and my first reaction was not to allow them to attend the conference championships. Ad and I met and decided, based on our existing policies, that they could attend, as no formal charges had been brought at the time. During that first meeting, it was I who argued for a harsher penalty.

The next day we departed for the meet with the offending athletes. As the day wore on, more information came out, and it looked as though the crime was more serious than originally thought. I phoned Ad from Spokane, updating him on recent developments about the charges against the athletes. Ad was pretty good about it, and he asked me how I wanted to handle the situation. I said we should send the athletes home, and probably should not have brought them in the first place. He agreed, and we made arrangements to send them home with the basketball team, who'd been eliminated early in the tournament and planned to fly home the next day.

Late that evening the school paper called, asking me to comment on the situation. I responded that the athletes had been sent home, that I was focused on the meet at hand and didn't have anything further to say.

Upon our return, Ad asked for my final national travel recommendations. One of the offending swimmers was a national qualifier, and there remained the question of whether he should attend the meet. At this point the college administration stepped in, and the dean made a decision on the day of the entry deadline. The qualified athlete would not be entered. I was fine with the decision, but it didn't end there. The athlete in question was a very accomplished swimmer and was likely to score points and earn All-America status; he was at the time ranked number one in the nation in one of his events. His parents had hired an attorney and later that evening (after the entries had been completed and mailed) the athlete's attorney called, saying the charges would be dropped by 9:00 A.M. the following morning. The dean ruled that this changed things, and I was instructed to contact the NAIA to request that it accept a faxed entry reinstating the athlete. We would then meet to discuss whether he would be allowed to attend and compete.

The dean, Ad, and I met on February 28. I had mixed feelings, but the dean felt the athlete should go. Ad, however, had now decided that the athletic policies didn't go far enough. He did not feel the athlete should be allowed to attend or compete in the national meet.

At this point I was worn down by the whole thing and didn't care much one way or another. What annoyed me was Ad's waffling. He seemed willing to support policy only as long as the swimmers were penalized.

A decision needed to be made. The dean was on one side, and Ad was on the other. Ultimately, the dean reinstated the swimmer against Ad's wishes.

The meet was held in San Antonio, Texas, and ran Thursday through Saturday. On Wednesday night, at approximately 11:30 P.M. Texas time, a reporter from the school newspaper called to ask about the swimmer attending "against school policy." This was a nightmare that wouldn't end, and I wondered where the reporter had gotten the idea that I was acting against school policy. I was half-asleep and responded that, to my knowledge, he was not at the meet against school policy, that the charges against him had been dropped, and that it was the dean, not I, who had made the final decision. At that I hung up.

Seventeen swimmers attended those national championships, and of those, fifteen earned either All-America or Honorable Mention All-America honors, four earned Academic All-America Honors, and four won six national event titles. Overall, the men's team placed fourth and the women's seventh. Interestingly, the offending swimmer was one of the few who performed poorly at the meet, placing well below his potential.

Upon our return I completed and submitted my expense report. Soon after, Ad called with questions. I had to go over the meet time line and every meal expense. On a more humorous note, while Ad was scrutinizing my expenses, his wife and secretary, Joan, was complimenting me on how wonderful I was. She said she wanted to "clone" me, because I was so quick and accurate with expense reports.

The story did not end there. On March 12 the swimmer contacted me to tell me he'd been recharged. Apparently, his lawyer and family had negotiated a temporary deal that would drop the charges for the period he was at the meet and then reinstate them. I was furious. I hadn't known anything about this, probably because the swimmer knew me well enough to know I wouldn't have allowed him to compete. The swimmer claimed he hadn't known the charges would be dropped only temporarily. I suspected he was lying.

I told him I felt it was wrong for him to have gone to the meet and explained that skirting policy was not the same as complying with it. I also called the swimmer's attorney to follow up. When I asked how it was that the charges had been dropped, the attorney smugly replied, "Good lawyering." This incensed me! I called Ad and the dean to tell them what I'd learned. I also asked the dean if he'd known all along that the dropped charges would be reinstated. He replied that he guessed "theoretically" the charges could be brought again.

The dean was not upset about the turn of events. He told me that at the time his decision was legitimate. He went on to say that after we'd left for the meet, "some members of the community had gotten to the district attorney" and, as a result, the district attorney had changed his mind. I wondered how people in the community were made aware of the situation and spurred to action.

A few days later the *News-Register* pounced on the story. The paper portrayed Ad as the "conscience" who knew the matter wasn't resolved and advised against sending the swimmer to the meet. Jeb, who had previously acknowledged he was one-sided, implied from the tone of his article that he'd actually been at the meeting with Ad, the dean, and me. He hadn't been there and must have been fed inside information from somewhere. According to Jeb's article, I'd argued strongly that the athlete be allowed to attend the meet, which simply wasn't true.

Ultimately, the swimmer and the others involved had to pay restitution and do community service. The affair had been blown out of proportion—not that what they did wasn't bad; it was. However, the issue wouldn't end and the truth had been distorted and leaked for public scrutiny, which was without doubt a response to its involvement with the swim team, which by association meant me.

In a similar vein, my long-standing complaint about the assistant coach salary schedule developed by Ad reached a head in February. Despite the length of the swimming season, its coach-to-athlete ratio, which was almost double that of any other sport, its many practice hours, and its squad size of at least eighteen women and eighteen men (making only football and track larger), Ad's idea of fairness dictated that swimming needed minimal assistant coach support.

The administration had even consulted again with Lynn Snyder from Sports Services. According to Lynn, the fact that I was no longer acting as assistant athletic director freed up considerable time, and therefore the support needs he'd previously identified were no longer valid. It failed to occur to anyone that my load had not simply been reduced. I'd been assigned additional teaching duties. I didn't have extra time to put into coaching. I'm not sure if it was arrogance or ignorance; it was probably both. Ad's salary schedule was approved and enforced, except when it came to select men's sports such as baseball.

As the year trudged on, other repercussions from my lawsuit began to surface. I had for many years run a very successful summer swim camp. In preparation for the coming summer, the conference services office was becoming concerned. The office had been receiving calls from as far away as Idaho from parents wondering whether there'd be a swim camp, and who'd be running it. Rumors had circulated across state lines, throughout the swimming community, ranging from assertions that I'd been fired to queries about the status of my lawsuit against the college. It was irritating, but most alarming was the potential loss of the swim camp's significant income—which was not to be taken lightly.

On and on the little things mounted. The longer I held out, pursuing the lawsuit, the more vicious and annoying the repercussions became. One can never really know what another is thinking or intending, but actions are revealing, and it seemed clear from his actions that Ad was not about to relent. I wasn't about to, either.

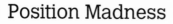

20

Position Madness

During this time, now that Scott had been announced as the heir apparent to Ad, the department turned its attention to other matters. On February 14 we had a department meeting to discuss position announcements. The HHPA department members were present, along with Barbara Seidman, the newly appointed Title IX compliance officer and associate dean of faculty.

The meeting focused on the teaching and coaching needs within the department. Three positions were announced, which was something quite unusual and special. It isn't typical in small colleges, or any colleges for that matter, to create positions routinely. The normal faculty process involves applying through faculty committees or the college administration for a position, providing extensive justification for the position, and then maybe, a small percentage of the time, having a position allocated. In our case the administration was simply giving the department new positions; there was not a faculty process involved at all. I think this was an attempt to assuage some of our departmental dysfunction and discontent. It was also, perhaps, an attempt to address Title IX "deficiencies" (as the administration liked to call them).

The positions were as follows: (1) a senior faculty position as department chair; (2) a one-year, nontenure-track junior faculty position with assistant football and baseball coaching attached; and (3) a women's athletics administrative position that included coaching two women's sports and teaching activity classes.

Following the announcements, departmental discussion ensued. Tara asked if one of the positions could be advertised to include the senior woman administrator post, as she didn't want to continue with that label added on to her existing job responsibilities. Ed argued for writing the job announcements so that people currently in the department could apply for the department chair position. This generated a fair amount of discussion, and I suspect Ed wanted to apply. Once Scott was athletic director, if Ed, the head football coach became department chair, any threats to the continued domination of men's sport interests could be easily quelled. I too was interested in the department chair position, but I had little doubt about how popular that idea would be.

Barbara Seidman spoke to the "very special" opportunity that hiring an outside senior faculty member presented, and urged the department to "seize" upon it and thereby strengthen our academic focus. Laura too spoke up. She emphasized the need to put academics above athletics and to hire teachers who coached and not more coaches who taught. This sparked quite a bit of comment. Ad especially wanted to make sure that there was balance. But his idea of balance was looking for coaches who taught. He followed by saying that it was the dean's job to let the department know if our teaching wasn't up to par.

The meeting went on, identifying many departmental needs, including health education teaching, department leadership, coaching, internship supervision, athletic administration, facilities supervision, and intramurals organization. The meeting ended with George wrapping things up and asking anyone interested in applying for the department chair position to let him know. I responded in writing, indicating I was interested. George and I had a brief conversation after the meeting. He told me that any perceptions I had that my application for athletic director had not been well supported by the department were misplaced, that indeed I'd had considerable support. I wasn't quite sure how to take that. Did it mean that in addition to ignoring the Faculty Forum input, the search committee also ignored the departmental input? It was hard to tell what anyone meant by anything at that point. George volunteered that he would be happy to share my intent with members of the department and then give me feedback about the support I could expect.

The next meetings were held February 26 and 27. Interestingly enough, during the first meeting the department had favored internal candidates' applying for the department chair position. After people learned that I was interested, they changed their tune. The department's new stance was that the search should be defined so as to limit the position to a health educator with all appropriate certifications and background, effectively precluding me from applying.

The administration added to this by sending a memo to the department arguing that if we recommended a search that effectively excluded an internal hire, they would support the three positions as previously outlined. If, however, the department did not comply, then the administration's support for all three positions would not be firm. The department might get only one hire or two junior faculty hires instead of the three positions originally described.

By mid-March the department chair job description was finalized, distributed, and worded in such a way that I could not be a viable candidate. The junior faculty football and baseball coaching description was put together by Jay and written as a three-year post. At the time I remember being confused as to why Jay was writing the position description, and how he managed to turn a one-year position into a three-year position.

By the first of April the search for a department chair was under way. Amazingly, during our first meeting the job description and evaluation materials made no mention of Title IX. This puzzled me; if the department chair was to serve in a supervisory capacity over the athletic director and athletics, it seemed fairly obvious and important that he or she be knowledgeable about, or at least interested in, Title IX.

At that point, I shared with George some research by Acosta and Carpenter that dealt with mobility of senior positions for women in physical education and athletics. I feared that we were defining the position in such a way that we wouldn't be able to generate a viable pool of female candidates. George and I discussed the materials briefly. He commented that he appreciated the information and then volunteered to serve as a reference for me at any time, should I want to leave Linfield and go elsewhere.

As our conversation closed, George expressed his dismay that the department was not taking advantage of the opportunity to strengthen our academics by framing the junior faculty position as something other than a football and baseball coach. George went on to say that this position had been negotiated by Jay and Scott when they assumed their respective promotions. (When Ed had stepped down from his head football coach post, Jay had been elevated from defensive coach to head coach.) George did not feel this was best for the department.

On April 10 the department held a meeting to discuss Jay's junior faculty position. As it worked out, the load allocations for this position included nine load credits for coaching football and four and a half load credits for coaching baseball. In essence, another assistant football coach would receive as many load credits as the head coach of any other sport. Laura was upset about this and pursued the matter in the meeting. She asked how the load allocations were decided. Jay simply responded that full-time assistant football coaches had always received load credit equal to other sport head coaches', and the head football coach received double the load of any other head coach. Jay continued by saying it had "always been that way" and so wasn't an equity problem. I wanted to get a tape recorder, record what he said, and play it back to him so he could listen to himself. Laura was bold and asked that the matter be pursued. George responded that he didn't want to "touch it," but reluctantly agreed to talk with the dean.

Later that evening I, along with the rest of the department, received a memo announcing a financial aid meeting for the next day. This was an important annual meeting. About a week before I'd seen an e-mail to Scott scheduling the meeting. Timely communication wasn't one of Scott's strengths.

By the end of April we had a candidate pool for the department chair position. Many of the applicants did not appear even minimally qualified, and quite a few strayed from or stretched the health educator qualifications. I spoke with Barbara Seidman about this. Her response was that the screening committee had decided not to screen. The committee had decided to let the department narrow the candidates based on its view of what a "health educator" was. At that, I let her know that I would again be interested in becoming an applicant if the plan was to adjust the search to allow candidates without health education backgrounds to reach the final applicant pool. Of course, that wasn't a well-received idea.

On April 26 the department members met to review the candidates. Two emerged as highly qualified. Three others were identified as second-tier applicants, one of whom did not have a health education background. Although I was opposed to this, it didn't seem to matter. No matter what I said or how ridiculous their position needed to become to stand contrary to mine, they seemed set on opposing me.

During this meeting I followed up on Laura's question about football coaching load credit. George replied that the nine load credits Jay had mentioned was a mistake. The load would be six. Jay was not happy.

The junior faculty position search didn't yield anyone other than two football coaches already in the department. On May 6 we started interviews. Joe Smith, a Linfield graduate, ex-football player, and current assistant football coach, was interviewed first, and Bob MeWhinny was second. Joe was more academically prepared than Bob, and he was preferable—at least he didn't publicly endorse *Plessy v. Ferguson*. But when asked about Title IX, Joe responded that he didn't know much about it and thought it was an "equity law for athletics" that dealt mostly with "D-I type schools and issues." I wondered where Joe'd been these past months.

On May 8 Bob was interviewed. Bob had no relevant academic preparation, but, according to the football staff, was a "good coach," and they reasoned that if one was a good coach one could learn to teach anything. Sadly, the department opted to hire Bob. Here we were hiring an applicant who, from his own statements, seemed to believe that laws supporting racial discrimination were good. I suspect the horror of this may have been lost on some of the football coaches, as Jay had recently taken a public stand at a faculty meeting, informing people that revising the antidiscrimination statement in Linfield's mission statement to include sexual orientation would hurt football recruiting.

As for the department chair search, we ended up interviewing three candidates: two planned, Peggy Holstedt and Dawn Graff-Haight, and one unplanned, John Fisher. Peggy didn't have a terminal degree, but was dynamic and energetic.

John Fisher was an interesting interviewee. He was from Australia and happened to be in the area, so Barbara set up an interview. One of John's questions was particularly amusing. He wondered why the department had tied health education to the department chair position. To him it seemed to make more sense to tie it to physical education, as physical education frequently included health education, but not typically the other way around. He continued by saying, "it seems a business gamble to hire a department chair from the outside." I almost laughed. It was obvious to a complete stranger that the position alignment was questionable.

The next interviewee, Dawn Graff-Haight, called me in advance requesting a meeting. We met at lunch on May 17. Dawn was from Portland State University (PSU), the school from which I was completing my doctorate. We talked a bit about PSU and her teaching. She then asked how I "felt about being [at Linfield]." She indicated she was aware of my lawsuit, and that she knew things had not been pleasant for me. She told me she'd asked a few questions about the lawsuit, but no one would talk much about it. I responded that I couldn't talk about it either.

She went on to ask if my Title IX concerns about Linfield athletics had something to do with proportionality. This was annoying. Linfield had tried repeatedly to portray me as fixated on proportionality. I explained to Dawn what proportionality meant, and that my position on the matter of gender equity in athletics was much broader and not so one-dimensional. We talked briefly about Title IX compliance, and I told her that I did not regret my role as a catalyst for change.

Over the course of the day, Dawn's interview presentations went well, although interestingly neither Scott nor Jay was present. They wanted Peggy for department chair. It was perplexing to me that people who didn't attend both candidate presentations would rate them both. This seemed especially odd with regard to Scott, as he would in effect be rating his potential supervisor.

On May 20 we met to discuss the candidates. During those discussions the pool was narrowed to Peggy and Dawn (I guess John asked too many relevant questions). Both appeared qualified, although I thought Dawn was the stronger candidate, particularly from an academic standpoint. The next day the search committee shared information from the reference check calls, and the department reached consensus to offer the job to Dawn. I was mildly surprised and felt very good about the decision. I believed she could be a good leader and would be an outstanding teaching addition to the department.

As the 1995–96 academic year drew to a close, the final touches were put on the departmental restructuring. On June 14 the department got a memo from the dean stating that the department chair would also be appointed as the senior woman administrator for "purposes of NCAA compliance."

Wes Suan (yet another football coach) was promoted to assistant athletic director and facilities director. With his new elevation, he became the number-two man in athletics, and I would have to deal extensively with him on facility issues. Larry Doty, the men's basketball coach, was reassigned as assistant facilities director (Wes's old job).

As a result of the departmental restructuring, with the exception of the department chair, the men's major sports—football, baseball, and basketball—controlled everything.

Part VI

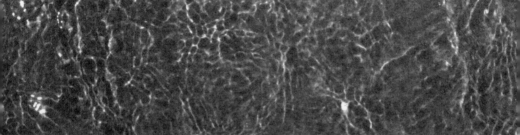

21

Ups and Downs

Over the course of the year, I continued work on my doctorate. Typically, students working on advanced degrees get their course work out of the way and then concentrate on a dissertation. My doctoral path was atypical. My course work and dissertation reached completion within a term of each other.

During the winter of 1995–96 I conducted my first dissertation workshop program, and in March 1996 I was ready to field-test again. Unlike the first workshop field test, the second was conducted at a college with a football program, in theory a more significant challenge.

The workshop went well. In fact, comments from those who attended praised my presentation as unbiased, informative, and evenhanded. My favorite comment came from the football coach, a man who'd been at the institution more than twenty years. He approached me saying he wanted to share just one complaint. I was nervous and ready for what I thought would be an attack. I was pleasantly surprised. His complaint was that he didn't understand why his school hadn't had a workshop like this years ago. He liked it, learned a lot, and especially appreciated the delivery, which he characterized as "broad-minded." With this second field test complete, I moved forward to the analysis stage of my research and prepared to complete my dissertation.

Also during this time, I received a phone call from Judy Marshall, a representative of the local American Association of University Women (AAUW) Legal Advocacy Fund. She'd gotten my name from someone at a recent AAUW meeting and contacted me to inquire about my potential financial needs regarding the lawsuit. She explained that people involved in suits like mine could apply for support through the AAUW Legal Advocacy Fund. In exchange, the AAUW expected recipients to give AAUW talks. Judy said she'd forward information to me, and I thanked her for the call.

I then contacted my attorneys and asked their advice about pursuing AAUW financial support. The costs of the lawsuit were mounting. I was receiving monthly bills ranging from a few hundred dollars to more than a thousand dollars for legal costs. I wasn't sure how much longer I could keep it up and was nearing the point of having to ask my family for financial assistance, something I very much wanted to avoid.

On April 10 I got a call from the Pacific University athletic director, Judy Sherman. She asked that I consult with her on an internal Title IX audit. Pacific's president had requested the audit. I agreed to help the department free of charge and asked for compliance assessment information as outlined in the Office for Civil Rights *Title IX Investigator's Manual*. I thought it best to do the audit by the book.

Interestingly, when Judy told her president that I was the one consulting on their audit, her president contacted Vivian Bull. According to what was relayed to Judy, Vivian indicated she'd been pleased with the Title IX process at Linfield and especially with the compliance information gathering I had initiated. How weird to have a person I'd named in my suit, a person instrumental in firing me as assistant athletic director, telling another college president

I'd done good work. I couldn't help wondering why, if Vivian really felt that way, she had left me to take the heat for Linfield's gender-equity fallout.

Throughout the lawsuit, I sent periodic updates of my documentation log to Liz and Lory. The purpose was to apprise them of what was going on and sometimes ask questions. On April 11 I sent such an update, again asking their advice about the AAUW Legal Advocacy Fund, along with a recent *News-Register* editorial that had been uncomplimentary.

On April 23 I got a call back. Lory updated me on the trial schedule and indicated she'd check into the AAUW Legal Advocacy Fund application. She also said there was probably no way to tie the HHPA department chair position into a discrimination suit (Linfield had hired a female). As to the *News-Register* editorial, Lory's advice was to "let it go."

On May 10 we received another offer to settle. I responded as before; I had no interest in settling. As far as I was concerned, we were pursuing right and Linfield was defending wrong. Settling wouldn't right the wrongs. I just wasn't interested in settling. I wasn't interested in money. I was too naive.

In mid-May I had a disappointing conversation with Laura. One of the saddest things about my Title IX ordeal and lawsuit was that people quickly forgot the struggle for equity once they perceived they were getting what they wanted. Laura was one of those people.

Softball had been a big winner from my Title IX efforts. Before I rang the Title IX bell, there had been a huge disparity between what baseball enjoyed and what softball endured, especially in terms of equipment and facilities. In response to compliance pressures, the softball field was undergoing a complete transformation. In most ways it was wonderful. Sometimes, when I'd feel depressed, I'd drive or walk by the softball field and marvel at the changes under way. It would remind me that I was making a difference.

Sadly, Laura and the players had bought the Linfield line,

which was that the softball field renovation would have occurred regardless of my Title IX efforts. As far as I was concerned, that was just not true. For years little had been done, despite repeated requests. It was only after I held a gun to Linfield's head that things began to change.

Laura's position had shifted. She supported Scott as the new athletic director and felt that the department needed to move on with new leadership. She also told me that, given the political situation and departmental climate, it was best that new leadership came from outside the department (meaning the outside hire as department chair), and that Scott was the "right choice" for athletic director. Scott's earlier actions toward her seemed to have slipped her mind. Scott, in Laura's view, was the man for the job. She continued by saying she wanted to get out of being an assistant athletic trainer, she chafed under Tara's authority, and wanted to move instead into athletic administration. Laura saw herself becoming the assistant athletic director for women's sports. She wanted the job I'd been fired from and seemed to believe she and Scott were the leadership team of Linfield's future.

Perhaps Laura had been bought off with vague promises of leadership, or maybe she simply changed her mind. Either way, I'd evidently served my purpose, and she seemed willing to step on me and over me to get to what she wanted. That conversation made me feel very sad. It also made painfully clear the realities of time, and how time was in Linfield's favor. With time people forget. With time the bad doesn't seem so bad. With time people convince themselves that it is easier to move on.

Also during this time Mary decided to fight back in response to her tenure and promotion denial, claiming irregularities in her tenure review process. The college agreed to investigate.

Howard Leichter, a senior faculty member, was in charge of the investigation. He called me in early May and asked about my recollections regarding various alleged irregularities. My response corroborated Mary's version of the story and was in conflict with the dean's. According to Howard, it came down to Mary's and my word against the dean's. The investigating committee couldn't determine who was telling the truth. Even so, they found in Mary's favor and, to remedy the situation, instructed Scott, Jay, Ed, and Ad to rewrite their colleague appraisals, disregarding any negative information they'd found when they invaded her file.

It was absurd. They didn't get reprimanded for violating school policy and were instead invited to evaluate Mary again. In the best of circumstances it would be ridiculous to expect people to be able to discount prior knowledge, and these were not the best of circumstances. As for Mary, she had less than a day to respond to four new, negative colleague evaluations before the RTS Committee would resume her review. A few days later the dean called. Mary would not be awarded tenure and promotion.

One would think a good lawyer would have a field day with Linfield, with its differential treatment and irregularities in policy and practice between male and female faculty, and jobs lost and reassigned over "he said, she said" versions of truth. But being right means little more than being right. The legal issue is can you win, and can you win big enough to make it financially worthwhile.

Mary spoke with George, and his comment was that he "just didn't understand it." He went on to suggest that she talk with Scott about a positive letter of recommendation and begin looking elsewhere for employment. Mary inquired about the Faculty Redress Committee, and George told her he thought if she took that route and didn't go quietly, she would not have support from members of the department or the college administration.

Mary asked what I thought of her situation. I was careful to tell her what was important was what *she* thought and pointed out that a decision to fight back was not to be made lightly. In the end, she did fight back. She threatened to sue and had an attorney represent her in settlement talks. Ultimately, she received some kind of settlement and moved on.

Mary fought back and had to leave. Laura joined the majority and stayed.

As the school year closed, the final issue of the school newspaper was released. This issue was traditionally a spoof called the *Linquirer*. In fairness to the students, I should say that most of it was pretty funny and meant to be taken tongue in cheek. But some of it bothered me. Perhaps I was just too sensitive after all that had gone on. I was referred to throughout the paper, often in an uncomplimentary light.

On June 5 I received some good news. My presentation proposal on Title IX had been accepted by the National Girls and Women in Sports Symposium. At Linfield I'd been fired for stating the truth, and systematically denied leadership and voice, but nationally I was gaining an audience.

About this time I sent another query to Liz and Lory. I wanted to consider filing an official in-house grievance regarding violations of personnel policy and to pursue Title IX compliance issues in regard to our recent departmental staffing decisions. Finally, I wanted the go-ahead to put together an application for the AAUW Legal Advocacy Fund. Liz and Lory didn't respond. Maybe they felt our plate was full enough and didn't want to heap more upon it. Maybe they didn't want the added publicity. Maybe they weren't aware of how close to the brink of financial disaster I was teetering.

Another opportunity presented itself June 20. On that day I had a conversation with a local bank manager. He was a notary public, and I'd had him notarize various legal documents over the past months. McMinnville is small community, and I was uncomfortable having to go to him, or anyone for that matter, but I had little choice. During this visit, he questioned me about Linfield's move from the NAIA to NCAA Division III, Title IX compliance, and booster donations. I was careful to be blandly informative in my responses.

He was critical of Linfield's administration and voiced his opinion that the recent "problems" seemed rooted in the college's leadership and communication. He went on to tell me about a Lion's Club luncheon he had attended at which a "recently promoted member of [my] department" was speaking. He'd been surprised and concerned about some of the comments made, calling them "off-color." He didn't reveal the name of the individual, but it was obvious it was Scott. I suggested to my attorneys that if it was Scott, then his "off-color" remarks in a public setting would be consistent with his sexist remarks to me. We didn't pursue this.

Other little annoyances within the department cropped up throughout the summer. In a July conversation with Ed, I was informed that football camp money would be used to purchase televisions and videocassette recorders for all the football coaches so they could watch game videos in their offices: a new verse in his TV and VCR song. This would have been fine—except if the ability to watch game videos in one's office was something only the men's sport teams benefited from. According to Title IX, it doesn't matter where the money comes from, it's what the money buys, and whether a disparate accommodation results.

We'd take a step or two forward and then leap backward. This development showed that many still didn't understand what Title IX compliance meant. If they were shut down in one area, they just routed their efforts in another direction. There was no gender equity or Title IX buy-in, and there was little administrative support, supervision, or regulation, just a haphazard mess of fits and starts.

When I speak on Title IX, people often ask how it's possible that compliance with a 1972 law remains largely unrealized. Even more remarkable is that after countless Title IX lawsuits and a virtually unblemished win record in favor of women and girls, the burden of compliance still falls heavily on athletes, coaches, and parents willing to pursue litigation. Schools feign surprise and offense at gender discrimination accusations, often holding fast to claims of innocence long after suits have been settled or run their courses.

I can't count the number of times people have said, "Oh, I'm all for gender equity, as long as we don't have to take away from the boys." Ideally, elevating sport for women and girls to the level men and boys have enjoyed for generations is a great solution. However, fiscal realities often make that ideal impossible. Much like a family into which a second child is born, unless there is a dramatic influx of new resources, what used to take care of one now has to cover two. Most people wouldn't say to their second child, "No, you don't get new clothes or a bike to ride. We only have enough for your older brother." Instead, parents must figure out ways to make their fixed resources fill the family's expanding needs and in the process, it is hoped, teach their children about the benefits of sharing.

Although I didn't say anything to Ed at the time, I later pursued the issue through the new Title IX compliance officer, Barbara Seidman. In response, without admitting anything, the administration purchased TVs and VCRs for all coaches, which was overkill, as not all coaches needed the same equipment. Equitable accommodation of comparable needs is different from a costly knee-jerk reaction where all people are treated identically, even if they do not need the same things.

Reactions like this are exactly what opponents of gender equity cite when making disparaging comments about Title IX. These are the types of reactions that fuel the false impression that gender equity is about women being given what men in sport believe they have earned. It's like employers blaming affirmative action for "quota" hires, when in fact quotas are not part of affirmative action and are generally illegal.

In the midst of everything, July 3, 1996, was a happy day. It was the day I defended my dissertation. My defense was a wonderful success. The only feedback I received was that I should copyright the material. It was a day filled with support from family and friends. As of July 3, 1996, I was (unofficially—graduation wouldn't take place until early August) Dr. Cynthia Pemberton! My degree in Educational Leadership–Higher Education Administration was complete. I felt an immense sense of accomplishment and relief. It was a milestone in my educational journey.

On July 17 I met with Barbara Seidman at her request to review the athletics department manual. Barbara was supposed to have a working version of the manual by fall 1996. We talked about the organizational chart and the demotion in status and reporting authority of my position as aquatics director. Barbara went on to describe how she perceived her work as Title IX officer progressing and asked to see the consulting work I'd done for Pacific University. Seemingly, my work was good enough to serve as a model, but I was incapable of participating in the leadership of our own gender-equity efforts.

Other tidbits of information circulated over the summer. Mary was told by a coaching colleague that, according to Laura, "Cindy and Mary were being blackballed, and so she felt she had to go along with the majority or it would happen to her too." Laura was probably right. An administrator in the College Development Office stated that everyone in her department knew Scott was incompetent, but they were hopeful he'd do better in his position as athletic director than his past history hinted.

On August 20 I received an annoying memo from Wes Suan. As the new facilities director, he was instructing me to process all aquatics work-study time cards through him. To understand how irritating this was, one would have to know Wes. Although not a bad guy, Wes has little to commend him. He was a Linfield football graduate with a bachelor's degree in physical education. Up to this point, he'd been the equipment room manager, and, during the football season, he, like the other football coaches, was typically unavailable—he generally didn't return messages, memos, or e-mails.

Wes was essentially a "good old boy" assigned duties beyond coaching to justify full-time pay.

A few days later, Wes followed this memo with a memo to the entire department asserting he was in charge of all facilities. I interpreted the word "all" to include aquatics. I sent a message to the new department chair, requesting a meeting to discuss this development. I also suggested that she involve Scott, Wes, and any other administrators necessary, so we would all be on the same page.

On September 4 Dawn, the department chair, replied. She informed me that Scott was writing up an aquatics job description for me. This too was news. I already had an aquatics job description. I called Dawn and left a message asking why Scott was writing up something I already had.

A day later Dawn told me she hoped I wasn't concerned. She felt there were some miscommunications, and she assumed at least part of the responsibility. She assured me that Scott would not be writing up an aquatics job description and agreed that she, Scott, Wes, and I should meet. She told me that Wes was probably eager to do his new job and didn't realize he was stepping on toes.

The totality of the list of little abuses that made my job difficult, along with the repeated efforts to diminish my job responsibilities, pointed unmistakably to whistle-blower protection violations. Many states, Oregon among them, have laws designed to protect employees who point out employer wrongdoings. In general, these laws make it unlawful for an employer to discharge, demote, or in any manner discriminate or retaliate—in terms of promotion, compensation, conditions, or privileges of employment—against an employee who has in good faith "blown the whistle." These laws are nice in theory, but the reality is that whistle-blowers proceed at their own risk and often, as I did, face on-the-job discrimination and retaliatory harassment.

Later that fall I made a presentation on Title IX during the National Girls and Women in Sports Symposium in Baltimore, Maryland. It was a nice trip, a good symposium, and my presentation went well. It felt good to get some positive reinforcement. Sometimes, despite knowing what I was doing was right and my understanding of gender equity accurate, being surrounded by so many people telling me I was wrong made it hard not to doubt myself. When I did get positive reinforcement, it was very powerful and important to me. Of course, those good feelings were usually short-lived, and this instance was no exception. While I was out of town, Jeb Bladine of the *News-Register* wrote an editorial titled "A New Prez for Linfield."

The September 28, 1996, editorial insulted me because I'd amended the lawsuit following the announcement of Scott's promotion to athletic director, and again after the new department chair was hired. The article portrayed the lawsuit as a frivolous attempt to "cash in" on a big payday. Jeb wrote:

> Yes, indeed, I think we've found the next best president for Linfield College. Dr. Vivian Bull is doing a dandy job, but surely, if the Selection Committee had been given the option it would have named Linfield Associate Professor Cindy Pemberton to the presidency. I think the courts should require Dr. Bull to step aside in favor of a more qualified candidate.
>
> OK, so I'm being a little bit sarcastic. But it was too much to resist after reading Pemberton's amended $2 million dollar lawsuit against Linfield, President Bull and Vice President of Academic Affairs Marv Henberg.
>
> Pemberton, a champion of equality in women's athletics, claims that Linfield discriminated against her on the basis of her sex in June 1995 when she lost her position as assistant athletic director. But that's just the beginning.
>
> Pemberton's lawsuit claims that when Ad Rutschman retired, she was "the most qualified to accede to the position of athletic director." Linfield's decision to hire Scott Carnahan

was sex discrimination, according to her lawsuit, and she is entitled to "reinstatement to the position of athletic director."

It gets worse. Linfield later named a new chairman of the Department of Health, Human Performance and Athletics. A woman, Dawn Graff-Height [*sic*] was hired, so Pemberton couldn't claim sex discrimination. Instead she is charging Linfield with "intentionally manipulating the selection criteria" to exclude her. And of course, she is entitled to "reinstatement to the position of HHPA Department Chair."

Like so many alleged victims seeking a big payday from the courts, Pemberton suffered "physical pain and substantial emotional distress." Presumably, that would be eased if she can get $500,000 in compensatory damages, $1 million in punitive damages from Linfield, and $250,000 each in punitive damages from Bull and Henberg.

Who knows . . . she may win. Juries around the country are making sex discrimination cases a tremendous growth industry within the legal system. And knowing how much this kind of litigation costs, Linfield's insurance company will probably offer a big fat settlement.

But Pemberton, if we are to believe her lawsuit, will not be happy unless she has $2 million in her pocket and is crowned athletic director and chairman of HHPA. And we can only guess what might follow—after all, Dr. Bull can't last forever. It would be a laughingstock if it weren't for the fact that cases like this are high on the list of what's wrong with America.

So much for feeling good. Jeb mischaracterized me, the lawsuit, and the legal system. He offhandedly discounted the many lawsuits, like my own, that are valid, grounded in what is moral and right, that either don't get filed because of lack of strength, support, or resources, or fizzle in settlement because the pressure against continuing becomes too great.

In early October I met with Dawn to review my professional goals. During this meeting she told me that she saw me as better suited for graduate school teaching. In her words, I was being "wasted" at Linfield. She thought I should be teaching more and not managing the aquatics facility and agreed that my education and expertise were being underutilized.

I told her about my repeated efforts to get out of aquatics and coaching, and Linfield's refusal to consider my requests, despite persuasive rationale. Dawn replied that she'd heard good things about my coaching and was surprised I would be willing to leave it behind. I wondered if I'd ever escape the label of coach, a label I was not proud of wearing, despite my accomplishments. For me, being a coach meant being lumped with Ad, Scott, Ed, Jay, and Wes, and that was not any company I was proud to be keeping. The meeting ended with Dawn telling me she was one of my "biggest cheerleaders" and would support me in any way she could.

Normally, such a meeting would have been a positive thing. In many ways it was, and I did feel better. But I couldn't help being skeptical. Maybe others wanted Dawn to manipulate me; perhaps this was just another Linfield tactic to get me to move on voluntarily.

The school year moved along with various department meetings, another professional opportunity to make a presentation on Title IX, at the American Education Research Association—Special Interest Group on Women in Education, and the start of depositions.

22

Depositions

Throughout the late summer of 1996, the lawsuit began to move into a new phase: preparation for depositions. The process began with my watching some videos and proceeded with numerous conversations with Liz and Lory, trying to coordinate scheduling. My deposition would be the first, and was scheduled for August 6 and 7, although it would end up stretching out over August 15, 29, and 30.

In a way, I was excited. I thought that finally the lawsuit would really begin to go somewhere, that we'd start getting to the truth. I expected some television-style Perry Mason moment. But that wasn't what happened. What I got was a final crushing blow to whatever shreds of innocence I still possessed.

Depositions are awful things. They are long, personal, and insulting. They are seemingly endless question-and-answer sessions, in which every query is an attempt to incriminate. They aren't about detailing the truth. They're about digging for dirt and working to find ways to twist the truth and use it as a weapon.

Day one started with my swearing in. We proceeded with a series of personal history questions—where I grew up, my competitive swimming background, and so forth. The questioning progressed to my early career in coaching, my marriage to Mike Anderson, and our move from Virginia Beach, Virginia, to Reno, Nevada. From that point the questioning focused for a long time on my decision to leave Reno, move to Oregon, and begin working at Linfield, as well as how that played into issues related to my marriage and ultimately my divorce in 1992.

One of the most irritating aspects of the deposition process was that the attorneys could ask anything they wanted. Personal privacy was immaterial, and relevance to the issue at hand could be stretched almost as far as the opposing counsel wanted to stretch it. It was a fishing expedition.

We spent an amazing amount of time with the opposing counsel's trying to understand why I got a divorce. They asked questions about romantic involvement outside my marriage, wanted me to describe my feelings for my ex-husband—whether I had loved him—and wanted me to give a list of the reasons that had led me to seek a divorce. To me it wasn't an incongruity to love someone yet not want to be married to him. I hadn't sat down one afternoon and created a laundry list of reasons to justify my decision to get a divorce. Mike and I had been together since I was seventeen years old. That was enough of my life lived in that partnership: end of story. There was nothing terribly dramatic to tell. We'd had good times and bad times. There was growth and joy, but there was also pain and a mounting divide between us. Eventually it became clear that our relationship was at its end. It took half a day of the deposition to get through my decision to end my marriage. It was an exhausting and invasive process, and I resented it.

We then moved on to a chronology of my work experience at Linfield, with various exhibits introduced into evidence. Much time was spent questioning the development of my job description, my role as assistant athletic director, and my interest in Title IX. The job description questioning was pointed and accusatory. I think the attorneys wanted to show that I'd had some master plan all along and created my own job description so as to mandate investigating Title IX, which just wasn't true. I had been asked by the Linfield administrators to work on the development of my job description and they'd provided me with a model. At the time I hadn't even known Title IX existed, let alone what it meant.

I'd been ignorant about Title IX until the summer of 1992. I testified that I'd first received Title IX information from a regional women's sports newsletter called *The Inside Track* and had seen some articles in the *Oregonian* newspaper. After reading this information, I had simply decided to look into it. There was never any master plan.

When I became aware of Title IX it seemed obvious that I'd been living in a bit of a void and needed to become informed. Pam Jacklin (Linfield's attorney) couldn't seem to get beyond this. She questioned me for what seemed like hours. At one point, referring to a summer 1992 memo I'd sent to Ad and various college administrators informing them that I planned to begin researching Title IX, the questioning went like this:

Q. *Why was it at that point in time you thought it was so important to let them know that you had found a topic you were now going to inquire about and become more knowledgeable about?*

A. Because Title IX has institution-wide implications.

Q. *Wasn't it possible, based on what you knew at that point in time, that it had institution-wide implications but that there was no problem whatsoever at Linfield College?*

A. Yes, that would be possible.

Q. *Then why would they care about your new interest in this issue?*

A. If that was the case, they might not care.

Q. *I'm still trying to get at why you were so enthusiastic about sharing your anticipated learning curve.*

A. There isn't another reason. Because I thought it was an issue that could have institution-wide implications. And if that's the case, then the people in those positions would need to know about anything that I might find out about that might impact the institution. There isn't another answer.

Q. *Okay. Isn't it true that you had already concluded that Linfield College had Title IX problems that needed to be addressed and you wanted to start a process for addressing them and this was the method you chose?*

A. I had no way to know that.

Q. *Okay. Did you make an assumption at the time you wrote this that the people you wrote to were not knowledgeable about Title IX?*

A. I made no assumption whatsoever.

It continued like that, questioning every aspect of every possible motive underlying my behavior and intentions, behavior and intentions that had occurred years earlier. It was exhausting. After eight hours, day one ended.

Day two began with a clarification of the previous day's testimony and a discussion about conversations I'd had with Tim. Before he came to Linfield, Tim had been a practicing attorney. The attorneys bantered back and forth about the notion of attorney-client privilege regarding conversations between Tim and me. It was silly really. As far as I was concerned there wasn't anything I'd said or done that I was ashamed of or felt needed to be hidden. At this point I still thought the truth would prevail. Tim wasn't concerned either. To him it was just lawyers posturing and had more to do with lawyers' egos than any real evidence that might be uncovered.

At one point, Pam stooped especially low and drafted a letter stating that she was duty-bound to report Tim to the Oregon Bar Association for giving legal advice while on inactive status. Although I knew that this was just one more attempt to get at me through someone I cared for, it still bothered me a great deal. Tim, however, was not bothered. He hoped she'd pursue the issue and looked forward to the opportunity to respond. In the end, it was just a bluff and never went any further than a tasteless letter.

Another tactic used throughout the deposition was to bombard me with questions about various memos, conversations, dates, and orders of events, expecting me to accurately recount what happened when, and why I did particular things in a specific order. Then, after Pam thought she'd cornered me, she'd produce documentation, such as memos I'd written, that clarified exactly what I'd said or done and when. I suspect the goal was to trip me up and make it look as if I was lying under oath. Even so, I kept thinking that it was a tremendous waste of time to have me stumble along attempting to remember details about things that happened two to four years back, when they could answer their own questions with information they had in their possession. It took a while for me to realize that efficiency wasn't a priority. The priorities were to make me look bad and run up the cost. The longer it took, the more money spent.

We consumed much of that second morning discussing various aspects of my communications and relationship with Ad. I was repeatedly asked to explain why I had followed the procedures outlined in the Linfield *Faculty Handbook* regarding my request for an academic leave of absence, as opposed to talking with Ad first. Either Pam didn't understand the reporting structure detailed in my job description and the *Faculty Handbook* instructions, or she was looking for examples of my insubordination and evasiveness with Ad.

We then had a long conversation about a meeting at which Ad told me that if Linfield had any Title IX problems it was my fault, that I was to blame because it was my responsibility to address the needs of the women's sports programs. In a way I agreed, and I responded to Pam's questions with some ambivalence. I told her that I did feel it was my responsibility to look out for the interests of women's athletics, but I didn't feel it was right to blame me for failings when I hadn't even known the law existed. At one point the questioning became quite heated:

Q. *What do you remember about [Ad's] mood?*
A. That he was angry.

Q. *And did you think his anger was justifiable?*
A. No.

Q. *Did you understand the source of the anger?*
A. Not really.

Q. *You say here that he, quote, said Title IX [was] my fault, un-quote.*
A. Correct.

Q. *Is that something you specifically remember him saying?*
A. Yes. Blamed me.

Q. *Blamed you for what, though?*
A. He said that if there were any Title IX problems—I'm paraphrasing—that it was my fault; that it was my responsibility as women's athletic director—he frequently referred in those terms—to take care of those things. So—and again I'm paraphrasing, but he was angry at me.

This exchange went on for a long time. We went back and forth about what I perceived my job responsibilities to be in regard to Title IX, what I had been aware of, and who was to blame for Linfield's Title IX problems. Finally, Pam seemed to reach a breaking point. In what appeared to be frustration and anger, she rose and leaned forward across the table, her jaw tight and her face red. Then, with my three-hundred-plus-page dissertation sitting on the table in front of her, she caustically asked, "You don't know how to read?!"

That was the clincher for me. She was apparently incapable of accepting that, despite my athletic background, education, and occupational experience, prior to the summer of 1992, I simply hadn't known about Title IX. At this point I too was flushed in anger. There was no way to take her question as anything but a malicious attack. There seemed to be no limit to how low she would stoop, and in my view, her spiteful personal attacks only made her look bad.

A particularly humorous exchange occurred when Pam produced what she thought would be a damning piece of evidence. It was an excerpt from my documentation log with names blacked out. Early on, when Pam had been consulting pro bono for Linfield, she'd asked for, and received, information from my documentation log that reflected issues of departmental climate. I was the one who'd sent her the document she was holding, and I'd done so at her request. She obviously didn't remember, and I got quite a chuckle out of what came next.

Pam asked about the document, what it was and what it was about. I calmly told her it was part of my documentation log. Her eyes narrowed, as if she was closing in on the kill, and she proceeded to ask about the blacked-out names, who they were and why they'd been obscured. I told her that they were blacked out because I'd been instructed to do so. Pam could hardly contain herself. It seemed clear she thought she had me. She hunched forward and in a lowered tone asked who had instructed me to black out the names. I too hunched forward and looked her carefully in the eye, then calmly replied, "You did." The look on her face was priceless: surprise, shock, and disbelief. Her mouth dropped open, and after seconds that seemed to stand still, she asked, "I did?" I then reminded her of her early Linfield consulting, and as the realization of the documentation source dawned on her, she slumped back, crumpling in retreat. Pam moved on to other questions.

The questions and answers moved along to specific areas in which I thought women's athletics had been denied equity. As Linfield's many Title IX deficiencies had been pointed out not only by me, but by consultants on multiple occasions, herself included, this line of questioning seemed a complete waste of time.

The other part of the puzzle that Pam just couldn't seem to understand was that, over the years, I'd submitted budget requests for equipment, supplies, facility upgrades, JV teams, coaching support, and other necessities, and that those requests had repeatedly been denied or only partially accommodated. In fact, my requests for women's sport program upgrades were most often deleted by Ad even before being forwarded to the administration. I had been working to achieve gender equity before I was aware there was a law that was supposed to guarantee it.

After a while, with question upon question about what I remembered doing, during which the opposing counsel sat with copies of memos and even my Franklin Planner notes in hand, reading day-by-day entries, I became annoyed. I began responding to questions such as "Did you make a note about that conversation?" with "You could look in the diary to know if I did." At that point Pam shifted focus, and we thankfully went through my notes together, instead of carrying on a ridiculous cat-and-mouse game, guessing when and what I'd noted in a diary I hadn't looked at for some time.

We spent much of the remainder of that day going laboriously over pages of my notes and correspondence, and recollections of conversations and meeting content. It became clear that the deposition process would take significantly longer than first anticipated, which meant more time, more energy, and more money.

Day three lasted only half a day. As before, we began by reviewing my testimony from day two and then resumed going through my Franklin Planner entries and notes. By this time I was beginning to figure out the deposition process.

For example, it was typical after a series of questions for Pam to say something like "isn't it true that," and then rephrase the scenario. The apparent goal was to make me and my actions look bad, and the other person, typically Ad, Scott, or President Bull, and his or her actions look good. Well, it wasn't "true," and despite Pam's desire to cast everything in a pro-Linfield light, that wasn't the reality I lived, and I repeatedly said so.

Another difficulty was that often I'd have to recall what I was thinking at the time of a particular notation or meeting, what emotions I'd felt, without letting the anger and hostility that I was feeling at the moment interfere with my recollections about the past, which was not an easy task.

Much of day three focused on various changes in policy and practice Ad implemented after I raised Title IX issues. The day concluded with a series of questions about my professional development meeting, comments made, how I'd felt, and my interpretation of the event.

Days four and five were long and grueling. Unlike the first three days, day four opened without Pam's presence. Her assistant counsel, Per Ramfjord, began the inquiry.

We spent a fair amount of time going over my early professional development meeting with Ken Goodrich, Jay Locey, and Vince Jacobs. This was the meeting at which Vince expressed the thought I'd be doing everyone, myself included, a favor by voluntarily removing myself from a tenure track faculty position, and Jay expressed concerns about collegiality in response to my raising Title IX issues.

I'd been very upset at that meeting and testified to that fact. As I look back now, it could be that people were conspiring even then to fire me. Getting rid of me would have been easier and cleaner had I been an administrator rather than a tenure track faculty member.

From there we moved on to a discussion of my leave of absence and the various events, meetings, memos, and conversations that ensued about how my position would be covered. Next we launched into a series of questions to try to show that the problem wasn't that I'd raised Title IX issues; the problem was me and the way I'd raised them. But the reality was that there was nothing inflammatory about what I'd done or how I'd done it. What I'd done was confront long-standing traditions, norms, and values, which was controversial by nature. As to going around the chain of command and my supposed violation of Ad's trust by sending copies of my first Title IX report to others, those charges too were without merit. I'd informed him verbally and in writing of what I'd planned to do. I'd followed Ad's directions when he made his demands explicit and not sent copies of my subsequent report to others. I'd acted in good faith and I'd been persecuted for it.

When that line of questioning didn't bear out the way he wanted, Per launched into a series of questions asking about "other complaints" regarding my communication style. He latched on to an issue involving a former women's coach. I had to go into considerable detail about my interactions with this person and why, when it came time to recommend contract renewal, I, as her immediate supervisor, did not support her renewal.

The questioning progressed to speculations about the way various Linfield employees (Ad particularly) might have reacted to Carol Bernick's letter on my behalf; the changes I perceived in the way I was treated by Ad; the early dialogue Linfield initiated about mediation possibilities; my discussions with President Bull; the college's series of efforts to engage external Title IX consultants; the internal gender-equity subcommittees and reports; and incidents of alleged harassment and retaliation against me and the swim program.

We quibbled over what exactly I meant in the reports I'd written, and what I viewed as examples of harassment and retaliation. Like Pam, Per repeatedly tried to get me to agree with his rewording, which always seemed to slant things to make me look uninformed, overzealous, or just plain wrong. By day four I was savvy enough not to fall for his little traps. I'd repeat myself, making my position clear, and, in the end, would simply say there wasn't another answer; the best he was going to get was the response I'd given. We ended the fourth day with questions about my tenure and promotion decision.

My fifth and final day of testimony opened with the issue of the department chair position and search. My belief was that the department would be best served by a person who had an academic and athletic background, but who clearly put academics before athletics. From the tenor and wording of Per's questions, I suspected he wanted to trap me into testimony that could be used to show that, by my own admission, I wasn't qualified for the job.

Next, we hit on my allegations of discrimination that resulted from Linfield's hiring Scott over me as athletic director. We discussed the members of the selection committee and my perceptions about their affiliation with athletics and potential biases against me, as well as my personal knowledge of colleagues' intimations that Scott was the lesser candidate.

I recounted conversations and comments made by various Linfield faculty and staff. We then talked about other ways I thought the search was biased against me. I responded with information about the weighting of the candidate evaluation criteria and the issue of collegiality.

The conversation about collegiality continued for some time. Per seemed determined to get me to affirm the appropriateness of collegiality as the most heavily weighted evaluation criterion. I repeatedly acknowledged the importance of collegiality as a leadership asset, but stood firm in my view that given the context, its weighting was an attempt to bias the process against me.

Q. *Would you view ability to lead in a collegial fashion as a prerequisite to being able to function effectively as an athletic director?*

A. I think leadership takes a variety of forms and that effective leadership is in itself adaptable, evolving, and flexible.

Q. *So effective leadership, in your mind, if it's going to be flexible, does involve collegiality or doesn't? I don't understand.*

A. Collegiality would be an asset to one's ability to perform in such a position.

Q. *So what you're saying is that ability to lead is a prerequisite to performing well as an athletic director, correct? Didn't you just say that?*

A. I believe that's probably true, yes.

Q. *And that collegiality is not in itself a prerequisite, but it's something that can help the ability to lead? Is that fair to say?*

A. Collegiality would be an asset to one's ability to lead. It would be—as would other factors or characteristics—assets to one's ability to lead.

Q. *In other words, it would help the ability to lead?*

A. "Help" is your word. "Asset" is mine.

Q. *And meaning that it's an asset, it's not a prerequisite in and of itself?*

A. A conclusion relative to prerequisite status is not a testimony—not a discrimination I can give. That's a definitive discrimination you want to make. My testimony is that it's an asset to one's ability to function in such a position.

Q. *I'm not asking you to make a distinction. I'm just asking what your view is on that point.*

A. You've received it.

Various objections from counsel ensued. Per didn't want to relent until I said his words, which I simply wasn't going to do. His words did not relay my meaning, feeling, or intent. We haggled back and forth a bit more, took a short break, and finally Per moved on.

Per next went over a list of Linfield names, people who I presumed had written comments in support of Scott's candidacy. The gist of the questioning was whether I had any reason to believe they'd be biased against me. In some cases I thought there might be connections or relationships that could contribute to bias, in other cases not.

Next we addressed why I thought I was more qualified than

Scott for the athletic director position. We covered everything from my superior organizational skills to past experience at Linfield administering athletics, from academic preparation to leadership potential. We discussed the broader community climate and how I felt Linfield had intentionally and repeatedly cast me, and my position on Title IX compliance, in a false light. We reviewed various local news articles, editorials, and gender-equity talks I'd given on campus and beyond and, as we had many times before, returned to my perceptions about what Title IX compliance meant.

It seemed Linfield was determined to make it look as though my view of compliance was myopic and single-mindedly focused on proportionality. But that just wasn't true. I was the one person at Linfield, after studying it since 1992, who knew what Title IX meant and fully understood the complexities of compliance. I believe Linfield and its attorneys thought it was vital to their position to discredit me and my expertise. They seemed intent on painting me with the brush of proportionality, perhaps so they could maintain ire against me.

Proportionality is the aspect of Title IX compliance most resisted. But no matter how much they wanted me to be obsessed with proportionality, I wasn't. Without doubt, proportionality is important. It is the ultimate outcome of developing women's sports and, for that matter, cutting men's sports. It's what we get to eventually, when equity is achieved. But knowing it is the result is not the same as being obsessed by it.

As we concluded my final day of testimony, we focused on specific allegations in the complaint. I was asked about examples of retaliation and ways I had been personally and professionally harmed by Linfield's actions. We talked about the physical symptoms I'd experienced: the problems with my teeth and jaw, my headaches and nightmares, the medication I was taking, and the counseling I was undergoing. We also discussed the harm I endured regarding my dissertation and having to change focus two-thirds of the way through the process. The day concluded with an agreement that my deposition would remain open for further inquiry, pending the ongoing review of discovery documents. My deposition ordeal was temporarily halted, but not officially over.

In the course of my deposition, we deposed Bill Apel. What I learned was that not only did I have to be available to give my own testimony, but I needed to sit in and be available throughout the testimony taken by my counsel. The rationale is good. Who better than the plaintiff to give input about what others say, especially when that testimony centers around the plaintiff and her legal complaint?

Bill's testimony was an eye-opener and a disappointment. Bill was evasive and at times, I thought, less than accurate in his testimony. I remember being shocked by this. He was, after all, the college chaplain. He, of all people, I expected to be completely truthful. After a day of testimony, Bill, who suffers from a neurological disease, was able to get out of further testimony on medical grounds. Apparently, the stress was just too much for him. I think the stress of the conflict between his principles and his testimony was too much for him.

In the midst of these endless days of depositions, I attended my doctoral graduation. It was a good day and a needed relief from the grind of the lawsuit. Family and friends were in attendance, and my mother hosted a get-together to celebrate. I can't help wondering how much more joyous the occasion might have felt had I not been embroiled in a lawsuit.

On September 28, the *News-Register* printed its "New Prez" editorial. There were many phrases that sounded suspiciously similar to what I'd said in my deposition. It seemed to me that someone was leaking information. A day later, the *Oregonian* followed with an article highlighting Linfield's winning tradition and mentioning the hiring of the "most qualified" person, Scott. Again, the timing and wording seemed suspicious.

The swim season got under way October 1. However, that did not influence the deposition schedule. Originally, the depositions were to have been scheduled in the winter and spring of 1996. The idea was that this would minimize interference with my doctoral work, preexisting summer plans, and, later, the swim season. That schedule didn't pan out. The deposition had conflicted with my dissertation defense, my doctoral graduation, my summer plans, and now was conflicting with my coaching responsibilities. That was another thing I hadn't expected: that the depositions would be such a huge added burden to my life. They didn't occur instead of other things. They necessitated my attention and involvement and took place in addition to everything else.

We deposed President Bull on October 14 and Marv Henberg on October 15 (and I think maybe into October 16) and resumed with Marv on October 29 and 30. Ad was deposed for at least part of a day on one of those October dates. Although I attended much of these depositions, I didn't get a copy of the actual testimony, as it was not transcribed. From what I remember, Vivian came across as timid and seemed to shift blame away from herself and onto Marv. Marv's testimony was mostly accurate. But there were times I remember whispering to Liz and Lory, suggesting follow-up questions; and there were instances where, based on my recollections, I felt he wasn't being exactly forthcoming. I don't remember much about Ad's testimony, other than being surprised that Liz and Lory were so gentle with him. He wasn't put through the wringer as I'd been, and it seemed that many areas of inquiry were left untouched.

At that point the deposition process stopped. There was talk about further scheduling, but for the most part the process was simply put on hold. It was strange. I expected something, I'm not really sure what, but something more than just stopping. There wasn't any big denouement, and after giving and listening to days of testimony, resuming business as usual seemed unjustly anticlimactic.

Perhaps I did get my turning point, at least in regard to my own awareness. If nothing else, I could no longer deny reality. The truth didn't seem to matter anymore, if it ever really did to anyone but me. The lawsuit wasn't going to deliver justice. It was about saving face and winning. It was about money: how much the costs could be run up, who could last the longest, how big the damages might be, and, ultimately, who would have to pay. That's it, nothing more and nothing less. Equity and truth were lost asides.

It was an awareness that stuck in my craw, a bitterness I taste still.

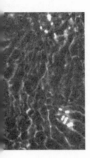

23

Business as Usual

During my years at Linfield, the swim program had grown considerably, and my repeated requests for assistant coaching help had been denied. Wanting to find a way to increase women's sport participation without further overloading the swim program, I proposed the addition of junior varsity swimming for women. I created a proposal detailing current participation numbers, a plan for increasing female participation, a competition schedule, and a budget outlining the costs associated with implementing the program.

In mid-November Scott asked me to survey conference swim coaches regarding practice expectations. I'm sure this request arose because the JV swimming proposal suggested participants have lesser practice and competition expectations than varsity swimmers. My rationale was that the research, as well as my own experience in coaching, suggested that in many cases women participate in sport for different reasons than men. Women are sometimes more motivated by the social aspects of sport as well as by associated fitness and health benefits. With this in mind, I'd crafted the JV proposal to meet the needs of some of the less-competitive female swimmers.

Within the current culture of sport, the benefits of participation for women and girls are often outweighed by the associated costs. In the early 1900s medical doctors and female physical educators thought that vigorous activity would endanger a women's reproductive capacities and result in the development of "unsightly" muscle. In response, early sport endeavors were limited to activities such as archery, dancing, croquet, golf, swimming, and tennis. To a degree, those same myths and stereotypes have a lingering effect on women in sport today.

A 1988 study by Mary Jo Kane found that when given a choice, high school males most wanted to be remembered as star athletes, while less than 10 percent of high school females wanted to be remembered that way. Kane also found that both females and males gave girls who participated in sports traditionally considered more feminine (such as tennis, golf, and volleyball) higher social status than those who participated in less sex-appropriate sports. In 1994 Alyce Holland and Thomas Andre reported similar findings in their study *Athletic Participation and the Social Status of Adolescent Males and Females*. Girls who played sports considered sex inappropriate (such as basketball and softball) were seen as less desirable as dating partners and friends.

In addition, the role of the successful competitive athlete and the espousal of stereotypically masculine sport values are often perceived by both women and men as incompatible with the role of women in society. Although there is evidence of change, women who are overly competitive risk being socially stigmatized as unfeminine. As a result, females in sport struggle with balance, acceptance, and success in a field characterized by the very attributes that the broader sociocultural context discourages and, at times, even punishes them for. It is unlikely, even in the few sports where professional opportunities for women do exist, that females participating at the collegiate level will ever play sports professionally; young women tend to view the perceived benefits as far outweighed by the practice demands and time commitment required for success at this level.

Thus it was that the JV swimming proposal included modest practice and competition requirements and flexibility to move, depending on commitment level, between the JV and varsity programs. This was not in keeping with sport as Scott understood it, and he was not for it.

Besides the fact that Scott appeared to be looking for evidence to use to deny my JV sport request, he and Ad had long thought that I exaggerated the training requirements for the sport of swimming. In the midst of conducting my survey, I got a call from Jim Johnson, the Pacific Lutheran swim coach. He'd been approached by his assistant athletic director asking questions about his swim practice schedule. He was being asked the same questions Scott was requiring me to survey. According to Jim, the source of the questions was Scott. Just like his predecessor, Scott was assigning me a task and then doing the same thing on his own. A few days later, Don King, the Lewis and Clark swim coach, called to respond to my questionnaire verbally. He told me he too had been approached with the same questions by his athletic director. It is a credit to my colleagues in coaching that they didn't get annoyed. It seemed obvious that they and their programs were being subject to scrutiny in their own departments because of what was going on at Linfield. Lesser people would have developed a bad attitude about the whole thing, and it would have been understandable if they'd directed some of that anger toward me.

That fall, the Equity in Athletics Disclosure Act (EADA) was enacted as part of the Higher Education Act. The EADA requires schools to report various gender-equity related numbers in areas such as sport participation, athletics-related financial aid, operating expenses, coaches' compensation, recruiting, and revenue and expenses. That fall marked the first reporting year.

I'd followed the progress of this new legal requirement and knew that although it didn't specifically address Title IX compliance, it did give a snapshot of equity issues in athletics. I'd reviewed the *Federal Register* and kept up to date about the EADA requirements. The people at Linfield who would be filling out the report (Scott and Barbara) were not so well informed. They bumbled along, making various mistakes and omissions in reporting, mistakes and omissions that I questioned.

During a November 26 department meeting, Barbara and Scott presented the public aspects of the report. They deemed that some information was public and other information private. The report specifies that the worksheets used to formulate various calculations need not be open to public inspection. Since that first reporting year, students in my classes have been requesting and collecting EADA reports from schools throughout the Pacific Northwest. Most schools don't distinguish between the required public and optional private information and disclose all aspects of the report. To this day Linfield releases only what is legally mandated.

At this meeting I pointed out errors in participation counting. Scott replied that he had just followed the report directions. I read the directions pertaining to the issue out loud. Scott reached over and grabbed my copy for himself. Despite the clarification, Scott persisted, claiming he'd just "followed along" with the directions. Barbara stated that it was no doubt a "simple error" and could easily be made right.

My second question centered on how coed sports had been defined for the purpose of composing the report. Scott replied that he'd used the NCAA definition. I asked if he'd looked beyond this definition. At that point Barbara got irritated and asked why I was asking so many questions. I replied that I'd read the *Federal Register* and *Congressional Record* regarding this legislation, and, as a result, I believed there were discrepancies between the way Linfield filled out the forms and the congressional intent. Barbara asked if I was saying the NCAA wasn't a credible source of information for the report. I wasn't saying that, or that the NCAA intentionally made a mistake in the reporting instructions. I was merely suggesting that

maintaining the impossibility of a mistake was being overly optimistic. Also, the legislation originated with Congress and not the
NCAA; therefore, it seemed reasonable to me that congressional intent would be the appropriate final authority.

Barbara and Scott indicated that they felt the NCAA directions
were misleading and unclear, and at this point things got heated.
I'd seen EADA reports from other colleges in our conference, and
Linfield was the only one that hadn't figured out how to count participation correctly. Scott and Barbara went on complaining about
the report directions, and, after listening to them, I asked what their
understanding of the EADA was. Barbara became furious. She
turned to me with venom dripping from each word: "Why don't
YOU tell us what it means!"

I wasn't quick enough in my thinking at the time. I should
have said I wasn't the one filling out the report and my understanding wasn't at issue, but I didn't. I answered her question and despite
the heat pressed on. Scott became annoyed and stated he had "a lot
to do [and] . . . better things to do with [his] time" than sit and
answer my questions. Barbara concluded the discussion by stating
that they'd completed the reporting in "good faith," and that although there may have been some "oversights," they operated according to what they were able to discern from the directions.

A few days following this meeting Barbara issued a memo titled
"Emendation of the Gender Equity Disclosure Report." It wasn't
clear who received the emendation, although its purpose was to correct some of the reporting errors I'd noted. Over the past few years,
the EADA reporting directions and forms have evolved, their clarity
has improved, and some of the questions I raised regarding the
NCAA interpretation of how and what to report have been resolved.
The early NCAA directions were not as accurate or clear as needed,
and reporting information has been revised and corrected to reflect
the legislative intent more accurately.

Besides the described incident, the EADA reports resulted in a
fairly comical incident. In June 1997 the Women's Sports Founda-

tion (WSF) released a "Gender Equity Report Card" based on EADA reports from colleges and universities across the country. Schools received grades based on enrollment percentages, scholarship allocations, recruitment, and overall budget resources. Five years after my first Title IX reports and after tens of thousands of dollars spent on consultants, Linfield's 1997 grades were published as follows: Enrollment D+, Recruitment D, and Budget D+ (since Linfield did not give athletic scholarships, it was not graded in that area). The sad truth was that those grades reflected the progress we'd made since 1992!

When the "Report Card" came out, Linfield was not pleased. The public disclosure of Linfield's reality was horrifying, but for the wrong reasons. Linfield was upset about what they viewed as a statistical misrepresentation of their gender-equity progress and status; and the administration appeared much more upset about the image the grades portrayed than the reality they reflected.

Barbara and Scott quickly went to work. Evidently there had been some problem associated with the way Linfield interpreted the instructions for counting coed sport participants. Barbara wrote a lengthy clarification correcting the participation count problem, among other things, and then noted how "[w]hen football [was] extracted from the mix, there [was] only a $4000 difference in 1995–1996 expenditures on male and female athletes, and only 22 more men than women in the program overall." In spite of all the professional and legal input the college had received, Linfield persisted in trying to define gender equity on its own terms. The law is clear: football is not a third sex and cannot be excluded from gender-equity considerations.

Linfield's revised grade was raised to a glowing "C," an achievement Linfield heartily applauded. I'm not sure why average is something to be proud of, especially when in this case only an "A" meant equity.

That November was a busy time, and, I have to admit, I'd become fairly fed up with Linfield and its gender-equity abuses. So I took it upon myself to point out the equity issues every chance I got, which, given Linfield's knack for Title IX blundering, was pretty often.

On November 21, 1996, I sent a memo to Barbara, Dawn, and Scott. The memo addressed possible Title IX issues and concerns, including TVs and VCRs, coaching uniforms, cheerleading, news coverage, coaching load allocations, and media publications.

Football had purchased TVs and VCRs for their full-time staff, which, as I've already said, resulted in Linfield's buying everybody TVs and VCRs. As to the coaching apparel, it seemed that many of the men's sport coaches wore uniforms of sorts, and I questioned what our policy and practice were in that area. In regard to cheerleading, the Linfield cheerleaders, like many schools' cheerleaders, focused their attention almost exclusively on football and men's basketball. I questioned this. As for news coverage, I'd done a study, with the cooperation of students from the school newspaper, analyzing the school paper's sports coverage during the 1992–93 and 1993–94 years. I suggested that we continue to review sports coverage and encourage more gender-equitable representation. I also queried, once again, the load allocations for head and assistant coaches.

In addition, I also expressed concern about equity in sport media guide resource allocations. Our sports information director had recently come to me asking which part of the swimming section in the winter media guide I wanted to cut. Swimming shared space with women's and men's basketball, both of which had six pages of coverage. Women's and men's swimming combined had a total of five pages and I was being asked to recommend cuts. It seemed that swimming was once again being singled out.

I received a partial reply from Barbara on November 27. She had not finished her inquiry into all the concerns I raised, but was willing to address those she'd looked into. In regard to the cheerleading issue, Barbara informed me that the cheerleading squad functioned during the fall, and that although it had offered to cheer at volleyball games, that offer had been declined. According to Barbara, the culture of volleyball excluded cheering. (As I sat recently at an Idaho State University volleyball game, with the band playing and cheerleaders cheering, I couldn't help wondering which culture of volleyball Barbara was referring to.) Because of what Barbara deemed as the cultural inappropriateness of cheering at volleyball matches, only football received the benefits of the cheerleading squad. It apparently hadn't occurred to her to consider soccer or cross-country, two other fall sports.

Barbara then tackled the issue of the school newspaper. She'd talked with the paper's advisor, and he'd replied that the paper, in accordance with an edict from the Board of Trustees, had the "absolute right to determine for itself the coverage it [would] provide on any given subject, in other words, . . . [it is] in total control of . . . [its] own editorial policy, independent of the college administration." Barbara thus determined that "sports coverage accorded by the student paper does not fall within the scope of the HHPA Department or the Athletic Program, which have no authority to dictate or interfere with its choices." She pointed out that the most recent issue of the paper featured a female swimmer in its photo coverage. Once again, someone from Linfield seemed compelled to twist issues and concerns I raised into what she perceived to be personal attempts for self-gain. She just couldn't accept that it wasn't about me. It was about being fair and equitable to women in sport.

Regarding the coaching issue, Barbara informed me that the school had made a distinction between what it deemed to be equitable distribution of coaching resources based on "basic level[s] of coaching . . . AND the amount of coaching an individual may choose to provide above and beyond the basic mandatory efforts." Once again, despite my swimming expertise; my survey of other conference schools, which had confirmed that morning and afternoon workouts were the norm in swimming; and the knowledge that Barbara could have asked any other swim coach in the country and received a similar answer, she apparently knew better. Adding salt to the wound was the fact that no other Linfield coach was being told what was basic or optional where his or her sport's practice and competition needs were concerned.

Finally, when she came to the winter sports media guide, Barbara simply responded that it wasn't a gender-equity issue. Basketball was being treated equitably across genders and so was swimming—which, in fairness to her, was true. The fact that swimming once again took a hit wasn't a Title IX issue.

It would be some months before word would finally come regarding the TV and VCR issue and coaches' clothing. The TV and VCR issue ended up being an ordeal and did not win me any points with the football staff. The coaches felt the equipment was their personal property. The Linfield administration didn't see it that way. And since the cost of the equipment had not been reported as income for tax purposes, Barbara noted, "[i]n order to protect the coaches legally, should they desire to keep the machines, they would need to correct the reported salary they filed on their tax returns for that year and pay the appropriate back taxes." Barbara recommended that the machines be considered HHPA property. Then they would need to be considered in light of Title IX and gender-equity issues, which is what resulted in the departmentwide equipment purchase.

Barbara's reply concluded with the determination that, with the exception of baseball, any coaching uniforms were purchased by individual coaches and were therefore not a Title IX issue. Whether that had been true in the past was questionable. However, I was fairly confident that it would be true as we moved forward, which at least addressed equity as Linfield worked to move from its historically biased past through a painful present and into the future.

Toward the end of November, I had my coaches' budget meeting with Scott. We'd actually scheduled to meet previously, but Scott had two commitments at the time and my meeting had to be moved. The stated purpose of the meeting was to discuss with each coach specific budget requests and to answer questions so that Scott could better defend requests to the administration. During the meeting Scott asked me three questions. The first had to do with latex tubing used to construct homemade stretch cords for resistance training. The second addressed why I'd listed three coaches on my travel requests when, as Scott was quick to clarify, I wasn't getting another coach for swimming. The third asked why my awards request was double the amount prescribed by policy. At first I was puzzled by this last one, and then responded that it wasn't double the prescribed amount. The request was for women's and men's swimming—two sports, twice the budget amount.

Following these questions, Scott and I had a brief conversation about the JV swimming proposal. He admitted that he'd been querying athletic directors throughout the conference about their swim programs. He then asked me if I would consider our program comparable to that at the University of Puget Sound (UPS). I said yes. He pounced on that, and stated that UPS had only two hours of practice for women and two for men (a total of four) and did not hold morning workouts. His point was that they practiced less than we did. I informed Scott that his information was wrong; UPS had morning practices. He was adamant that they didn't, and he wanted to know why we did. I repeated that the UPS athletic director was wrong and that the survey information I was submitting to him showed that all conference teams had morning and night practices. I told him I would be happy to supply him with the actual surveys filled out by the coaches, along with the coaches' phone numbers.

Scott's point was to imply that I chose to have morning and night practices, and that daily doubles went beyond "basic level[s] of coaching." Scott, who had no background in swimming, apparently felt perfectly comfortable telling me what was needed for success. I wonder how he would have felt about me giving input on how much baseball should practice?

Scott went on to tell me that UPS had only two coaches and it did just fine. UPS was, at that time, considered the strongest team in our conference. However, unlike all other conference schools, during that time UPS had athletic scholarships to award for swimming. I responded, telling Scott that, unlike me, the UPS head coach was virtually a full-time swim coach. He had very limited teaching duties and managed the swimming pool with an assistant. In contrast, my coaching responsibility totaled just over a third of my contract; the remaining two-thirds of my responsibilities were allocated to teaching and aquatics. I further informed Scott that the UPS assistant coach was paid more than double what our assistant was paid. At that he dropped the issue.

Scott's next line was to tell me he did not support the idea of JV swimming. By then I was exasperated and told him it really didn't make any difference to me one way or another. Scott seemed disappointed and confused.

It never ceased to amaze me the lengths to which people at Linfield were willing to go to disregard or discredit ideas, opinions, and suggestions I put forward. They couldn't imagine that I'd propose to do something because it was good for the school or the athletic department. Perhaps that was the problem all along; they couldn't seem to see that I wasn't the one to gain from my efforts. Linfield and the student-athletes were the potential winners.

Shortly after this meeting, Mary told me that during the 1992 football play-offs, a corporate vendor had given the Linfield players free turf shoes. When Ad was still at the helm, he had taken issue with my requests for national team suits. Everyone in swimming knows that racing suits for championship meets are different from in-season suits. In a sport where great effort is expended to minimize surface resistance (for example, swimmers shave down and wear body suits), a tight-fitting competition suit, especially for championships, is imperative. Not only did the football players get free shoes, but those who stood on the sidelines and didn't play later returned their shoes for cash.

Recruiting is a year-round effort in swimming, but fall and winter are particularly busy times. Given my job responsibilities, except during summers I rarely had time to attend recruitment meets. I did most of my school-year recruiting by mail and phone. In December Scott paid me a visit, asking about the cost of using college stationery to send recruitment letters. He wanted me to use plain paper instead. Later that day he circulated a memo directing all coaches to use college stationery for special correspondence only. This was not in any team's best interest and was particularly harmful to teams such as the swim team that didn't have multiple assistant coaches to travel and recruit in person.

In January 1997 I received a phone call from *Advancing Women in Leadership,* a new Internet publication. The caller wanted to know if I could put together a paper on my earlier American Education Research Association—Special Interest Group presentation on Title IX. I was pleased and flattered, and quickly complied. Despite being stonewalled at Linfield, I was able to get out general information about Title IX and gender equity in athletics, which felt very good. I also sensed, in regard to the lawsuit, that I was gaining the credibility that would qualify me to serve as my own expert witness regarding Title IX.

Also in January, the department launched its search for a new women's basketball coach. The first meeting was scheduled for a time the department chair knew I would be unavailable. Also, the position had been demoted to nontenure track and was to exist on a one-year renewable basis. I was against this and thought it would lessen the department's ability to attract high-quality candidates.

Barbara responded to my concerns, stating that some coaches might find a tenure track position "unwelcome," as she supposed strong coaches would want their evaluations to be based on their coaching "acumen." Barbara, who'd never coached, was evidently an expert on the career aspirations of strong collegiate coaches. The search committee met on February 25; although Linfield claimed to be an affirmative action employer, it seemed unwilling to institute affirmative actions to get a diverse applicant pool or award bonus points for qualified minority applicants who might emerge. I questioned this. I was relentless, if nothing else, or maybe I was just a glutton for punishment. I crafted a lengthy memo outlining and quoting the college's affirmative action policy, reviewing recent court cases, and tying things back to Title IX. Despite my arguments, Barbara sent me an e-mail reply on March 3 saying, "I will say in closing that I do not find myself rethinking my statements of last Tuesday—I continue to believe that I represented the current status of the law as various 1990's rulings have left it." She went on to say, "We are not in the same world regarding affirmative action as we were in the 1980's."

In a way Barbara was right. In 1978 the Supreme Court had issued a landmark decision in *Regents of the University of California v. Bakke*. In this ruling racial quotas were outlawed but consideration of race allowed. Over the course of the next decade, a series of affirmative action cases emerged, honing the focus of permissible preferential treatment to a standard of strict scrutiny. This meant that affirmative action programs could be justified when they served a compelling governmental interest and were narrowly tailored to achieve that interest. In essence, affirmative action plans are allowable only if they address documented discrimination, do not have an undue negative impact on the majority group, and are crafted as temporary remedies that continue only until the underlying discrimination has been adequately addressed.

By 1996 the pendulum had swung back a bit, and a ruling by the United States Court of Appeals for the Fifth Circuit (*Hopwood v. Texas*) found that using race to achieve a diverse student body in college admissions was not a "state interest compelling enough to meet the steep standard of strict scrutiny." Recently, affirmative action has again made headlines. In the state of Washington, where the Ninth Circuit held in favor of affirmative action, the court ruled that the University of Washington acted legally when it considered race in its now-abandoned admissions policy. In two cases involving the University of Michigan, one regarding undergraduate admissions and the other law school admissions, the courts have reached two different decisions. In the undergraduate case the judge upheld the concept of affirmative action in the university's admissions policy. However, in a similar case involving the university's law school admissions policy, the court ruled against using race as a factor. Both cases are headed to the Sixth Circuit Court of Appeals.

Most recently (September 2001), the Eleventh Circuit invalidated the University of Georgia's freshman admissions policy, which added bonus points to minority applications. Whether this case will be appealed remains to be seen.

The disagreement among various lower court decisions indicates it is likely that the Supreme Court will address affirmative action in higher education in the not too distant future.

Barbara's formal response came a few days later in the form of a departmental memo:

> The matter in question concerns whether a search committee may give added weight to the gender of an applicant for a particular job where it might be deemed desirable to have an individual of one gender rather than another for purposes of role modeling, or to correct underutilization of persons in a protected group. At the meeting where I spoke to this issue I stated that an individual's membership in a protected category (gender, race, disability, etc.) should not be part of the weightings by which candidates were evaluated and compared. Since receiving Professor Pemberton's memo, I have had conversations with quite a few individuals, several of them attorneys and one of them the College Attorney. Following all of those conversations, I have come to the conclusion that my advice in February should stand. Whether the law would permit the College to do more and expressly favor a candidate because of her gender, it does not require such pref-

erence. More importantly many successful affirmative action
hiring efforts are based upon positive recruitment efforts and
fair but gender neutral evaluation of candidates.

Barbara continued, stating that affirmative action applicant recruitment efforts were appropriate, and that with a strong candidate
pool the committee would be empowered to select the best coach
for the women's team. Barbara advised the committee to consider
issues of sensitivity to women's sports and role modeling in devis-
ing its gender-neutral criteria.

What she wrote is good and true, to a degree. However, it ig-
nores the historic bias against women in sport and does not suffi-
ciently recognize the importance of female coaching role models
for female athletes. It also gave the committee the opportunity to
hire whichever male it pleased.

The history of women in coaching since Title IX has been bleak.
According to a twenty-three-year study by Vivian Acosta and Linda
Carpenter, in 1972 over 90 percent of the coaches who coached
women's sports were female, but by 1999 just over 45 percent were
female. And, although coaching opportunities for men in women's
sports have increased dramatically, there has been no corresponding increase in opportunities for women coaching men. Only about
2 percent of NCAA men's programs have a female coach at the
helm.

I could only hope a strong female candidate would emerge. To
my delight, one did. She interviewed successfully and was ultimately hired.

In February I heard rumors, through class comments and discussions, that Linfield football players were giving students in my gender issues class a hard time for taking the course. According to the
football players, their "accounts had been frozen" because of Title
IX, and their program was suffering. Their coach, Jay, reportedly

told them swimming was suing football because football got more money than swimming.

The rumors were quite silly. However, they were being spread and were beginning to have a negative impact not only on the swim program, but on my ability to perform in the classroom. Apparently, attacking me through swimming was no longer enough.

Throughout this time, I'd been continuing to see Etta. I'd gone as often as every week at times, and our shared time had been a lifeline. However, I'd quickly used up the insurance maximum for counseling and was having to pay the entire bill for our visits. With mounting legal costs, I couldn't afford to go as often as I had been, wanted to, and probably still needed to.

24

Closure?

As the school year progressed I muddled along with various aspects of my job. The deposition process stalled as Linfield became increasingly intent on settling the case. I'd stopped recording everything in my Franklin Planner and made less-frequent notations in my documentation log. Liz and Lory felt I documented too much and advised against continuing to write everything down. From a legal standpoint, anything written down can be considered hard evidence and, as a result, presents more material to defend against. It was a hard habit to break.

After a series of phone calls, I agreed to attend a judge-mediated settlement negotiation during the spring of 1997. I hadn't changed my mind. I still wasn't interested in settling, but I could tell my position was becoming increasingly untenable.

This wasn't the first time we'd been approached by Linfield's attorneys and cornered into settlement talks. Early on, in October 1996, Linfield had asked what it would take for me to settle. Not wanting to settle, and intent on seeing that right prevailed, I put together a settlement response outlining terms and conditions I would consider. That early memo to Liz and Lory read: "I can't say

I am not pleased that I may have an opportunity to 'get my life back' sooner rather than later. However, I want to make very clear that any settlement must be true to the things I value relative to the issues raised and pursued through this legal action. . . . As I have stated many times . . . I do not want to settle."

I outlined my demands, which included Linfield's acknowledgment of its wrongdoing, a public apology, a promotion to women's athletic director, a position equal to Scott's as men's athletic director, my designation as Title IX officer, and relief from my responsibilities as swim coach and aquatics director. I also stipulated that Linfield would pay all related legal expenses, as well as my associated medical expenses, agree to support a sabbatical request for me to further my education in educational leadership, and pay damages for pain and suffering. It was a lengthy list, and I expected Linfield would have little interest in it.

In December 1996 Stoel, Rives, Boley, Jones, and Grey (the firm Pam was affiliated with) responded with a counteroffer, the details of which I cannot go into for reasons of confidentiality. I can say, however, that I rejected the offer, and that was when we moved on with discovery and depositions.

Another earlier attempt involved mediation with a supposedly neutral party. I don't remember the exact date; it might have been that fall. As things turned out, the mediator had worked with Pam before, and, because of past working and social relationships, it was questionable whether neutrality was possible. That effort failed too.

As I look back, I wonder why I even bothered to talk with the enemy. Since 1992 I'd been given no reason to believe they were in any way interested in what was right. Even so, I repeatedly responded to their requests to try to negotiate some middle ground. I was trying to make sense of it all and to find a way to get on track with the issues of gender equity and Title IX and get beyond Linfield's obsession with focusing on the personal. I was not the problem. As far as I was concerned it was never about me, Ad, Scott, or any one person. It was about women in sport and equity.

In a book called *Women in Power: The Secrets of Leadership*, Dorothy Cantor and Toni Bernay describe a study in which they interviewed twenty-five female government leaders to determine which qualities and strengths enabled them to get elected and persevere in positions of power. Repeatedly, the women attributed their success to a combination of competence, creative aggression, and something they called woman power. They linked these qualities to sport participation as a "training ground" for effective participation on the "playing field of power." I wanted both sons and daughters to reap these benefits.

So it was that through the winter and early spring of 1997, with depositions left incomplete, Linfield's counsel again began pushing for a settlement resolution, and my counsel began listening intently. The bottom line is always money. The attorneys' hourly charges were fast accumulating. Bennett, Hartman, Reynolds, and Wiser (the firm Liz and Lory were affiliated with), although of considerable size and stature, was a smaller firm than Stoel, Rives, Boley, Jones, and Grey. Smaller typically means shallower pockets, and this instance was no exception. I was strong, capable, and relatively resilient. I was able to come to work each day and perform well. My emotional, psychological, and medical damages were, to outside appearances, under control. Linfield had been smart about not firing me entirely and thereby minimizing any negative impact on my income. I hadn't (despite considerable effort on Linfield's part) succumbed and crumpled. For all these reasons, the question of how much money my damage claim might be worth was unclear.

Realistically, from the attorneys' point of view business is business, and when the costs exceed the potential payout (assuming a win), it's time to reevaluate, which was exactly what I think happened.

In fairness to them, I understand the financial pressure Liz and Lory were under, as well as the broader concerns of their firm. What I struggle with even now is how those concerns outweighed pursuing what was morally, ethically, and legally right. We had an opportunity to make an example of Linfield and of my case, and not only remedy wrongs at Linfield, but increase the odds that wrongs elsewhere might be avoided or at least addressed. We had a chance to make a difference. I knew, despite all the trauma, that I was strong enough to follow through with the lawsuit. I knew I could continue to find ways to manage financially. I knew we were right and Linfield was wrong. But it didn't matter.

My attorneys talked with me and always said it was my decision, but then they'd rattle off all the reasons we should try to settle and not carry the case forward. There was always a chance we'd lose, the damages award might not be big enough, and people at Linfield would never admit they were wrong or say they were sorry. Liz and Lory told me that all we could hope for was a sum of money. In their minds settling was the most likely way to get the most out of the situation. It was a very disappointing time. Once again the message came through loud and clear: it was all about money, money and winning. The issue that started the whole thing, the cause I believed in, was lost amid facts and figures, files and piles of paper, and damage assessment potential.

Settlement proposals and counterproposals were passed back and forth in January and early February 1997. After considerable time, paper, and expense, the process stalled a bit, and a judge-mediated settlement conference was scheduled for March 12, 1997.

The judge was briefed with "personal and confidential settlement" correspondence from each side. The meeting started in the late morning and went on late into the night. In some ways it was a good thing. I trusted the judge and believed he intended to act fairly. Many of my thoughts and feelings were validated through that experience, and I remember feeling that the judge came to understand the issue and my position.

But in other ways it was not a good experience. It was like an endurance test, a relentless interrogation session in which the victim isn't allowed to rest until she finally gives in and signs a confession. The session went till well past midnight, and still we hadn't reached an agreement. The judge went back and forth between rooms. In one room I sat with my counsel and in another Linfield with its counsel; back and forth, back and forth, proposal and counterproposal.

Regrettably, eventually I gave in and (more or less) bought in. I found myself saying things such as "where's the middle ground?" and looking for some point of convergence where Linfield and I could coexist. Late that night we hammered out a sort of rough draft settlement, and over the course of the next weeks various aspects were further detailed and specified.

On April 8, 1997, a "stipulation of dismissal with prejudice" was filed with the court, and over the next few days the last few settlement details were finalized. The long battle ended, anticlimatically, without much fanfare and certainly without a sense of triumph.

It was a weird feeling really. It was like training all season for a singular peak performance, sacrificing, persisting, and enduring, becoming ready and poised for the start, taking my mark, and then just when the gun was supposed to sound, the race was called off. It was over without the feeling that it ever had really started. It left me with a haunting sense of incompleteness, a nagging wound of wrong.

Because of the terms of the confidentiality agreement, the details of the settlement cannot be disclosed in this book or any other forum. What can be disclosed is that Linfield had to admit, at least indirectly, it was wrong and in some way say it was sorry. Linfield's official statement was lengthy and appears in full in the appendix. Excerpts read as follows:

PEMBERTON'S PUBLIC STATEMENT

McMinnville—Associate Professor Cindy Pemberton has been named Senior Woman Administrator for athletics, according to Marvin Henberg, vice president for academic affairs and dean of faculty at Linfield College.

The Executive Committee of the Board of Trustees reports that the lawsuit brought by Pemberton against Linfield challenging certain decisions made by the college, including her reassignment and elimination of the assistant athletic director for women position, has been settled. Dean Henberg regrets any negative perceptions that may have been fostered as a result of the reassignment and position elimination. The parties have agreed to keep the terms of the settlement confidential.

Professor Pemberton will begin her new duties on September 1, 1997 as Senior Woman Administrator. As Senior Woman Administrator she will interact with the Health, Human Performance and Athletics leadership, and the Title IX Officer, and represent Linfield at regional athletic conference and NCAA levels. Also, in this capacity Professor Pemberton will chair a faculty committee charged with planning projects to try and facilitate increased opportunities, and interest and abilities for women in sports at Linfield. As chair of this committee, Professor Pemberton will be charged with the administrative oversight and implementation of projects designed by the committee. Additionally, she will continue as the head swim coach for the women's and men's teams and as an associate professor in the Health, Human Performance and Athletics department.

"It is good for the college that Professor Pemberton has agreed to serve in this pioneering role," Henberg said. "This is a challenging position and she is well qualified for it. I trust that under her leadership Linfield will develop innovative approaches to expanding opportunities for women in athletics. These efforts along with the implementation of our five-year plan to increase opportunities for women, should put Linfield in the forefront among institutions devoted to a strong athletic program for all students."

Through her work in the role of Senior Woman Administrator, Professor Pemberton will help Linfield promote athletic opportunities for women by working to increase interest in athletic participation among women students, and, where appropriate, work to facilitate opportunities to develop their abilities to compete at the club sport or intercollegiate level. In addition, Professor Pemberton will focus campus-wide attention on efforts to enhance athletic opportunities for women consistent with the college's institutional goals and its Title IX plan. This position allows the college to utilize Professor Pemberton's leadership abilities and experience in athletic administration, as well as her enthusiasm for promoting opportunities for women athletes.

Pemberton served as assistant athletic director for women under former athletic director Ad Rutschman from 1989–1995. In her new capacity she will report directly to the HHPA department chair.

The statement went on to extol my various career highlights and accomplishments. And that was that. The seemingly endless invasion and disruption of my life was over. Was I glad? Yes, in a way I was. I couldn't help it. I would finally begin to get my life back. Was I disappointed? Yes, very much so. I always will be. Regardless of the terms of agreement, I do not consider settling an honorable option. Settling was buying silence. As far as I was and am concerned, settling was ugly and dirty. Did I win? Maybe in a way, but nobody ever really wins in these things.

25

Getting On with My Life

Just releasing information doesn't mean anyone will print it, and that's pretty much what happened. Linfield released the statement through a campuswide e-mail, as well as to the local paper and the *Oregonian*. What appeared in print didn't include any of the many accolades put forth in the press release; the articles simply pointed out the lawsuit had been settled and I'd been appointed senior woman administrator (SWA).

Even so, I received much positive feedback from people across campus and beyond. (As I noted earlier, the names have been left out in deference to their privacy.)

From a dear friend: "This is no small achievement. . . . your determination, hard work, and I dare say your very daring spirit have been rewarded and I am so very proud of you. Congratulations!"

From my doctoral advisor: "Wow—once one scrolls through all the public relations verbiage which purports that all of this was the Linfield administration's idea in the first place, it is clear to me that YOU WON!!!!!!!! Congratulations for sticking in there, for your courage, for your ethical behavior, for your leadership. I'm sure that the 'good old boys' are having a chew on this one."

From a swimming alum: "Congratulations! I'm glad to see they saw things your way."

From a Linfield administrator: "CONGRATULATIONS!!! You go girl!"

From another Linfield administrator: "Once again, congratulations. I do so respect your courage, determination, and commitment to doing what is right. You have definitely made a contribution and impact. Thank god for women like you!"

From a coaching colleague: "What can I say, you are the greatest! Congrats! Anything I can help you with?"

The lawsuit was over. I remained at Linfield and began the process of trying to get on with my life. Most people probably would have left. Maybe I was stupid. Maybe I was stubborn. Maybe both, but I wanted to stay and work in earnest on advancing women in sport in my new role as senior woman administrator.

Oddly, that spring I received word from Associate Dean Barbara Seidman that I'd been nominated for an outstanding faculty award. How ironic. She needed permission from me to allow the review committee to look at my professional development file. I wanted to ask whatever for, and suggest the committee might simply gain access to what it wanted with or without my permission. But what I thought and did were two different things. I granted permission, and in May when the award was announced, I was not the winner.

One of my new duties as SWA involved chairing a committee that actually had a budget and would look at the issue of expanding women's sport opportunities. I was excited about this and began an extensive literature review to prepare for a study I wanted to conduct on attrition in women's sports.

During the summer of 1997 I took a much-needed vacation, attended a special faculty teaching and learning seminar, and ran swim camps. In July my mother, sister, and I took my grandmother on a road trip, driving from Salt Lake City, Utah, to Omaha, Nebraska. My grandmother had been diagnosed with terminal cancer and wanted to return one more time to the place she'd grown up. Late summer flew by with various weekend excursions visiting friends and family, as well as preparations for the coming school year. I was thankful that my summer was busy and I had little contact with Linfield. I remember feeling anxious, wondering what the coming year would bring.

When it arrived, the school year didn't bring much excitement at all, and I was glad. I kept busy coaching, teaching, and working on various projects. I met with Etta periodically. Things were winding down and our time together would soon come to an end. We worked to tie up loose ends and to help me prepare for life at Linfield.

The only thing significant that fall was my submission of a proposal, "Reassignment of Swim Coaching Load Credit." Nothing in the lawsuit settlement indicated that I was to be forever chained to coaching swimming. Even though coaching had been a source of strength, support, and respite for me during the lawsuit ordeal, I hadn't changed my original intent. I did not want to continue coaching or running the aquatics facility.

In early September I sent the proposal to the department chair requesting reassignment of my coaching load and discussing how my full-time load might be accommodated with other teaching duties. Our various conversations and correspondences spanned a number of months, and, in the end, Linfield rejected my requests. I was destined to coach as long as I stayed. I suppose that was smart of the Linfield administrators. They'd known for some time that I didn't want to continue coaching. One sure way to spur my disaffection (if it was possible for me to feel more disaffected) was to force me to do a job they knew I no longer wanted. That fact, more than all the Title IX trauma, caused me to consider carefully what I wanted my future to look like, and whether Linfield would play a part in it.

That year we enjoyed another very successful swim season, and, aside from teaching, I worked on the SWA sport attrition project, a project that quickly became a source of irritation. For whatever reason, as I began to prepare the research methodology, Linfield decided that we needed to hire an outside consultant to ensure the study's validity. Normally this wouldn't be a bad thing, but in this situation it seemed to me a pretext. Linfield appeared to be incapable of trusting that I would do the work I was assigned and determined to monitor what I was doing. I was forced to allocate some of the SWA committee budget to retain someone who was in effect a babysitter. It annoyed me no end.

There would be no getting past our shared Title IX history, and I'd never be viewed with anything other than suspicion, as an outsider and a troublemaker. No matter how many local, regional, and national presentations I gave, no matter what I published, people at Linfield had created their own image of me, and they appeared determined to maintain it.

In April I spoke at the American Alliance for Health, Physical Education, Recreation, and Dance national convention. It was a team talk with Dr. Sharon Shields from Vanderbilt University in Tennessee. We spoke on the cross-country undergraduate media research project we'd integrated into parallel classes. It was a bright spot and sent a powerful message to me. Only when I was away from Linfield was I viewed as an intelligent, capable professional. I'd been receiving that message for some time now. I just hadn't been ready to hear it.

In May I spoke at the spring 1998 NCAA Title IX seminar on coaches' compensation issues and Title IX compliance. This was quite a feather in my cap. Also during May, largely because of the research I'd done to prepare for the NCAA seminar, I once again attempted to raise issues of equity in regard to Linfield's recent coaching hires. The Equal Employment Opportunity Commission (EEOC) had come out with guidelines addressing issues of coaching compensation. Based on this information it seemed that Linfield had erred in its most recent coaching hires.

The EEOC guidelines indicated that compliance assessment would not be limited to like sport coaching comparisons, but could include a broad, programwide analysis. With that in mind, I suggested that Linfield's most recent position proposals and coaching load allocations be reconsidered. I suggested Barbara, Dawn, and Scott take a look at the Federal Register Rules and Regulations, the Policy Interpretations, the Office for Civil Rights *Investigator's Manual,* the EADA worksheet reports, and the EEOC notice regarding "Guidelines covering sex discrimination in compensation of sports coaches in educational institutions." I followed up a few days later with a second e-mail suggesting that the position proposals reflected a disparate allocation that favored men's sports, and that the component parts of the position proposals would favor male candidates.

The reply I received a couple of weeks later indicated that, once again, I'd been right. Frankly, I should have charged for all the free advice I'd been giving. The position proposals were reallocated, although I'm not sure that the reallocations were much better. They ended up identifying the positions as a football and baseball coach and a football and softball coach, with a little teaching sprinkled in for appearances. The e-mail reply concluded: "While we recognize your concern about the desirability of attracting women candidates to the positions we will be staffing, limited resources and our desire to increase the number of women's coaches employed on a full-time basis have necessitated combining football and softball in this way." Women's sports simply could not gain without throwing a bone to football.

The cost of all this progress was felt not only by me, the swim team, and my classes, but by women elsewhere in Linfield's sport leadership. With these pending new hires and what would occur over the the next year, Linfield continued to eliminate female coaching leadership in athletics. Ultimately, only women's basketball and softball would have a female coach at the helm (as of fall

2001 I believe only basketball has a female head coach at Linfield). All other head coaches for women's and men's sports would be male, as would almost all the assistant coaches. Since my firing as assistant athletic director, athletics at Linfield had become almost entirely male.

There comes a time when enough is enough, and it finally became clear to me that I'd reach that point. I'd made a difference at Linfield. There had been significant Title IX compliance gains, and women in sport had benefited a great deal. I could continue to plug away, making small inroads to further gender equity, or I could make a change. Late that spring I sent a letter and résumé materials to two colleges with full-time teaching positions open, one in Colorado and one in Idaho. I then left town for an extended vacation and didn't give the applications much thought until my return.

Within a few weeks of coming home I had an interview in Grand Junction, Colorado, and, in July, an interview in Pocatello, Idaho. Both were wonderful experiences, and it didn't take much for me to decide what to do. On July 30, 1998, Linfield College put out the following press release:

CINDY PEMBERTON LEAVING LINFIELD FOR IDAHO STATE

Cindy Pemberton has accepted a teaching position at Idaho State University and is resigning her position as Linfield physical education professor and swimming coach after eight years. She takes with her 20 years of experience as a swimming coach, including 11 years at the collegiate level.

Pemberton joined the coaching staff in 1989, the same year Linfield's 112,000-square-foot Health, Physical Education and Athletics complex opened.

In eight seasons, her men's teams compiled a 65–14 dual-meet record and won four straight Northwest Conference team championships from 1992–1995. The Linfield men also captured the NWC crown in 1997, edging out three-time defending national champion Puget Sound.

Under Pemberton, the Linfield women were 47–36–1 and won the conference title in 1993.

In national competition, she guided five Linfield swimmers to a total of 13 NAIA individual championships.

Selected as the NAIA women's coach of the year in 1993, Pemberton is one of the most successful small-college swimming coaches in the country. She was named men's Northwest Conference Coach of the Year three times and women's NWC Coach of the Year twice. In addition, she was also named NAIA District 2 men's and women's coach of the year three times.

In 1992, the American Swimming Coaches Association presented Pemberton with a certificate of excellence for outstanding achievement. She was one of only five NAIA coaches to be so recognized.

An All-America swimmer at Willamette University, Pemberton earned her bachelor's degree in 1980. She received her master's degree from Southern Oregon University and completed her doctorate degree in higher education administration at Portland State University.

Prior to Linfield, she was the head women's swimming coach at the University of Nevada in Reno, where her teams compiled a 21–16 record. In 1988–89, she was named Nevada's coach of the year.

I should have been pleased. It was after all a complimentary release. But it annoyed me that all Linfield could say was what great a coach I'd been. I felt I'd been so much more than a coach.

The *News-Register* also managed to run a satisfactory piece in the sports section of their paper on August 4, 1998, titled "Pemberton Moving On to Idaho State."

Three years after filing a lawsuit against the college Linfield's swim coach is leaving for academic pursuits.

Cindy Pemberton is giving up her job as swim coach, associate professor and head of women's athletics at Linfield College to take an assistant professorship in physical education at Idaho State University in Pocatello.

Pemberton will be remembered for leading Linfield's swim team to a series of successful seasons during her nine year tenure. . . . she will also be remembered for filing a $2 million sex discrimination suit against the college in 1995, culminating in a successful out-of-court settlement two years later.

I was quoted as follows: " 'I decided that Linfield college would be the last place I would coach swimming, that any positions I would look at once I completed my doctorate would be of a more academic orientation. . . . This is a step up for me in terms of academic career moves.' " The article discussed the lawsuit, then my swimming credentials and Linfield's swimming success under my leadership. Scott Carnahan "declined comment on Pemberton's lawsuit, or the Title IX issues she raised at the college. He termed the move this way: 'She found a position that suited her professional goals, was offered the job and elected to take it.' "

The article concluded:

Pemberton said she is proud of the work she did championing women's athletics at Linfield. She said she felt significant progress had been made since 1992, partly due to her efforts. "Where we are now in 1998 is reflective of positive moves forward. I can't help but be pleased for the athletes." This will be Pemberton's first absence from coaching in 26 years. She coached club and prep teams before moving to the college level. "I knew I would look to move out of coaching," she said, "but the move was quicker than I thought. I've coached novice swimmers through Olympic [trial] qualifiers. My most treasured friendships and relationships will be associated with swimming." In her new position, Pemberton will teach classes in athletic leadership, philosophy, administration and management. She also will deal with gender issues in athletics. "My professional interests lie in working on my writing and research," said Pemberton, who led a student study of gender bias in sports media coverage at Linfield. "Teaching at the graduate level will afford me those opportunities and allow me to grow academically."

I received feedback from various people in and out of the Linfield community. It reminded me of when someone dies, and only then people come forward with good things to say. Many found it easier to appreciate my presence once they knew I was leaving. All were positive, thanking me for my work on Linfield's behalf, remarking on the "positive difference I made," telling me what a great coach I'd been and how much I'd be missed.

I'd been concerned about how the swimmers would take the news. I'd always been one to harp on finishing what was started, and no matter what the timing, there would always be freshman, sophomores, and juniors on the team whom I would be abandoning. To my great relief, the letters and notes from swimmers, past and present, were heartfelt and supportive. One, from a swimmer named Eli, captured their sentiment: "I don't know what to do. My first inclination . . . was to get mad, but that didn't last long. I have a really hard time believing that this was an easy choice for you and that you didn't do what is best. I'm really proud of you and you got a good job, I hope this one appreciates you for what you really have to offer."

Epilogue

There are three things I am often asked. The first is how I was able to recall events in such detail. The answer is that I wrote everything down. I kept copies of e-mails, memos, notes, reports—all sorts of documents—and even recorded and transcribed voice mail messages. Early on, both Tim and Kenton Hill recommended I document what was occurring. That, combined with my own tendency to be meticulous, resulted in many pages of personal documentation and many files of records. The effect was twofold. On the downside, the paper mountain I created resulted in an equally enormous mountain of discovery documentation that had to be provided to Linfield's attorneys, often to the dismay of my attorneys. On the upside, however, it provided the material I needed to re-create the events that unfolded between the summer of 1992 and the present. As a result, although the process of writing this book has been long and sometimes tedious, with quotes and information checked and rechecked, I believe it to be a thorough and accurate reflection of what transpired.

The second and third questions are was it worth it and would I do it all again. Those are much tougher questions.

The real cost of equity, the price of Title IX, goes far beyond dollars and cents. I lost a significant part of my job, and, although it took me a while to come to terms with it, my life at Linfield was over. I lost any hope of a career in athletic administration, particularly in the Pacific Northwest, something at the time I thought I wanted. My academic work was hindered and disrupted, and my dissertation focus, after months of work, had to be redirected. I was publicly humiliated over and over again. My swimmers and assistant coaches were harassed and hurt. My reputation in coaching was tainted, my swim camps suffered, and my colleagues in coaching were badgered and scrutinized because of their association with me. Friends and colleagues at Linfield brave enough to stand beside me were also harassed and hurt. Tim was hassled professionally and personally, and I know, although he never complained, my constant neediness wore him down. My Title IX battle cost us both more than one long-standing friendship. I came to the brink of financial ruin. My physical, mental, and emotional health to this day are under repair. The emotionally strong, capable, and resilient woman I once was is less strong, less resilient, and much more vulnerable.

Contrary to popular myth, I haven't retired to a life of leisure in some tropical paradise. But benefits also reach beyond dollars and cents. I believe that women in sport at Linfield benefited from my efforts, and that they continue to benefit, although according to Linfield's annual EADA reports, progress seems to have slowed considerably since my departure. At least locally, awareness regarding gender equity was heightened, and surely there is value in standing up for what is right, not only because it's right, but because it's important to model that behavior for others. And perhaps through this account women and girls in sport will benefit more broadly.

Certainly, given the state of Title IX today and the force of renewed efforts to thwart gender-equity progress in the name of preserving men's minor sports, it is important that this story be told. It is important that we not give up our momentum in the pursuit of gender equity or be beguiled by politically loaded headlines claiming Title IX requires quotas, when it simply does not. It is important that we not let groups with names that sound fair-minded, such as the Independent Women's Forum, Iowans against Quotas, and the National Coalition for Athletics Equity, or the 2000 Republican platform supporting "a reasonable approach to Title IX that seeks to expand opportunities for women without adversely affecting men's teams" woo us into believing Title IX has gone too far. As I have said repeatedly, the problem isn't women's sport growth. The problem is decisions made to limit or cut men's minor sports instead of reining in men's major sports.

Great strides have been made in gender equity, and it is because of Title IX. But there remains much work to be done. We have not yet achieved equity, and we cannot afford to pull back.

So I suppose the answer is yes, it was worth it, and I would do it all again. But if I have regrets, they are that I remained so naively optimistic for so long and, as a result, was surprised, confused, and hurt, over and over again. Even now there is a part of me that doesn't understand, that just doesn't get it.

It should be a simple concept. Inattention and resistance to gender equity is morally, ethically, and legally wrong. The only way to make sense of Linfield's legacy of wrongdoing is to assume that, like me (before the summer of 1992), people at Linfield hadn't known any better, and that once they knew better, we would work together to make things right. The alternative is to assume that Linfield, and the hundreds of schools across the country that continue to ignore and openly resist gender equity do know better, and that their actions and inactions were and are intentional and willful.

I have a new life now. Today I am an associate professor, a graduate faculty member, and the chair of the Department of Education Leadership in the College of Education at Idaho State University (ISU). I teach and administer our graduate curriculum in educational leadership and very much enjoy my work. I haven't once missed coaching or working in athletics. And I especially haven't missed Linfield, although my experiences there provide plenty of examples of what not to do when it comes to legal issues in education administration.

For the most part I am comfortable writing, speaking, and teaching about Title IX, gender equity, and, more generally, social justice. I write "for the most part" because there are still times when I feel the weight of all that transpired.

In the spring of 1999 I was asked to serve on the ISU NCAA Gender Equity Certification Committee. I hesitated, not wanting to get involved or reveal my expertise. More recently, I was approached by a student-coach of an ISU women's club sport and asked if I would help pressure ISU into making it a varsity sport. My response was quick and clear. I told the student no. I did not feel ready to rejoin the fray.

Time, however, is the ultimate healer, and I have since agreed to work with the ISU athletic department exploring possibilities for women's sport additions and am part of a small team looking into the possibility of developing a case to support dance as an emerging NCAA sport. I believe ISU is taking the high road to gender equity.

On a personal level, the transformation I underwent upon leaving Linfield has been nothing short of miraculous. I rarely have nightmares anymore, and although it will take some time, two-plus years of braces, and some dental crown work, my jaw should eventually be put to rights.

I carry with me two photos, one taken during the start of my last swim season at Linfield (fall 1997), and the other taken during my first year at ISU (1998–99). The face in the Linfield photo looks lined and tired. The person is clearly older and more worn in expression. The ISU photo shows a different woman, a woman renewed, refreshed, and rested, with far fewer worry lines. They are constant reminders to me of what was and is.

Not long into the new millennium I received a note from a friend in McMinnville: "[D]o you know about the Linfield class of 2000 time capsule? I would say it is a pretty good bet that you are the inspiration for one of the items included. Read on. . . . You may have left Linfield, but you (and your good work) are remembered! Hooray!" Enclosed was a news clipping from the *Oregonian* dated December 30, 1999. The title was "Linfield Exhibit Puts 'Time in a Bottle.' " Among the items in the time capsule was "a woman's swimsuit, representing women's fight for equality in sports."

It made me smile.

Appendixes

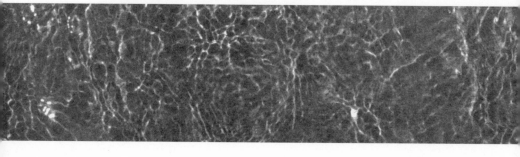

Time Line

June 1989	I arrive at Linfield.
Summer 1992	I first receive Title IX information and inform Ad Rutschman and various Linfield administrators about my intent to begin studying Title IX.
Fall 1992	I prepare and submit Title IX Reports One and Two.
Winter 1992–93	I have my first Title IX meeting with President Vivian Bull. She informs me that Pam Jacklin will be conducting a Title IX compliance audit for the college.
	I apply for, and am granted, a nine-month leave of absence for the 1993–94 school year.
Spring 1993	I hire my first legal counsel, Carol Bernick.
Summer 1993	Linfield wants Ad and me to participate in leadership coaching and mediation with Kenton Hill. Pam Jacklin collects Title IX information. Final details about filling my position responsibilities during my leave of absence are worked out.
Fall 1993	I begin my leave of absence and first year of doctoral study.

Winter 1993–94	Linfield appoints Bill Apel as Title IX officer. President Bull announces Linfield has decided not to receive a legal opinion from Pam Jacklin, and instead the college initiates its own internal compliance efforts.
Winter–Spring 1994	Work begins on the athletic department manual.
Spring 1994	I begin leadership coaching and mediation work with Kenton Hill.
Summer 1994	My leave ends and I resume work at Linfield. Ad and I move forward with our Kenton Hill mediation and meet to try to work out a "mutual success agreement." Kenton advises me to start writing everything down. Linfield contracts with Sports Services Consulting.
Fall 1994	Sports Services Consulting collects information. It issues its preliminary findings noting Title IX deficiencies.
Winter 1994–95	We begin "Linfieldizing" the Sports Services Consulting report.
Spring 1995	The "Linfieldized" consultant report response is released through the Linfield library, as is my "Response Clarification." Our internal work on the athletic department manual is stopped. Lynn Snyder is contracted to write the manual for us. I give my first on-campus Title IX talk during women's history month.
Summer 1995	The *News-Register* begins its attacks. I am quoted out of context June 3. Marv Henberg, the dean, points specifically to these articles and quotes when he informs me I've been "reassigned" and will not continue as assistant athletic director. I make a contract for legal representation and file a lawsuit against Linfield.
Fall 1995	I try to learn to live with a lawsuit. Departmental restructuring discussions take center stage.

Winter 1995–96	The athletic director search is conducted. The position goes to Scott.
Winter–Spring 1996	Searches for a department chair and two junior faculty/administrative coaching positions are under way.
Summer 1996	I defend my dissertation and graduate with an Ed.D. degree. In late summer we begin the deposition process.
Fall 1996	Depositions continue and move beyond me to include Ad, Vivian, Marv, and Bill.
Winter 1996–97	The deposition process stalls. Settlement efforts are engaged in.
Spring 1997	Settlement terms are agreed upon. The lawsuit ends.
1997–98	I try to come to terms with living and working in the aftermath.
Summer 1998	I leave Linfield.

E-mails about the Faculty
Perspectives Series

The following is Marv Henberg's final e-mail to me about the Faculty Perspectives Series, with my responses to his points given in all capitals; I e-mailed my response to him on December 6, 1994.

Dear Cindy,

Thanks for your candid reply to my request. I'll be equally candid in response. You see your presentation as strictly related to your professional interest and educational achievement, and I don't question the validity of your offering your thoughts on the subject to your faculty colleagues.

THANK YOU FOR SUPPORTING THE VALIDITY OF MY INTENT. I REMAIN COMMITTED TO THE VALUE OF SUPPLYING GENERAL TITLE IX INFORMATION IN AN EDUCATIVE CONTEXT TO AND FOR MY PEERS.

None-the-less, Title IX issues are larger than any of us. They are also highly politicized at this time and on this campus. LBJ used to say that "politics is getting everyone under the same tent." To do so we all need allies, and my modest suggestion of Bill Apel as a co-presenter is designed to do exactly that, build alliances. Nothing more, but certainly nothing less.

I AGREE THAT TITLE IX ISSUES ARE LARGER THAN ANY OF US, AL-THOUGH IT CONTINUES TO ASTOUND ME THAT SO MANY PEOPLE HAVE SUCH DIFFICULTY ACCEPTING THE REALITY OF FEDERAL LAW,

WHICH IS AFTER ALL . . . ONLY THE MORAL MINIMUM. I AGREE THAT COALITION BUILDING AND "ALLIES" WOULD BE VALUED AS WE CONTINUE TO ADDRESS TITLE IX ISSUES ON CAMPUS. I AGREE THAT BILL'S ROLE NEEDS TO BE CENTRAL AND FEEL THAT LEADERSHIP NEEDS TO COME FROM THE PRESIDENT, THE DEAN (YOU), THE COMPLIANCE OFFICER (BILL), AND ATHLETIC DIRECTOR (AD). I PERSONALLY HAVE NO DESIRE TO CONTINUE "ON POINT" AND FEEL I HAVE "SUFFERED" MORE THAN ENOUGH IN THE NAME OF THIS "CAUSE." THAT SAID, I WOULD GLADLY ATTEND A PRESENTATION PUT FORWARD BY BILL, AND/OR YOU, AND/OR THE PRESIDENT, TO ADDRESS THE COLLEGE'S COMMITMENT TO TITLE IX. I DO NOT FEEL IT IS MY PLACE TO DO THIS AND I AM NOT COMFORTABLE WITH THE IDEA THAT A PRESENTATION OF MY ACADEMIC WORK WOULD BE PUT TO THIS END (EVEN WITH SUPPORT—WHICH TO BE HONEST HAS BEEN TERRIBLY LACKING OVER THE PAST 2 AND A HALF YEARS).

Your own example to me of the fulminations against Title IX that Irv Wiswall was privy to convinces me that Bill's cooperation is important. How do we reach that particular audience?—the audience that is apriori convinced that Title IX will be the ruination of football. I suggest that a Perspectives presentation by you alone will attract none in that group. Bill, however, brings not only his official designation as Title IX Officer, but a status as a guardian of the institution—20 years—that neither you nor I as relative newcomers can command. I urge you to look at the importance of him as an ally, divorcing the suggestion from any sensitivity you may have because you have assimilated it to your "denial" by Ken Goodrich to give a Faculty lecture this year.

I AGREE THAT THERE ARE MULTIPLE AUDIENCES. AND, AS STATED ABOVE, FEEL I CAN BE COMFORTABLE (AND SAFE) ADDRESSING AN ACADEMIC AUDIENCE FROM THAT FRAME. THE OTHER AUDIENCES YOU ALLUDE TO NEED TO BE MET BY SOMEONE OTHER THAN MYSELF, ALTHOUGH (BEING CANDID), I QUESTION WHETHER EVEN "GOD," OR KNUTE ROCKNE OR EVEN VINCE LOMBARDI, COULD GET THE MESSAGE ACROSS TO SOME. . . . READINESS AND RECEPTIVITY MAY INDEED BE UNATTAINABLE.

On the later point I think you are overreacting. I have heard from two other faculty members that they had proposed a lecture and were not invited to proceed. What looks like "denial" from one perspective (yours) looks more like allocating scarce spaces from another (mine).

AS TO OVERREACTING . . . YOU MAY BE RIGHT, YOU MAY NOT BE RIGHT, WE CAN NEVER REALLY KNOW. BUT REGARDLESS, WE CAN AGREE TO DISAGREE AND LEAVE IT AT THAT. MY ONLY ADDED COMMENT WOULD BE THAT PARTICULARLY IN THIS SITUATION, AT THIS COLLEGE, WITH THIS ISSUE, AND OUR 2.5 YEAR TITLE IX HISTORY, WE ARE AT THE LEAST TO A DEGREE CONTEXT EMBEDDED RELATIVE TO ANY INTERPRETATION.

Finally, let me say that in suggesting Bill as a co-presenter, I do not seek to control the content of what you have to say. I do seek to get two messages across: 1) that Title IX is an institutional commitment, and 2) that Cindy Pemberton does not carry the weight of progress on that issue solely on her shoulders. There are multiple audiences for these messages. Some will be in attendance and some will not.

I AGREE, AS SAID BEFORE, SOME WILL AND SOME WILL NOT ATTEND, AND REGARDLESS OF ATTENDANCE, SOME WILL AND SOME WILL NOT "GET IT." REGARDING AN INSTITUTIONAL COMMITMENT—WELL . . . ACTIONS SPEAK LOUDER THAN WORDS, AND I REMAIN PATIENT (IF PARANOID). RELATIVE TO "WEIGHT" AS I SAID, I HAVE NO DESIRE TO CARRY THIS BURDEN FURTHER . . . HOWEVER, AS I BECOME LESS NAÏVE, AND MORE AWARE OF THE REALITY IN WHICH I AM LIVING, I BECOME INCREASINGLY CONVINCED THAT REGARDLESS OF WHETHER I WANT TO OR NOT . . . SOMEONE HAS TO BEAR THE BRUNT OF WHAT MANY PERCEIVE AS THE DEMISE OF LINFIELD'S GREAT ATHLETIC TRADITION, AND I FULLY EXPECT TO BE THE ONE WHO ENDS UP: (1) THE TARGET (ONGOING), AND (2) TAKING THE FALL . . . (I WONDER IF ANITA HILL WOULD BE PROUD . . . OH HOW GRANDIOSE OF ME).

WELL, ALL THAT SAID, AS YOU MAY KNOW, I WILL BE MAKING A SIMILAR PRESENTATION TO THE LINFIELD WOMEN'S CAUCUS (I.E. LOCALLY), AND THE AMERICAN ASSOCIATION OF UNIVERSITY WOMEN'S GENDER EQUITY SYMPOSIUM (I.E. NATIONALLY). AS FOR THE FACULTY PERSPECTIVES SERIES, ALTHOUGH I AM DISAPPOINTED, GIVEN YOUR CONCERNS MY PRESENTATION MAY NOT MEET THE NEEDS YOU DESCRIBE. PLEASE LET ME KNOW: (1) IF THERE MIGHT BE ANOTHER LINFIELD FORUM BETTER SUITED FOR AN ACADEMIC PRESENTATION OF THIS NATURE, AND (2) WHEN BILL WILL PRESENT SO I CAN ATTEND AND SUPPORT HIM.

Stipulation of Dismissal Agreement
(April 1, 1997): Excerpt

PEMBERTON'S PUBLIC STATEMENT

McMinnville—Associate Professor Cindy Pemberton has been named Senior Woman Administrator for athletics, according to Marvin Henberg, vice president for academic affairs and dean of faculty at Linfield College.

The Executive Committee of the Board of Trustees reports that the lawsuit brought by Pemberton against Linfield challenging certain decisions made by the college, including her reassignment and elimination of the assistant athletic director for women position, has been settled. Dean Henberg regrets any negative perceptions that may have been fostered as a result of the reassignment and position elimination. The parties have agreed to keep the terms of the settlement confidential.

Professor Pemberton will begin her new duties on September 1, 1997 as Senior Woman Administrator. As Senior Woman Administrator she will interact with the Health, Human Performance and Athletics leadership, and the Title IX Officer, and represent Linfield at regional athletic conference and NCAA levels. Also, in this capacity Professor Pemberton will chair a faculty committee charged with planning projects to try and facilitate increased opportunities, and interest and abilities for women in sports at Linfield. As chair of this committee, Professor Pemberton will be charged with the administrative oversight and implementation of projects designed by the committee. Additionally, she will continue as the head swim coach for the women's and men's teams and as an associate professor in the Health, Human Performance and Athletics department.

"It is good for the college that Professor Pemberton has agreed to serve in this pioneering role," Henberg said. "This is a challenging position and she is well qualified for it. I trust that under her leadership Linfield will develop innovative approaches to expanding opportunities for women in athletics. These efforts along with the implementation of our five-year plan to increase opportunities for women, should put Linfield in the forefront among institutions devoted to a strong athletic program for all students."

Through her work in the role of Senior Woman Administrator, Professor Pemberton will help Linfield promote athletic opportunities for women by working to increase interest in athletic participation among women students, and, where appropriate, work to facilitate opportunities to develop their abilities to compete at the club sport or intercollegiate level. In addition, Professor Pemberton will focus campus-wide attention on efforts to enhance athletic opportunities for women consistent with the college's institutional goals and its Title IX plan. This position allows the college to utilize Professor Pemberton's leadership abilities and experience in athletic administration, as well as her enthusiasm for promoting opportunities for women athletes.

Pemberton served as assistant athletic director for women under former athletic director Ad Rutschman from 1989–1995. In her new capacity she will report directly to the HHPA department chair.

Pemberton attended high school in Medford Oregon. She attended Willamette University from 1976–1980, earning a bachelor's degree with a double major in biology and psychology. As an undergraduate her academic achievements included receipt of the "Peck" Biology Scholarship, and the Hannah Keenan Undergraduate Scholarship. While at Willamette, Pemberton earned All American swimming honors all four years, and was recognized in her senior year as Willamette's outstanding female student-athlete.

Pemberton completed her master's degree in Interdisciplinary Studies in 1983 from Southern Oregon State College, in the areas of physical education, sport psychology and nutrition, and was a nominee for Southern Oregon State College's outstanding graduate student award.

Immediately prior to Linfield, Pemberton was the head women's swimming coach at the University of Nevada in Reno (an NCAA Division I intercollegiate athletics program), and an instructor in the recreation, physical education, and dance department. In her final coaching season she was named Nevada's women's coach of the year.

Pemberton began her work at Linfield in June of 1989. As assistant athletic director she oversaw the development of the women's athletics' participation numbers from 97 (June 1989) to 169 (June 1995), as well as a two-fold increase in the women's athletics non-salaried operating budget. During her tenure as assistant athletic director Linfield's women's athletics overall NCIC (conference) all sports rankings improved from seventh (out of seven 1989/90), to second in the 1991/92 season, and third in both the 1992/93 and 1994/95 seasons.

In her HHPA teaching capacity, Professor Pemberton has taught HHPA courses in Organization and Administration of Physical Education and Athletics, Gender Issues in Education and Sport, and Foundations of Physical Education, as well as participating in the HHPA Professional Activities core courses for physical education majors, and teaching various aquatics instruction courses. And, she is currently teaching in the Linfield Honors program.

While coaching at Linfield, Professor Pemberton has been named NAIA national women's coach of the year once (1993), NAIA District 2 men's and women's coach of the year three times, and NCIC women's coach of the year twice. In June of 1989 when Pemberton arrived at Linfield, the swim program boasted two female and four male swimmers, with no recent history of dual meet, conference or national level success. Since that time she has coached nine Linfield swimmers to a total of 13 individual national event championships, 123 All America or honorable mention All America swimmer honorees, and 17 Academic All Americas. Nationally, both the women's and men's teams have consistently placed in the top 10 since 1992, with the women's team achieving a 4th place finish in 1993 and 1995, and the men's team placing 4th in 1995 and 1996. She has compiled an impressive winning dual meet record of 60/12 for the men's team, and 42/29/1 (win/loss/tie) dual meet record for the women's team.

In August of 1996 Professor Pemberton completed her doctorate degree in Educational Leadership—Postsecondary Education Administration from Portland State University. Her dissertation work was entitled: "An Educational Gender Equity/Title IX Workshop for Intercollegiate Athletic Personnel." Based on this work, over the past two years Professor Pemberton has presented and published at both regional and national levels. Some of her recent presentations/publications in this area include: The American Educational Research Association—SIG on Research on Women and Education (October 1996), the National Association for Girls and Women in Sports (symposium September 1996), the American Swim Coaches Association (world clinic September 1996), and the American Association of University Women national symposium (June 1995). Professor Pemberton has just completed an invited publication for an international on-line journal "Advancing Women in Leadership." This publication focuses on Title IX as an American education gender equity intervention strategy. External to her work at Linfield, she has also done Title IX consultation and intercollegiate athletic audit work, and serves as the Oregon State Coordinator for National Girls and Women in Sports Day.

Index